THE SINGLE MOTHER'S COMPANION

Essays and Stories by Women

edited by
Marsha R. Leslie

SEAL PRESS

Cover design by Kris Morgan
Cover art by Christopher Baldwin
Book design by Clare Conrad

Acknowledgments:
"Route 23: 10th and Bigler to Bethlehem Pike" from *Lovers' Choice* by Becky Birtha. Copyright © 1987 by Becky Birtha. Reprinted by permission of Seal Press. "New Shoes" by Linda Hogan from *A Gathering of Spirit: Writing and Art by North American Indian Women* edited by Beth Brant. Copyright © 1984 by Sinister Wisdom Books. Reprinted by permission of the author. "Quality Time" from *Homeland and Other Stories* by Barbara Kingsolver. Copyright © 1989 by Barbara Kingsolver. Reprinted by permission of HarperCollins Publishers, Inc. "Operating Instructions" excerpted from *Operating Instructions: A Journal of My Son's First Year* by Anne Lamott. Copyright © 1993 by Anne Lamott. Reprinted by permission of Pantheon Books, a division of Random House, Inc. "Feeling Special" by Jenny Morris and "A Woman's Right to Choose" by Barbara Walker from *Alone Together* edited by Jenny Morris, first published by The Women's Press Ltd, 1992, 34 Great Sutton Street, London EC1V 0DX, reprinted on pages 94–106 and 161–176, respectively, are used by permission of The Women's Press Ltd and the authors. "Contingent Lives" excerpted from *Lives on the Edge: Single Mothers and Their Children in the Other America* by Valerie Polakow. Copyright © 1993 by Valerie Polakow. Reprinted by permission of The University of Chicago Press and the author.

Library of Congress Cataloging-in-Publication Data

The Single Mother's Companion: Essays and Stories by Women / edited by Marsha R. Leslie.
1. Single mothers. 2. Fatherless family. I. Leslie, Marsha
HQ759.915.S17   1994   306.85'6—dc20   94-10613
ISBN 1-878067-56-7

Printed in the United States of America
First printing, November 1994
10 9 8 7 6 5 4 3 2 1

Distributed to the trade by Publishers Group West
Foreign Distribution:
In Canada: Publishers Group West Canada, Toronto, Ontario
In the U.K. and Europe: Airlift Book Company, London

Editor's Acknowledgments

Just as "it takes a whole village to raise a child," as the African proverb states, it has taken a community to bring this anthology to fruition.

First, I am sincerely grateful to all of the contributors who found the time and energy to add their voices to this collection.

For being there when all of life happened at once and for ever nudging me toward the finish line, my heart-felt thanks to my dear friends, passionate companions, and loving family. Special thanks to Sharon Babcock, Easter Baylor, Dick Birnbaum, Julia A. Boyd, Marilyn Fullen-Collins, Valerie Griffith, Kathryn Hunt, Michael Leslie, Lynn Pruzan, Charlotte Watson Sherman, Mary Ellen Smith, Edna and Martin Westerman, Evelyn C. White, and Carletta Wilson. Somehow they always appeared with just what I needed to keep going—a hug, a meal, a run, a shoulder, a laugh, a word.

My deep appreciation to Holly Morris and Faith Conlon, my editors, who guided me through this process with great patience, understanding and skill. Thanks to all the women of Seal Press who have made working on this first book an incredibly nurturing and satisfying experience.

Lastly, I am forever grateful to Michaela Leslie-Rule and Mary Pat Hess for their love and support always.

To my mother, Versa L. Rule;
my sisters—Sheila Rule and Diana Rule;
and my daughter, Michaela Leslie-Rule

and

In memory of my father,
William Rule

and my spiritual mentor,
Ruthelma Johnson

Contents

Introduction

I grew up in St. Louis, a midwestern town with southern sensibilities. During my childhood, being a single mother was equated with being an unwed mother—one of the worst labels a woman could wear. It was akin to being stamped with a scarlet letter. A person who found herself in such straits was thought to be immoral, destined to a life of poverty as a social outcast. Divorce was probably the next worst label—after all, what woman in her right mind would leave her husband? (There was the consideration that it might be the other way around. But if a man did leave his wife, it was often thought to be her fault.) Being a widow with children was an enviable position for which the community might have compassion—at least for a while.

My parents believed in family, in working hard and staying together, even through the most turbulent marital trials and stressful economic challenges.

Ironically, or perhaps not so, each of their daughters is a single mother—by choice. I left a marriage which should have been a friendship in the first place; one sister adopted a child after an adventurous career; and my youngest sister made a decision to have a child even though she did not want to get married.

When we made these choices, I'm sure somewhere in our souls we asked ourselves: but what about the statistics? Will we become yet another statistic of pathology and fall into the stereotype of "single mother"?

Fortunately, we, like many women, have since come to question the institution of marriage, the nature of our relationships and the meaning of family, in the broadest sense. Women all across the nation are redefining family and what it means to be a single mother. The media have even expanded their image of "single mother," primarily into two camps: either the hard news version—welfare, fraudulent, pathetic, and usually black, or the sitcom Murphy Brown version—upper middle-class, sympathetically humorous, and usually white, but sometimes black. You choose!

A mother is a mother is a mother—with or without a partner—and a child is a child is a child—with or without two parents. We each come to this particular relationship differently.

Some single women make calculated decisions to have children through alternative insemination or through adoption. Others fall into it; they are single mothers by accident, by divorce or by death.

For many of us in America, the image of mother and child may bring warm feelings of adoration—as long as we know that there is a father somewhere in the shadows. If there is no father in the picture, the image of mother and child, at least as portrayed in the media, becomes flawed and grim. The single mother is often set up to be despised or pitied and her children are often characterized as "at risk."

There are real issues and concerns that surround single mothers: the lack of such basic needs as adequate wage compensation, child care, health care, education, housing. In addition, the forces of racism, homophobia, sexism and poverty all exert a tremendous pressure on the lives of single mothers.

However, these issues also surround other people's lives as well—they are born out of a culture that places little value on community and a lot of cachet around individual prowess, power, competitiveness and the bottom line. Ours is not a culture that is founded on the common good. Very few people hold the nation's wealth and power, women earn only seventy cents to every dollar earned by their male counterparts, and children still are not securely anchored on the national agenda.

In 1992, the number of single mothers in the United States rose to more than 9 million—nearly 4 million of whom, along with their children, live in poverty. Of the 35 million-plus Americans who lack health care insurance, nearly 10 million are children. Because of a lack of affordable or low-income housing, many low-income families spend more than half their income on housing, or end up homeless or in temporary shelter.

The issue of child care holds many low- and middle-income women hostage to a system in which it is hard to get ahead financially. Child care costs may consume twenty-five to sixty percent of a single mother's income. If the mother is on welfare, she may find that the cost of child care does not justify the income she would receive from working at a minimum-wage job.

The U.S. lags behind other industrialized nations in acknowledging the unique position of women as workers and mothers in establishing public policies that strengthen all families. While countries in Western Europe have offered family-centered subsidies for such basics as health care, housing, child care, and education, the U.S. has just begun the debate in earnest. The human and economic toll of our failure to support all families is enormous.

There is nothing inherently wrong with being a mother without a partner. All families need support and a network of economic and community connections to survive. Unfortunately, many of the current local, state and federal practices and policies only support narrowly defined notions of family.

It is time for us to speak out and for the realities of our lives to be recognized. Filled with words of joy, hardship, humor and support, *The Single Mother's Companion* is a place where single mothers have spoken and will be heard.

When I first explored the idea of an anthology by single mothers, it was the summer of 1992, not long after former Vice-President Dan Quayle accused television character Murphy Brown of bringing down America's morals by being portrayed as a popular, happy, single mom. I knew that this national fracas and debate was symptomatic of America's schizophrenia around the notion of motherhood. Only in America could the situation of a fictional television character grab and hold the attention of our elected officials and media, while real women struggle off-stage in the shadows to be seen, to have their stories heard and to effect real change. Where were the realities and voices of real single mothers being heard?

A call for manuscripts went out to national women's newspapers, writers' magazines, organizational newsletters as well as to friends, family, colleagues and acquaintances. I solicited fiction, essays, non-fiction narratives, interviews and articles that, when placed together, would portray the reality and diversity of the experiences of single mothers. I wanted this collection to explore relationships, creativity, spirituality, history, and economics through the voices of mothers without partners.

The Single Mother's Companion provides a forum for single mothers to read and to write about their lives from their own varied and unique perspectives. This anthology moves beyond media hype, beyond stereotypes and beyond academic and legislative microscopes to encompass the lives of women who have experienced the singular act of mothering.

Some of the contributors' voices are young and face dilemmas from the outset. Mary Plamondon, for example, reflects on being an unwed mother in the seventies: "The first feeling when I awoke was a heavy, slow realization that I was pregnant. . . . He wrote that he wanted me to have an abortion. I wrote him a second letter and told him I felt too Catholic to get an abortion. . . . "

Others, like Sheila Rule, are in mid-life and longing for a parenting experience. After spending years as a foreign correspondent for *The New York Times*, Sheila decided at forty that she must fulfill her life-long dream of mothering: ". . . the yearning to be a mother fights long and dies hard. It was that yearning as much as anything else that threw me against a wall and blocked my exit until I examined my life. What I saw was a life made up of years of longing to be a mother . . . a longing to be tied to routine, stability and responsibility for someone else's well-being."

Some, like Bonnie Tavares, welcome the solitude that comes after leaving an abusive relationship: "As I lie in my bed my first night as a single mother, I am struck by the silence—the wonderful silence. . . . The silence brings wonderful solace—a sense of peace and long overdue calm. It is not the calm before the storm—the next round of screaming and accusations, but rather a true calm. This calm is almost tangible in its depth."

Others struggle economically, as in the story, "Loosestrife," by Carol Weir: "We were out of money by June. Carl had left in April when the lilac bush in front was still full of tight purple clusters, not yet flowers. . . . I tried to find something else besides my hours at the convenience store, but the bakery needs someone early in the morning, and the coffee shop only has an opening for lunch. If I have to pay a sitter I might as well not bother working."

Some single mothers, such as United States Senator Carol Moseley-Braun, are working within the system for change: "We have an opportunity, and an obligation, to demand that our governments prioritize a family agenda, concrete and specific responses to a host of issues as they affect families. A first step lies in defining families comprehensively and realistically."

Still others take on the topics of unconventional parenting. Mayumi Tsutakawa explores divorce and nurturing children of mixed heritage: "The children are growing up with a continuing sense of their *tricultural* heritage (Japanese, Chinese and whatever American is). . . . One year, I filled out a public school application that asked my son to 'ONLY CHECK ONE' and the choices included Japanese or Chinese. In my presence, he chose Japanese. Perhaps with his father, he would have checked the box 'Chinese.'"

Young mothers speak about the hardships of poverty in Valerie Pokalow's compilation of interviews, "Contingent Lives": "I don't want to be on ADC [Aid to Dependent Children] but I had to get back so I could get caught up on my rent and get Medicaid for my baby. . . . I hate being on ADC, they make you feel so belittled. I hate that! I hate going to the office and I hate dealing with the social worker and dealing with every worker that has something to say about my life."

A recovering alcoholic, Anne Lamott, gives an intimate, honest, and humorous account of the ups and downs of single mothering: "I had these fears late at night when I was pregnant that I wouldn't be able to really love him, that there's something missing in me, that half the time I'd feel about him like he was a Pet Rock and half the time I'd be wishing I never had him. So there must have been some kind of a miracle. ...I never ever wish I hadn't had him....But I do sometimes wish I had a husband and a full-time nanny."

No matter what the relationship or personal story of single mothering—there always comes that moment of separation, as Diane Lutovich poignantly observes: "Raising a child as a single parent is a lot like riding a roller coaster. Frightening, exhilarating, exhausting—certainly not boring. And as we sink into the rhythm, the ups and downs, the expected and the surprises, it's easy enough to stop thinking about the end of the ride. And then the time is up. Ride is over."

We each come to the mother-child relationship in our own way and we are uniquely shaped by the experience. It is important to allow into our lives those who would willingly give of themselves to nurture our children and ourselves. Parenting is not the sole job of one or two people. It is a gift of community—the giver and the receiver are mutually benefitted. I hope that in *The Single Mother's Companion* women find a part of that community reflected back at them and that they find strength and encouragement to organize their lives around their own truths, not around others' myths about who they are. It is important that we speak for ourselves and share the real stories of our lives. Only then will we have the power to change the myths and policies that affect the landscapes of our lives.

Marsha R. Leslie
Seattle, Washington
April 1994

THE SINGLE MOTHER'S COMPANION

◆

ANNE LAMOTT

Operating Instructions

◆

Some Thoughts on Being Pregnant

A man told me once that all men like to look at themselves in the mirror when they're hard, and now I keep picturing Sam in twenty years, gazing at his penis in the mirror while feeling psychologically somewhere between Ivan Boesky and Mickey Mantle. I also know he will be someone who will one day pee with pride, because all men do, standing there manfully tearing bits of toilet paper to shreds with straight and forceful sprays, carrying on as if this were one of history's great naval battles—the Battle of Midway, for instance. So of course I'm a little edgy about the whole thing about my child having a penis instead of a nice delicate little lamb of a vagina. But even so, this is still not the worst fear.

No, the worst thing, worse even than sitting around crying about that inevitable day when my son will leave for college, worse than thinking about whether or not in the meantime to get him those hideous baby shots he probably should have but that some babies die from, worse than the fears I have when I lie awake at three o'clock in the morning (that I won't be able to make enough money and will have to live in a tenement house where the rats will bite our heads while we sleep, or that I will lose my arms in some tragic accident and will have to go to court and diaper my son using only my mouth and feet and the judge won't think I've done a good enough job and will put Sam in a foster home), worse even than the fear I feel whenever a car full of teenagers drives past my house going 200 miles an hour on our sleepy little street, worse than thinking about my son being run over by one of those drunken teenagers, or of his one day becoming one of those teenagers—worse than just about anything else is the agonizing issue of how on earth anyone can bring a child into this world knowing full well that he or she is eventually going to have to go through the seventh and eighth grades.

The seventh and eighth grades were for me, and for every single good interesting person I've ever known, what the writers of the Bible meant when they used the words *hell* and *the pit*. Seventh and eighth grades were a place into which one descended. One descended from the relative safety and wildness and bigness one felt in sixth grade, eleven years old. Then the worm turned, and it was all over for any small feeling that one was essentially all right. One wasn't. One was no longer just some kid. One was suddenly a Diane Arbus character. It was springtime, for Hitler, and Germany.

I experienced it as being a two-year game of "The Farmer in the Dell." I hung out with the popular crowd, as jester, but boy, when those parties and dances rolled round, this cheese stood alone, watching my friends go steady and kiss, and then, like all you other cheeses, I went home and cried. There we were, all of us cheeses alone, emotionally broken by unrequited love and at the same time amped out of our minds on hormones and shame.

Seventh and eighth grades were about waiting to get picked for teams, waiting to get asked to dance, waiting to grow taller, waiting to grow breasts. They were about praying for God to grow dark hairs on my legs so I could shave them. They were about having pipe-cleaner legs. They were about violence, meanness, chaos. They were about *The Lord of the Flies*. They were about feeling completely other. But more than anything else, they were about hurt and aloneness. There is a beautiful poem by a man named Roy Fuller, which ends, "Hurt beyond hurting, never to forget," and whenever I remember those lines, which is often, I think of my father's death ten years ago this month, and I think about seventh and eighth grades.

So how on earth can I bring a child into the world, knowing that such sorrow lies ahead, that it is such a large part of what it means to be human?

I'm not sure. That's my answer: I'm not sure. One thing I do know is that I've recently been through it again, the total aloneness in the presence of almost extraterrestrially high levels of hormones. I have been thinking a lot lately of Phil Spector and Wall of Sound, because to be pregnant is to be backed by a wall of hormones, just like during puberty, and the sense of aloneness that goes along with that is something I have been dancing as fast as I could to avoid ever having to feel again. For the last twenty-some years, I have tried everything, in sometimes suicidally vast quantities—alcohol, drugs, work, food, excitement, good deeds, popularity, men, exercise, and just rampant compulsion and obsession—to avoid having to be in the same room with that sense of total aloneness. And I did pretty well, although I nearly died. But then recently that aloneness walked right into my house without knocking, sat down, and stayed a couple of weeks.

In those two weeks, tremendous amounts of support poured in, as did baby clothes and furniture. My living room started to look like a refugee relocation center, but the aloneness was here, too, and it seemed to want to be felt. I was reminded once again that the people closest to me, including my therapist, function as my pit crew, helping me to fix blownout tires and swabbing me off between laps, and the consensus, among those individuals who make up my pit crew, was that I was probably just going to have to go ahead and feel the aloneness for a while. So I did, and I'll tell you it didn't feel very good. But somehow I was finally able to stand in that huge open wound and feel it and acknowledge it because it was real, and the fear of the pain of this wound turned out to be worse than the actual pain.

As I said, though, it didn't feel very good, and it brought me up against that horrible, hateful truth—that there wasn't anything outside myself that could heal or fill me and that everything I had been running from and searching for all my life was within. So I sat with those things for a while, and the wounds began to heal.

This all took place a few months ago, at age thirty-five. I mean, I'm old and tough and I can take it. But Sam is just a baby. Sam, in fact, hasn't even come out of the chute yet. I guess when he does, there will be all these people to help him along on his journey; he will have his pit crews, too, but at some point he will also have to start seventh grade. Maybe he will be one of those kids who gets off easy, but probably not. I don't know many who did. So he will find himself at some point, maybe many times, in what feels like a crawl space, scared of unseen spiders, pulling himself along on his elbows, the skin rubbed raw, not knowing for sure whether he will ever arrive at a place where he can stand up again in the daylight. This is what it feels like to grieve a loss that is just too big, the loss of a loved one, or of one's childhood, or whatever. (And it is sometimes what it feels like to be in the middle of writing a book; and also what it feels like sometimes when you've lost your hormonal equilibrium.)

Yet we almost always come out on the other side, maybe not with all our *f-a-c-u-l-t-i-e-s* intact, as Esmé put it, but in good enough shape. I was more or less okay by ninth grade. I am more or less okay now. I really love my pit crew, and I sometimes love my work. Sometimes it feels like God has reached down and touched me, blessed me a thousand times over, and sometimes it all feels like a mean joke, like God's advisers are Muammar Qaddafi and Phyllis Schlafly.

So I am often awake these days in the hours before dawn, full of joy, full of fear. The first birds begin to sing at quarter after five, and when Sam moves around in my stomach, kicking, it feels like there are trout inside me, leaping, and I go in and out of the aloneness, in and out of that sacred place.

October 23

My friend Orville dropped by yesterday with a beautiful red and green satin stuffed fish from China, embroidered with all sorts of things that the presence of this fish will protect us from: scorpions, spiders, snakes. I kept trying to convey to Orville how wasted I am by the baby's needs, while the whole time Sam lay there doing his baby Jesus routine. He's so beautiful you can't take your eyes off him. But Orville, who raised a baby son fifteen years ago, says he remembers clearly how insane things get with an infant around. He said that even with a mate, it's like having a clock radio in your room that goes off erratically every few hours, always tuned to heavy metal.

Sam sleeps for four hours at a stretch now, which is one of the main reasons I've decided to keep him. Also, he lies by himself on the bed staring and kicking and cooing for fifteen to twenty minutes at a time. I had these fears late at night when I was pregnant that I wouldn't be able to really love him, that there's something missing in me, that half the time I'd feel about him like he was a Pet Rock and half the time I'd be wishing I never had him. So there must have been some kind of a miracle.

I never ever wish I hadn't had him.

But I do sometimes wish I had a husband and a full-time nanny. And that I could still have a few drinks now and then. I am coming up on three and a half years clean and sober. The memories are still very clear of how lost and debauched and secretly sad my twenties and early thirties were, how sick and anxious I felt every morning. I thought at the time that I was having a lot of fun, except that the mornings were really pretty terrible. But there are still times when these movies start to play in my head, where I see myself putting the baby down to sleep and then sitting and sipping one big, delicious Scotch on the rocks. Just sipping, just sipping one fucking drink. Is that so goddamn much to ask? I just want that kind of relief, that smoothing of the sharp edges. The only fly in the ointment is that if I went to a liquor store and put some money on the counter for a bottle of good whiskey, I might as well put Sam on the counter, too, because I know I will lose him if I start drinking again. I know I would lose every single thing in my life that is of any real value. I couldn't take decent care of *cats* when I was drinking. They'd run off or get hit by cars or get stolen, because I'd forget to leave windows open for them or wouldn't come home for a couple of nights in a row. So I don't know, I guess I won't have a drink today. Maybe tomorrow, *probably* tomorrow, but not today.

Sam has this great roar now, like maybe he's about to cry, but then it turns out that he just feels like roaring because that's the kind of guy he is—he's a roaring kind of guy—and because he's coming into his own, like "I am baby, hear me roar, in numbers too big to ignore . . . " Then he burns his diaper.

Half the time I'm completely winging this motherhood business. I get so afraid because we are running out of money. We have enough to live on for maybe two more months. Also, I just had no idea I had so much rage trapped inside me. I've never had a temper before. I've always been able to be mellow or make jokes. But we went though a difficult patch this evening when Sam was being hard to please, whiny and imperious and obviously feeling very sorry for himself, and at first I could kind of roll with it, shaking my head and thinking, it's because he's a *male*, having an *episode*, this is very familiar stuff to me, he's already got testosterone poisoning. But I couldn't get him to stop, and it wore me down. It was one of those times when I desperately needed to be able to hand him over to someone, like, say hypothetically, a mate, and there wasn't anyone. So suddenly all this bile and old fear of men and abandonment stuff were activated in my head. All these furious thoughts about Sam's father. Sam was so exasperating that I could feel fury coursing through my system, up my arms into my hands, like charged blood. I made myself leave the room, just left him crying in his bassinet in the living room, which is what Bill Rankin said to do once before. I went to the tiny bedroom in the back, and breathed, and prayed for major help. The next thing I knew, I had decided to take him for a walk in the stroller in the dark.

It was warm and the stars were just coming out; the sky seemed unusually deep. I said to God, I really need help tonight, I need you to pull a rabbit out of your hat. One minute later Bill and Emmy and Big Sam came walking along the road toward us. So we stopped to talk for a few minutes. Big Sam is such a brilliant and gentle little guy, so artistic and tender with the baby that it helped me to breathe again. I felt completely back on the saddle by the time we all said goodbye.

Part of me loves and respects men so desperately, and part of me thinks they are so embarrassingly incompetent at life and in love. You have to teach them the very basics of emotional literacy. You have to teach them how to be there for you, and part of me feels tender toward them and gentle, and part of me is so afraid of any more violation. I want to clean out some of these wounds, though, with my therapist, so Sam doesn't get poisoned by all my fear and anger.

I nursed him for a long time tonight. He's so beautiful it can make me teary. I told him I was sorry for thinking such sexist stuff about his people. He listened quietly and nursed and stared up into my face. I wanted to justify it, tell him about all the brilliant but truly crummy men out there, and let's not even get *started* on the government, but then I began humming some songs for him until he fell asleep. Then it was perfectly quiet.

October 25

He's very brilliant, this much is clear. He's learned to comfort himself without the pacifier by sucking on his hands and fists, like a lion with a bone. I wish *I* could sit in public places slobbering away on my own fist. It looks very comforting. The colic is gone. I am still wheat- and dairy-free. Also, mostly shit-free. I am finally saying no when I mean no, which is a lot of the time, especially when people want me to come to their house for a party. People have been inviting me and Sam to their parties lately, for God knows what reason. Everyone knows I don't do parties or dinners. Everyone knows I don't do "do's." It's just torture for me. "Why is that?" people always asked, and all I can do is shrug. I think it's either that I'm not remotely well enough for that sort of thing or because I've gotten *too* well. Who knows, but I would honestly rather spend an hour getting my teeth cleaned than an hour mingling. I am absolutely serious about this. I get so nervous that I actually skulk, and then I get into this weird shuffling-lurk mode. It's very unattractive. I look like a horse who can count, pawing the ground with one hoof. I don't know why people would even bother inviting me.

But in the old days I used to get sucked in and say yes to everybody and be there for them, showing up at their parties, helping them move, or staying on the phone with them too long. I'd try to entertain or help or fix, nurse them back to health or set them straight. Now I do the counting-horse shuffle and shake my head and say I just can't do it, can't come to the party, can't do the favor, can't stay on the phone. I want Sam to understand when he grows up that "No" is a complete sentence. It's given me this tremendous sense of power. I'm a little bit drunk on it. I ended up saying no to a couple of things I really wanted to do with friends, then had to call them up and beg, "Take me back, take me back."

Also, it's great to be so taken up by Sam that I don't have to deal with men. It's like that beautiful old movie by Vittorio de Sica, *A Brief Vacation*. I have had a lot of men do stuff to me over the years, and I sanctioned it, but I did not want it. I have listened so attentively to the most boring, narcissistic men so that they would like me or need me. I'd sit there with my head cocked sweetly like the puppy on the RCA logo. On the inside I would feel like that old poem by Philip Levine, about waiting until you can feel your skin wrinkling and your hair growing long and tangling in the winds. It was like these men held me hostage. I'd think about chewing my arm off to get out of the trap so I could rush home and hang myself, but at the same time I'd need them to think well of me. Now I all but say, Oh, I'm so sorry, but I'm on this new shit-free diet. Now there's Sam, me, Uncle Jesus, Pammy, Steve, a few friends, a few relatives, and the kitty.

Sam has a Big Brother now named Brian. He has come the last two Tuesdays to take care of him for a couple of hours. He is married to my good friend Diane, who is in her mid-forties and does not want children, whereas Brian is ten years younger and adores them. He signed on to be a Big Brother in Marin last year and got assigned a kid who thought he was a total dork and who was ashamed of Brian's big land-boat Buick. They just couldn't connect at all. So when I was about to deliver, Diane came to me and asked if Brian could be Sam's formal and official Big Brother. Brian's another sober alcoholic, very kind and funny. It's been wonderful. He's already learned to change diapers and feed Sam bottles of pre-pumped breast milk and bathe him, and he puts him in the Snugli or the stroller and takes him to the park down the street. They discuss guy stuff. Brian gets tears in his eyes when he talks about Sam because he is so grateful and surprised they have each other. I sense that they will be together for life.

There are great men in Sam's life, the best men the world produces. It's another kind of miracle, that he has this devotion, that we both do, but still it will probably hurt beyond words someday that he doesn't have his dad in his life. I'm just going to have to tell him that not everybody has a father. Look at me, I will tell him: I don't have a father, and I don't have a swimming pool, either. But Sam will have a tribe. You can't help but believe that these other men will help Sam not have such a huge sense of loss. They'll be his psychic Secret Service.

◆

DEVORAH MAJOR

A Cord Between Us

◆

My daughter was lying long and hot near the wall. A persistent fever made her seek a dawn refuge in my bed where she rested quietly, having finally learned to leave me some covers. My son was wriggling around on the futon's other edge, ready for the morning to begin. After tiring of lonely cartoon watching, he had run up two flights of stairs and leaped into bed. I was enjoying the luxury of a morning when I didn't have to push, a morning that would meet me on my terms, slowly and lazily, without any pressing commitments, work responsibilities or household chores—not that they don't always exist, just that after four years of singleness, I had finally learned to "freeze-frame" all demands on my time and make room for myself.

Each child pressed against me—the one burning, the other cool—both taking comfort in the familiar closeness. We lay there, silently, until the morning was warm enough to chat. Then we told jokes to each other and traded stories about being sick, about children bothering their parents in bed, about cartoons, about war fears, about dreams.

Through my first years as a single parent, following the terror of an ugly and sometimes violent breakup and the painful death of what once had promised to be a wonderful life-long friendship, my children and I built a stronger and deeper kinship. It seemed as though in the painful lesson of learning that all promises could be broken and nothing could be taken for granted—not even the resiliency of love—we had learned how to be better friends to one another. Somehow we knit our lives back together, all of us taking turns falling into the hole that was left in our household and each of us pulling one of the others out of a tearful silence, dissatisfied grouchiness or thick loneliness. We created and discovered new ways to be—not just parent-to-child, but friend-to-friend. We became best friends.

They had had to learn so much, so much sooner than I was prepared to teach them. My children were left alone far more often than I would have liked. They learned to be more responsible, to cook simple meals, to nurse themselves while I worked, to take care of each other. They learned that this mother most certainly did get tired and was not even close to being a "super-woman." They learned to leave me alone, to give me space, to see that I was in one of my moods and wait for it to pass. They also learned, despite the seemingly bottomless children's world of taking and needing, and taking and needing, to give back—in huge portions—the love and care that I fed to them. So we drew even closer together, the three of us being both circle and triangle, reshaped our home and flourished.

I almost never lay in bed with my parents. Oh maybe when I was a baby, a time of which I have no memory. My parents shared their time with us in other ways. My mother worked, painted, loved her husband passionately, loved her children unswervingly and juggled each of our needs with a precision that defies imagination. My father, too, between his work, his writing and his rages gifted us with freedom and love, as he gave us the world in long drives and wilderness trips. Not until I was grown did I find the kind of friendship with my mother or father that I already share with my children.

Somewhere in between the hard questions which they

asked for years and the hard answers which I sought to give them, sometime in those months when I could not hide my fragility, my weaknesses, my pain, my imperfections, I had grown, we had grown into a stronger unit. I was, after all, the parent who stayed. I was the one who had not missed a birthday, who tried and usually succeeded in fulfilling, although often late, every promise I made, and I was the one who had learned, feet to the coals, how to be humble in the face of my children's clear-eyed perceptions. And I had, thankfully, remembered to remind them again and again that no matter what else, these two were always wanted, always loved, always desired by their parents. And so my daughter, my son and I lay cuddling the morning, finishing each other's sentences, jumping into corners of conversation, having all the time in the world to be friends.

I am not recommending leaving one's spouse because it forges a truer bond with one's children. I miss, most fervently, the support of another adult in my household and the passion of another regular mate in my bed. However, sometimes in that spouseless space there emerges room for a different kind of parent-to-child understanding. When two adults share the decision making, children have the luxury of being children longer. They don't have to consider as many sides of any given situation, shoulder as much responsibility, or be included in the mechanics of problem solving.

When the family is reduced and one adult has to make the decisions, there can be an opening where children are let in on issues and ideas they would have been protected from. Even simple decisions become different. When I was married, for example, my children's father and I discussed dinner menus. The children could put in requests for special dishes and always had a say on birthday dinners, but basically the adults planned and cooked. When I became single, I got tired of having to think of what to cook, what to buy, how to be different. I began to rely on my children for ideas. Of course, at first they took this as an opportunity to learn the breadth and shallowness of fast-food emporiums, but with persistent direction my son began bringing me recipe cards to look at and my daughter began to ask about dishes she had tasted at a friend's house. I couldn't be full-time entertainment coordinator on weekends, so they were forced to be more creative about finding ways to spend their time, offering me alternatives. That process of shifting the family weight more evenly made negotiations a constant in my home and forced us all to stretch to handle the load.

I know this special friendship with my children is something that is not unusual in single-parent homes. Recently I was reminded of this while taking care of my friend's daughter. I had to smile as the girl spoke wistfully of the times she and her brother and mother shared a room in their grandparents' house. She spoke of studying and laughing and telling stories before her mother had remarried. It was, she said, "just the three of us" and they were "so close" and it was "so nice."

Now, with the obligations of her mother's new relationship and the labor of knitting together a larger family, that time was diminished and, the child had noted, although there was plenty of time for her and her mom to be mother and daughter, there was little time for them to be friend and friend. It wasn't that their friendship was gone, the daughter continued, it was just that they didn't get much time to maintain it.

So when weeks later I lay in my bed on an ordinary, special morning feeling my daughter slowly cool, teaching my son to be quiet, laughing, I took the time to enjoy the rewards of my single life. I was friends with my children before my marriage ended. I am friends with my parents now. Friendship is not a reward for the courage or foolishness or even the necessity of single parenting. But there is a special friendship that grows, like adult friendships grow, from simply being together more of the time, from finding the answers, looking at the questions and leaning one on the other. We are closer and together our hearts have grown.

◆

BARBARA EARL THOMAS

A Parent Variation

◆

To be a parent is a special designation in any culture. It labels its carrier as someone who has passed through a sacred rite or a ritual of love which has brought forth a tiny miracle. Parents are a special breed. They have chosen to settle, to plant seed, to sacrifice their time and a portion of their lives to the tending.

There is an ideal that we each carry with us, like a snapshot inside our mind's eye—the ideal family that may or may not have been our own. We pull it out and hold it up as we make our way through the world. We measure all who come before us by this standard. For some it is one mother and one father, a house and a yard.

I grew up surrounded by relatives. Almost any of those early years I choose to remember are found peopled by the aunt or cousins living with us in our big old house in the center of the city. When the relatives would move out, my father would rent out the extra rooms to people we called roomers. And the roomers, after a time, would soon become relatives. Some stayed months, others for years. They would come and go, sometimes mysteriously and usually unexplained. My sister and I were the children who belonged to the house. Even then I knew we were special. If you rented a room in my house, you got a house, a room and two kids. We were the kids who belonged to the house. I like to think that we were the special feature of the house, not like the apartment house next door where you just got a room. There was Clarence, John H. Anderson, Uncle Willie and Ray; certainly not all by any means, but these were the special ones for me. And then there was the neighborhood, filled with the families who were our neighbors and formed yet another layer of familial extension: there were the Ruffins, the Wassons, the Jeffersons and Mrs. Smith who lived with her daughter and five grandchildren—and whom we all referred to as Mother. Even my parents called her that.

Finally, there was Emily who lived across the street with her husband GW. She was childless, except for me. I would go with her to church teas and luncheons and attend social functions that called for children. Other times, I would just sit in her house with her, listening to Dinah Washington records while she told me stories of Kansas City, where she was from. When I think back I realize that all of these people offered guidance or care in some way that I have now come to think of as parental.

My idea of a family was of an amorphous living thing that grew and contracted not necessarily by bloodlines but by some other mysterious rules based on who passes through and almost any unplanned circumstance one could think of. Mostly, families in my world were not planned.

My child, the only child that I will have, came into my life when I was a young college student. She was actually my sister's child. My niece. My sister was seventeen when her daughter was born, and she was having hard times, which persist to this day. It was clear from the very first moment that I was going to have more than a passing involvement. Although there was never a time when my parents said to me, "*Now* you know you are going to have to take some responsibility here and help with the raising of this child," there was the reality of a child who would be taken care of. In my family there were things you just understood that were based on unspoken connections. My parents were like that. They were always giving unspoken direction based on whatever was needed. From the moment my niece was born we all shared the responsibility.

It would make a more heroic, selfless-sounding story to say that this unspoken direction was clearly received with seamless intuition. Unfortunately, if it resembled anything, it was lurching and confusion interspersed with longings to be free—as I imagined all my classmates to be. It was hard to imagine that anyone else had a mother like mine who could make you call her just by "putting her mind on you." That's what she would say when I called home every other day or so from the dorm. "Hi baby, I knew it was you, you been on my mind all day. So, I put my mind on you so you would call." I would laugh, protest and tell her to keep her mind to herself. I'd hate to think that I could be in the middle of some crucial moment of my education, or worse, some romantic interlude when I would feel compelled to stop and say, "Excuse me, but I have to call my mother."

Early on it seemed that maybe my sister and her husband might actually be able to put some semblance of a life together. And, however inadequate, they would limp along as the family they were. The first code was: If the first-line family exists you support it no matter how inadequate it may seem to you. So in the early years, I bought milk and left money for food. I stopped leaving money when I thought it was being spent for something other than that. I would leave class early so I could visit and see that my young niece and my sister were well. I realize now that those were my first visitations as a single parent to the child that I would spend so much of my life with. I went, I think, like any parent trying to establish continuity and a relationship with a child who was not with me. There was a need for regularity, I thought, I will give that.

For the first few years of her life I would just appear. I'd go in between classes or for whatever emergency occurred. I would appear and provide what was needed, whether it was food, medical care or outings. Time passed and my sister's marriage dissolved. My sister and my niece lived as often with my parents as not. It was established, again unspoken, that my parents would provide the housing. My sister was still the mother to my niece—by definition, if not always by function. I would provide all else that was needed. It's hard to explain to anyone who doesn't already understand the theory of providing what is needed. I might argue with my sister, or even my parents, that this or that needed to be done. But in the end, something would be done.

It went on like this, for years. There came to be an established routine. I was the other parent who lived elsewhere but came once or twice weekly to do homework, go on outings, or to spend the afternoon. With amazement, I watched this child grow. She would tell me stories about her snakes that lived on the roof. During the seemingly endless visits where we would invariably end up in my mother's kitchen, she would wrap her arms around my legs and look up at me as if she had waited all week for my visit so she could recount to me stories about each of the snakes. There were lots of them. Each had a name. They were friendly good snakes. Then she would take me by the hand and lead me to the refrigerator where she kept her pet worms. Actually, they were my father's night crawlers, kept in ice-cream-like containers filled with cool moist earth. I remembered those night crawlers from my own childhood; I worried that they would somehow get out of the container, crawl around the refrigerator and get into the butter and leftovers and that we would unknowingly eat them. She didn't seem to have those fears. She was good at weaving the unexplained into some kind of coherent reality for the moment.

As a parent, who was not a parent, there were many moments when I was stymied by my ever-changing role. I could provide what was needed but couldn't really plan or have control. I wasn't there for the day-to-day. My directions only had so much influence, and of course, my parents and sister had their own ideas about what was needed. So we fashioned a dance of sorts, weaving in and out of our roles depending on the state of my sister's situation. There were moments, however fleeting, when my sister and niece had their own place. This motion out of and away from my parents' house was always one of hope and anticipation that this time she would be able to keep her job and that the specter of alcohol and drugs would not undo her as it always had in the past. It was a place where she would be the mother, not the daughter, as she was in my parents' house, which in turn made her into a version of sibling to my niece instead of the "parent." The idea that my sister and niece would finally achieve "a place" became our family code for talking about the hopes and dreams that we had for my sister. The talk about her future apartment or her getting to that mythical "place" was our way of referring to a sort of heaven where the ideal of family would finally work out perfectly for her and my niece. It was hard, no matter what my doubts, not to want to put the energy of my hope together with that of a young child who was longing for the biological source of her being and the mother symbol to be one and the same. She wanted what was normal and regular.

My sister and my family suffered from what my sister could not resist. There were times when all the energy of the family went toward trying to fix that one among us who was broken and spreading torment as if under the spell of some demon that could surely be cast out. My parents, though they would not say it in this way, always felt that they had somehow been the reason for how and why my sister was lost. They could not understand why my sister could not drink as they drank. After all they never missed work, disappeared or lost consciousness. The intravenous bag containing their drink dripped slowly during the week, flowing freely only on weekends. They kept their drinking, like their sadness, into that part of their lives which existed outside of their jobs. My parents were clearly baffled and unable to understand why my sister couldn't drink quietly at home and then fall asleep in front of the television like they did. It wasn't easy those first years. There was always the hope that something would happen to change my sister's luck. For me there was the balancing of college, work and time to spend with Michelle. She was a bright child, talkative sometimes beyond belief. It was all I could do some visits just to keep up with her questions. I often thought: She is doing this for me. She thinks I need these questions. She thinks that if I don't perceive that she needs me, I may not be back. My role was defined: I would be dependable to prove to her that she could rely on some steady plan.

My niece and I often spent Saturdays together. I would call during the week and appear Saturday afternoon like clockwork. One Saturday I showed, only to be greeted at the door by my mother who explained, with a little concern, that Michelle was hiding in the back of the closet in her room, crying and refusing to come out. I marched back to her room and, sure enough, found her in the closet whimpering. After checking to see that she wasn't physically ill, I put the question to her that was so often put to me by my parents: "Girl—what is wrong with you?" Her response was half real, half dramatized. She meekly replied that she had made other plans. Her friend, Erica, was coming over and they were supposed to go on some outing. To this I retorted, "You made other plans and didn't call to tell me?" She gave me her best nine-year-old "yes" without looking up.

I responded, "Now let me get this straight. You made this arrangement knowing I was coming over and you didn't call to let me know?"

"Yes," she replied.

I looked at her, and said, "Well, you know what you have to do."

She looked at me, unsure, and said, "What?"

With all my energy I said, "You have to call Erica and tell her you made a mistake—that you can't go with her right now because you already had plans." She cried, but phoned her friend. We talked. I felt bad. We both got through it. I wanted her to know that, while I was one of the parents, she also had responsibility in the relationship.

There were all those years. The planned and the not-so-planned visits and outings. One of my jobs was to oversee the yearly preparation for the new school year. This was my job because at this point, I was only a few years out of graduate school and still the only one in my family to have such an educational experience. I had domain over this part of Michelle's life—from school clothes to books to spending countless hours at open houses and in the principals' and counselors' offices those last years of high school. This was not like the more ordinary situation with parents who are separated. There was no custody arrangement, obviously, that spelled out how much my fair share would be. There was only our family's rule of thumb acted out as unspoken guides to be applied: As always, you will supply as much as is needed.

When my niece was really young it was relatively easy. I bought her what I thought she needed and what I thought was cute or attractive. I bought and read her books. There was a semblance of control. Then puberty set in, with all the temporary insanity that goes with it. This period was a lot like rodeo: lots of bucking and jumping, accompanied by hot dust, screaming crowds urging you on and shouts of excitement from the stands. I spent much of this period on my head trying to re-direct the unforeseen. There were clothes, there were boys, there was the mall.

The summer after she turned twelve, I remember being with her at one of our city's largest shopping malls, Southcenter. This may say more about me than the place, but this mall was large and horrible, filled with a series of open storefronts, all resembling gaping mouths. It seemed like a garage sale gone awry, a sanitary, plastic place filled with young people in the company of thousands of distressed parents in all shapes, sizes and colors. It was August. As I recall, my niece ended the school year that June still basically a child. Now it was August, and something was really different. It was clear she and all those other children were not like me: they were at home in the mall. There was a kind of hell-bent energy. There, she was not just my niece, my charge, but a soldier of fortune—shopping division—out to get what she was after. And, if she and the other young shoppers were soldiers of fortune, certainly we (the parents) were prisoners of sorts, present out of necessity rather than of our own accord. My niece and all those other young people having their "near teen" experience looked exactly alike to me. I remember thinking *I must memorize what she is wearing just in case we get separated.* That was the day I innocently went to pick out her clothes as I normally did, only to re-enter the dressing room to see, with surprise, that she now had the start of breasts and that these particular outfits were not going to work. Besides, she had her own ideas about what she wanted.

Buying shoes was also a part of this day; it was announced to me she could have only this one brand of shoes and in only one particular color. I stood there, in a well-known designer department store, dumbfounded. "I can't believe this," I nearly shouted. "I'm here in this store with a child who has somehow talked me into buying her a fifty-dollar pair of shoes (this was *some* years ago; the stakes are higher now), but we can't spend this money I have stupidly agreed to spend because the color is not exactly the one she wants." I'm shouting, I'm hysterical, and I know it. "Surely, there must be some child in this store on whom I can spend this money." At this point, my niece has her arms around me and is pushing me out of the door and out of my misery.

No shoes were bought that day. I realized there were possibly things this child and I couldn't do together.

Then there were the wonderfully funny moments like when my mother recounted to me, as she did weekly on the phone, her Michelle stories. I imagine that this is what cooperative co-parenting is like; one parent—my mother, my father, my sister—keeping me, the other parent, filled in and connected. This time, it was how Michelle had been lying on the floor, lifted herself up on her elbows and asked my mother, in emphatic earnestness while pointing to her newly forming breasts, "Grandma! Grandma! How are you suppose to sleep on these things anyway?"

I said, "So, Mommy, what did you tell her?" knowing full well that my mother was never the person to be specific about body parts. Hadn't she, in raising me and my sister, referred to our breasts as our little lily pads and our vaginas as little porkchops?! "So," I said again, laughing so hard I could barely stand it, "Mommy, what did you say?"

She retorted in her own self-amused way so as not to be undone, "I told her, turn over on your back, baby, and don't worry about it. You'll work it out."

There were lots of these incredibly funny moments, wrapped around the hard times when it was clear that my sister was not going to "get stable" as we all euphemistically referred to her difficulties. My niece was not unaffected by all of this in spite of extremely attentive grandparents and a would be know-it-all aunt. My sister was still the mother we all referred to and we continued to expect as much as we could from her in that role. I watched my niece at times become a parent to her own mother, trying to teach her to be the parent. I would hear my own words coming out of my niece's mouth as she would, in her fourteen-year-old voice, explain my sister's life back to her. In her childhood fierceness, she would try to shake my sister back into remembering "the place" that they were suppose to be going. During these periods she was like a boxing coach in the corner with her flagging fighter who was leaning against the ropes, threatening to go down for the count.

In these times, I was like the other parent, gingerly walking the tightrope of guiding the child while actively practicing to never estrange the child from the other parent. My mother had been my model in this. My own parents had separated often when my sister and I were growing up. My mother, sister and I would move in and out of the house based on whatever difficulties my parents were having at the time. No matter how often they argued or separated, my mother was always clear about my father's relationship to us. She told us often during these times, "You know, your father and I may not always get along, but there is no question that he loves you. Our problems have nothing to do with you or your sister."

I, in turn, would venture to assure my niece that no matter what difficulties our family might experience, she was indeed loved beyond all question.

There were so many difficult times to be navigated. My niece's high-school years, which often seemed impossible, co-incided with the drowning deaths of my parents—a sudden gulf that threatened to undo us. By this time, I was coupled with the man whom I would eventually marry. Fortunately for me and my niece, he was fearless in the face of this rather unconventional parenting arrangement that I brought to our union, both before and after my parents' deaths. He knew and accepted that my role and his would be to finish the work that my parents and I had started—the completion of the raising of my niece. In the way of this family, for both of us, it went without saying.

Her hormones and our collective grief carried us through the remainder of her teens. We found the public schools less than prepared to deal with our "family," although our arrangement could hardly be referred to as radical. At the close of the 1980s, the school system somehow managed to exist in a quasi-1950s mode. It only worked well with the nuclear family model: that is, a father and a non-working mother who was available at all times to move the child through a demanding series of school activities. There was no sense that the schools were aware of the times or the economic realities facing parents or that economics were issues of both time and money. We were saved in that system by the occasional exceptional teacher who recognized that my niece had needs that went beyond what the school system itself was able to conscientiously offer. I credit those exceptions—a French teacher and a sensitive counselor—as part of what saved us during that time.

In all of it, I wish things had been better. I wonder how this child might have fared had she been dealt a different hand: a mother, a father, whole, both functioning in one home. In thinking back now, I know that in my own way I overdid it. I replay particular times and incidents as they should have been and not as I lamely worked them out. A parent's worry is that no matter how much is given it will never be enough to sustain or show a child the way to the future. Then I think back to my own childhood and all the imagined childhoods that never were. I recall all of my parents, the real and the all important "others," who had a hand in the person I've come to be. There were no nannies nor day care as we now know it: these were neighbors, friends, relatives. And it was by that same magic that my husband, niece and I were aided. An amazing array of relatives, friends and neighbors appeared like angels to fill the spaces for which we had no experience or words.

These days I marvel at my niece—beautiful, bright and now over twenty-one years old—as she and her friends spend an evening with me discussing how they see their lives and view their past. We laugh about that day at the mall, and we continue to avoid shopping together. Because she was both overexposed to the harsh realities of life and overprotected, she seems both older and younger than I was at the same age. She speaks of her generation as being lost without a spiritual center or compelling social goals, essentially without ideals. She and her friends tell me that they think we babyboomers did it all in the sixties and seventies when we fought against the injustices we saw—those of race, gender, class and the war in Vietnam. I tell her that I think we had it easier—we spent that energy being against the system, working to take it apart. To the extent that we did, we managed and still manage to leave the hardest part undone: that is to muster the energy, persistence, and intelligence to put a better, truer, more just system in place. Underlying all of this is another irony—when we were doing our best to attack the system, the system was nevertheless there, by and large, to protect and carry many of us. That system, those safety nets, are far more tenuous now. It is also this realm of dis-ease that our generation is passing on to this younger one.

I see my niece and her friends making families, becoming parents to each other and now to their own children. The definitions we've known no longer hold. We fear for them as our parents did for us. These children, now adults, bring to mind parachuters in a free fall, holding tightly to each other as they float down. They are bringing their own definitions of family into the future by responding to the realities of their day.

To raise a child takes a mysterious mixture of many hands. As a parent who was not really a parent, I held on to more hands than I can count. And, I am grateful that there were so many hands to hold, and count on—it's hard to imagine that families or communities can survive without that kind of support. Raising a child without it, under any circumstance, would be too hard, too solitary.

CAROL WEIR

Loosestrife

◆

There was a sweet smell of molasses hanging over town that summer, especially when the wind blew from the east. It came from the feed and grain store near the railroad tracks, a block from our house. I liked the smell; it made me think of making cookies on a cold day with a fierce wind pushing branches against the window. I'd be standing at the kitchen island, flour all over the butcher block, while little Bobbie played on the floor, getting his stretch suit dirty at the knees. The kitchen would smell of cinnamon and cloves.

We were out of money by June. Carl had left in April when the lilac bush in front was still full of tight purple clusters, not yet flowers. He told me he had to go find some work, that there was nothing for him here. Maybe he'd try on the Canadian border, he said. There was a lot going on up there; they were building new shopping centers and Canadians were moving their factories across to Buffalo, things like that. He took all his hand tools and the chain saw which I guess he needed, and he took the VCR. He said he might have to take a room for awhile before he could get back. I didn't start to cry until after he pulled out of our driveway with the pickup all loaded and it was dark and I was tucking Janice in. Then I just sat on the edge of her bed, looking up at the ceiling where her night lamp made a small plate of light, so she wouldn't see my face.

I tried to find something else besides my hours at the convenience store, but the bakery needs someone early in the morning, and the coffee shop only has an opening for lunch. If I have to pay a sitter I might as well not bother working. Mom doesn't mind helping me out—she watches Bobbie and Janice while I do the four to twelve shift—but she can only do it weekends, when she's not working herself.

On Friday nights Mom waits up for me until I get home and then we have a cup of tea before she leaves. I try to make sure there's something in the fridge that she can make for herself and the kids, chicken or meat loaf, something nice, but last week was bad because of Janice getting an earache and going to the doctor (his nurse makes you pay before she gives you the prescription) so there was only spaghetti. I was getting dressed for work, brushing my hair, deciding whether to let it hang straight down or pull it back. Mom comes in the screen door and goes straight to the fridge to check it out.

"He's not sending you anything, is he?" she says.

"No, that's not true, Mom. He sends money when he can. He hasn't found anything steady yet, that's all."

"Why not?" she says. "I thought things were so good up there. Didn't you tell me how the Canadians are spending so much at the border and there was all this opportunity? He's a carpenter; there's always work for carpenters if there's building going on. Has he called?" She takes out some brown-edged lettuce and looks at it.

"It takes a while, he's new in town," I say. I hadn't heard anything from him in at least two weeks, but I wouldn't tell her that. "How does my hair look tied back like this? Isn't it getting long!" Carl loves my hair, it's my best feature, besides my boobs. He likes it when he's laying down on the bed and I'm bending over him, so he can grab me or use my hair to pull my head back. I turn away from the mirror to face her. "What do you think, Mom, tied back or down?"

"You look fine either way," she says, "considering you're

a big girl." I hate when she says that about me being a "big girl." I'm still saving my other jeans in the closet for when I get thin again. Statuesque, that's a better word, like a marble statue of a goddess. I lean over to give Janice a kiss and she hugs me tight. Her hair is shiny brown like mine.

"Ellen," Mom says, "I think you should go see a lawyer and make Carl pay support." Mom is standing by the back door, blocking me, her arms folded across her waist. No more nonsense, her body says. She makes me feel like I'm ten years old.

"I can't do that, Mom. He'll be furious. Besides, I don't have any money to pay a lawyer."

She persists, taking some bills out of her pocket and pushing them at me. "I know you don't have money, so your Pop and I are giving you this to hire someone. It's for Janice and Bobbie. It's for them, so you can get them what they need."

"What's for me, Gram?" Janice asks, her braids bouncing up and down.

"It's nothing," I tell her. "Mom, he'll take care of us, I know he will, as soon as he gets settled in with the new job. We'll be ok, Mom."

"Don't Mom me, Ellen. It's been three months and I've watched the fridge get emptier and emptier. You have two growing children here. You have to do something about this." Now she moves away from the back door to let me pass. I fly out, the money in my hand.

"Why did he leave, Ellen?"

I look down at my hands and twist my wedding ring. We're sitting on this colonial-looking wooden bench; Janice is holding Bobbie on her lap, and he's having his bottle. She's such a little mother. The money is still in my pocket. I could get up now, take the kids and walk out, forget the whole thing.

"I'm not exactly sure," I say. "There's not much work around here, you know." I can't imagine this lady lawyer knowing anything about the mill or the match plant where Carl used to work before he started his own carpentry business. She's wearing a heavy carved ring with some precious stones. Rubies? It's not a wedding ring, I can see that.

"Did he always work as a carpenter?" she asks, writing everything down on her yellow pad. Now Bobbie wants to be on my lap, and Janice starts to suck her thumb.

"Mostly," I say, shifting my butt around on her spindly bench. "He used to work for other people, when we were first married, but last year he went out on his own. Carl's Custom Carpentry. He has these cards, with a little hammer and saw." I pull one out for her. She staples it to the yellow sheet of paper.

"How much does he usually earn?" she asks. "I mean, how much *did* he earn, when he lived with you?"

"He still lives with us," I say. "He's coming back. I hope you understand that." Janice snuggles up next to me.

"Yes. But, how much?" she asks again.

How much? How much? Enough so we always ate good, enough to go out every weekend, to Dairy Queen or the speedway, the four of us squeezed onto the seat of his pickup, Carl's arm around me, sliding his hand down from my shoulder to touch my boobs. "*Wow, some knockers,*" he'd say. The radio would be playing old-time favorites from the sixties and Janice would be giggling at Bobbie. *Carl, watch the road, honey.*

"I don't know. Three hundred maybe. He took care of everything and paid all the bills."

"We'll ask the court for a hundred," she says, "but you'll probably only get seventy-five because you work, too." Bobbie reaches for the pencils on the desk, and I pull him back. "You have to give him visitation, you know," she says. "A father is entitled to visitation with his children, unless he's a danger to them."

I can still see us all in the pickup, and I feel like crying now. "Carl can see his kids whenever he wants. We don't have any problems about our kids. We both love them." Bobbie is getting restless; I have to get out of here. "Can't you just file some papers," I ask her. "Do I have to be there?"

She looks up at me. I wonder how she gets her hair to fluff back from the sides that way. Her earrings are probably real gold. "You have to be there, Ellen. Carl filed a petition for visitation. He wants to have the children with him every other weekend, starting this Friday night." I don't understand what she's talking about. Is he coming home this weekend? "I'll meet you at the courthouse around nine," she says. "Don't be late and try not to bring the children. It's not a good place for children."

I hand her the money from Mom. "I have to bring the kids," I say. "There's no one to watch them."

She seems annoyed and stands up. "Well, all right then, if it can't be helped." Now she opens the door to the reception area, and I stand up with Bobbie, whose bottle drops to the floor. I have to bend down, holding him to get it. My ass is so big, it bumps against her door. Janice is still sucking her thumb, waiting for me. We finally get out of the office.

The night before we have to go to court I'm sitting on the front steps waiting for Mom to come over and holding Bobbie while Janice rides her tricycle up and down the cracked sidewalk. In June it seemed the summer would never end. Now August is going faster and faster. Bobbie's just had his bath and smells good from baby powder. His hair is blond like Carl's and it's soft and clean from being washed. The molasses smell from the feed store is blowing this way again, mixing with the velvety purple-and-white petunias by the steps. All that sweetness. I bury my face in Bobbie's hair, and then Mom is here, getting out of her car, holding a package and a bunch of wildflowers. Bobbie reaches out to go to her.

"I saw this blouse at the store today—thought maybe you would like it, you know, to wear tomorrow. Your Pop sent the flowers over. He said to tell you 'good luck.'"

I put the flowers on the step and unwrap the box. It's a plain white blouse, polyester, size sixteen. "Thanks, Mom," I say. Then I look at the flowers Dad sent, phlox and black-eyed Susans, and something else.

"What's this purple flower in with the daisies?"

She sits down on the step with me. "Loosestrife," she says. "You know it's August when the loosestrife comes." I run my hands over the tall spiky purple plumes. "It's pretty. Is it a flower or a weed?"

"A weed," she says. "It's choking out the pond, but your father won't mow it down 'cause he likes the color. You and your Pop like flowers and pretty things, but loosestrife doesn't hold up as a cut flower; it falls apart right away, drops all over the table." She smoothes Bobbie's hair with her hand. I know she's thinking about the way he's going to look like Carl. "Have you heard any more from him?" she asks.

"No," I say, "Not since he called about wanting to see the kids this weekend. He's angry at me, I know it, about this court thing. He just started a new job and now he's going to lose a day's pay."

"Well, he has no cause to be angry. You should be the one that's angry, a man not supporting his family."

I don't want to fight with her. Tomorrow, when I see Carl, everything's going to be all right again. I just know it. He'll explain what's happening and hold me. Maybe he can stay over before he has to go back. I hope we can all be together this weekend.

She goes on. "You still don't even know exactly where he's working, do you? I mean the name of the company?"

Bobbie's eyes are closing, and I've got to get him in his crib. "He couldn't talk much, it's long distance. I guess I'll find out tomorrow when I see him."

Mom gives me the baby to put to bed. "I'll sit out here and watch Janice," she says.

Janice sees him first. I'm busy signing in with the guard and looking for my lawyer, plus trying to change Bobbie (there's no place to put him down in the ladies' room except the floor). Janice is leaning over the railing that goes all around the marble staircase in the center of the courthouse. She's got her tummy bent over the top railing, her panties showing. "Get down, baby," I tell her. "You'll fall down those stairs."

"There's Daddy," she says, turning around. "Daddy!"

Carl is coming up the stairs; his blond hair is slicked back and he's wearing a shirt I never saw. I just wait and hold on to Bobbie. He'll see me in a minute. Now Carl bends down and scoops up Janice, hugging her. Janice has her arms around his neck.

"Hey, hey, how's my princess? You're getting so pretty I almost didn't know you! How's Daddy's girl? You miss me, darlin'? Did you miss your Daddy?"

He sees me over Janice's head, I know he does, but I go on waiting. Now I see that a very young girl in tight red stirrup pants is standing next to Carl. She's short and suntanned; white hoop earrings dangle from under her black curly hair. "Janice," he says, "this here's my friend Marie. Marie, this is my little girl." Janice gets shy and keeps her forehead pressed against Carl's chest. He tries to pull her face up. "Janice, say 'hello' to Marie."

"Oh, Carl, she's so cute," Marie says.

Bobbie is getting restless again, so I take out his bottle. He doesn't even notice Carl. Five months is a long time for a toddler. I can leave him on the bench with his bottle and get up. He'll stay put. I smooth down my skirt—it's all wrinkled, and there's a damp spot on the front from the baby. "Carl," I say. "I want to talk to you."

He puts Janice down and she hides her face against his leg. "What is it? I don't have much to say to you," he says. The girl named Marie is making funny faces and finally gets Janice to turn her head and giggle.

"Who is this, Carl?" I say, pointing at Marie. Funny words are coming out of my mouth, not the words I want to say to him. I want him to see me with our kids, like in a picture frame, and remember the good times, us being just married and making love all the time. I want him to pull me to him so hard I can feel his belt buckle. *Carl, it's me, Ellen.*

Remember how you like my molasses cookies? Let's all get in the pickup. Do you see how long my hair has gotten? Those are my real words, stuck in my throat like ketchup or something. All that comes out is bitter little drops. "You said you were in Buffalo looking for a better job! Who is this girl? What is she doing here?"

"I have nothing to say to you, Ellen," he says. "My lawyer will be here soon. Let the lawyers handle it." He turns away and bends down to whisper something to Marie. The top of her head only comes up to his shoulder, even though she's wearing spiky heels. Carl puts his arm around her thin waist. I look at his fingers holding the wide black plastic belt. There's his wedding band. Janice is standing between us, watching them. Now I see my lawyer coming up the staircase. She was right; this isn't a good place for children.

It seems like hours before our case is called. The corridor outside the courtroom is filled with people and children. The crowd spills over to the staircase and landing, everyone talking. Sometimes someone starts crying. Our lawyers, Carl's and mine, keep their distance from us and wait down the hall near the library, "conferencing," my lawyer calls it. I hardly get a chance to tell her anything before she takes her briefcase and goes to talk to Carl's lawyer. Finally she leaves him and comes back to see me.

"Ellen, they have a proposal to make, to settle the case. Let's try to find a quiet place so I can explain it to you." She looks pleased with herself, as if she's done something wonderful.

"Who is the 'they?'" I ask. It better not be Marie; she's got nothing to do with all this.

"Carl and his lawyer," she says. "Come inside the courtroom. It's empty right now and we can talk in here." She leads me inside this huge courtroom. I'm carrying Bobbie. It looks like on TV, except there's no judge, only a uniformed guard who is reading his newspaper and looking bored. We sit down at a long mahogany table where lawyers usually sit. It's been polished so much I can see my face in its surface.

"This is the deal," my lawyer says, looking at her yellow

pad. "He'll pay seventy-five dollars a week child support based on his average income of three hundred dollars. I couldn't get them to talk about overtime, *but* he'll keep the children covered under his health insurance. He has a very good plan with his company."

"What company?" I break in.

"We'll get to that. Let me finish explaining the proposal." She turns over a page and reads some more. "His health plan covers dental *and* optical—even some psychiatric treatment if the children ever need it." I look at Bobbie and try to picture him at a psychiatrist's office. "*Plus,* he'll make the children the irrevocable beneficiaries of his life insurance."

I'm wondering what "irrevocable" means, but I don't interrupt her yet. "Now, on the visitation, twice a month like I told you, *and* he agrees to do all the transportation. He wants to pick the children up around seven on Friday nights, and he'll get them back by 6:00 P.M. on Sundays. Holidays are to be...."

Now I interrupt her. "Wait. Janice and Bobbie don't have anything wrong with their health, and Bobbie is just getting his molars; he doesn't need a dentist." Everything is happening very fast, like a high-speed train, and I have to slow it down. I put my hand over her yellow pad so she looks up at me surprised.

"Ellen, why are you so upset? It's a very good settlement."

"I don't know anything that's happening!" I say. "Where does he work? Where does he live? Is there a crib there? How can he take care of Janice and Bobbie? The baby doesn't even know him anymore." I'm squeezing Bobbie and crying.

She hears the part about Bobbie and stands up. "You're right, Ellen. There shouldn't be weekend visitation with the baby. He's too young. How about when he's three? We'll just let him have Janice for now. He can visit with the baby when he picks up Janice." She smiles brightly at me, another problem solved, and heads for the door. "Oh," she says, "The company he works for—very stable, a large construction company called Di Pasquale and Sons in Lockport, near Buffalo. Now don't get upset, but I think it's Marie's father. But it doesn't matter, they're a large company." I don't say anything, which seems to surprise her. "I'll get right back to you, don't worry," she says. "One more conference should do it, and then I think we have a settlement."

I wait at the mahogany table. The court officer puts down his paper. "She's a good lawyer," he says. "She's here a lot." I want to ask him if it always happens this fast—if people's lives get chopped up like this, in a hallway, with no time to sort it all out—but he starts reading his paper again, so I just wait for my lawyer to come back. I give Bobbie some cookies and a banana from the diaper bag. It's good I brought along food.

Just before one o'clock we go before the judge. Marie has to wait outside. "She's not a party to the action," my lawyer says. I let Janice wait outside with Marie. Janice is overexcited from all the people and is dancing around. I force myself to talk to Marie, but I don't really look at her; I'm looking at Janice wriggling.

"Please take her to the bathroom."

"Sure, honey," she says.

Carl blows a kiss at Marie as we go through the doors to the courtroom. I'm numb as I sit there and listen to the lawyers explain the settlement. Bobbie's tummy is full of banana and cookies, and he's smiling at everyone. The judge beams at him, "What a good looking little fellow." Then the judge asks me if I understand what's been "put on the record." This is my chance to say no, I don't understand any of it, but my lawyer whispers to me, "say 'Yes, Your Honor,'" so I do.

It's over very fast and then we're all standing outside again in the hall. The lawyers shake hands. Carl comes over to talk to me. "What time can I pick her up? It's a long drive back."

"Come by at four," I tell him.

"Why can't I just come get her now, follow you back to the house?" he asks.

"Because I have things to do, that's why." He drops his

head and doesn't argue. Imagine that! Carl not taking charge! Marie is holding Janice's hand and I go and pull her away. "Come on, Janice. We have to go now, baby." Janice has these pale blue smudges under her eyes that she gets when she's tired, and I know she'll fall asleep in the car.

The road back from the courthouse passes near Mom and Pop's place, and I decide to stop. Bobbie and Janice are asleep in the back, curled around each other. I go up on the side porch and knock but no one's home. They probably went shopping.

In back of the house where I grew up, there's this pond. When I was little, it was one of my favorite places. Pop kept goldfish in there for me, and each spring there were tadpoles that turned into little green frogs, and then by August they were big enough to play with. I sit down on an old webbed lounge chair by the side of the pond, facing west. I can smell the cut grass, and I lift my face to the afternoon sun, letting it burn my skin one more time before summer's over. Close to me, I hear the little splashes of the frogs. Far in the background are the sounds of cars and trucks from the road.

I'm almost asleep like a cat when Janice comes over and puts her head in my lap. Her hair is sweaty from sleep and there are creases on her face from the car upholstery. "Is Bobbie up?" I ask her.

"No," she says, her arms hugging me around my stomach. "Are we going to wait for Gram and Poppy to come back?"

I pull myself out of the lounge chair and look at her. She's never going to have anything like what I had as a little girl, that's what Carl has done; he's stolen a lot of good times from Janice and Bobbie. I want to hurt him so bad for stealing from my babies; I wish I could stick something in him. "We can't wait, Janice," I tell her, "We have to go home to get you packed, so you'll be ready for Daddy when he comes."

Janice looks at me. I can see she's scared and doesn't know what to do. This is all so new, so strange for her.

"Let's pick some flowers, honey," I say, "so you can give them to Daddy when he comes to get you."

In a minute she's off and running around the edge of the pond, picking handfuls of black-eyed Susans.

"Janice, take the tall purple ones and take the loosestrife, too," I tell her. "They're so pretty. You give some of those to your daddy."

MICHELLE RAMSEY

Kevin

◆

It had been warm, clear and sunny. The children and I spent the day playing in the pool and picking fresh vegetables from our garden. While I prepare dinner for my family, my gaze wanders out the back window and rests on my children, who are playing in the back yard. Beyond the children, our Golden Retriever is chasing the ball my son has just thrown with all of his might. As I turn to set the table, my husband walks through the front door. In his hand is a huge bouquet of sweet-smelling flowers he has just bought on his way home from work from the corner flower peddler. "Just because I love you!" he says with a big smile on his face. His job has always provided more than enough financially for all of our needs and wants. My job, by choice, has been to stay home and care for our children, decorate our newly built home, and volunteer at our children's private school.

Here is where I always wake up.

This fairy-tale scenario is a wonderful dream; it's not my reality. Here I am almost thirty, a single parent of a three-year-old boy and back living in my mother's home.

Sunny days are still beautiful and clear, but instead of picking fresh vegetables from my own garden, I'm usually picking weeds from Grandma's flower bed or mowing her lawn. Instead of preparing dinner for my family, I'm usually opening a can of Spaghettios or thawing a microwave dinner for my son, Kevin, as I rush off to another night class. Since I am living with my mother, I have traded the dream of a Golden Retriever for a furry hamster named Gus, a lizard named Puff and a fish named Fishy-Fishy.

Sometimes as I lie awake at night, worrying about our future, I wish there was someone to lie beside me, to hold my hand and worry with me. That reassuring someone, to let me know things will turn out all right. I spend those long nights alone, thinking about Kevin's college choices, who he will marry and whether or not he will blame me for his not having a father. I have all of those future worries on my mind, and last month I couldn't even buy him new socks.

My dream-life illustrates the gulf between what I want and what I have, but I feel the real loss in everyday happenings with my son. I always thought I would be able to coddle my children when they were sick—make them chicken noodle soup and warm Jello while we read book after book. Never in my wildest dreams did I imagine I would have to leave my sick child because I couldn't afford to take a zero on a "no make-up" midterm.

All of Kevin's friends have fathers at home, and these fathers are very active in their children's lives. They read to their kids, keep the peace when things get out of control and teach their sons how to play baseball. When I think about this, I usually feel sick to my stomach. I worry that Kevin is somehow being cheated.

Today as we played at the park, Kevin's friend told him about the baseball game he and his father had gone to together. Here it comes! I thought.

"Mom?"

"Yes, Kevin?"

"Where's my daddy?"

"I don't know, honey."

As fast as the subject popped into his mind, it was again forgotten. Kevin and his friend ran off to re-enact the baseball game his friend had vividly described. I sat alone thinking about what he had just said. As I watched the boys playing, I thought back to all of those warm summer nights Kevin and I spent in the back yard practicing baseball. I showed him how to hold the bat and told him when to swing. He missed and became so frustrated that he wanted to "just play catch instead." But as I watched these two playing, my little boy was hitting pitch after pitch! Soon after the game had ended, the friend's father came to take home his son. Kevin and I walked slowly to our car, hand in hand, watching his friend. Kevin's serious little face turned to analyze mine. I could feel his tiny mind working.

"Mom?"

"Yes, Kevin?"

"It's okay, we can find a new daddy tomorrow."

As I picked him up to hug him tight, I told him how proud I was that he had hit the baseball so many times. I had never dreamed a mom could teach a little boy how to play baseball—and how to play it successfully, too!

Baseball coach, nurse, mud bug collector, the role of a single parent is never clearly defined. It is not something you can teach, nor is it something that can be learned. The special relationship between a parent and a child going it alone is one you must experience to understand.

The special relationship between Kevin and me began nine months before he was born. It was an unplanned pregnancy and a time of gut-wrenching fear and late-night crying. I knew there was no choice. No decision to be made. I would have the baby! Alone if my boyfriend didn't want to be a part of it. From that first bright blue, positive pregnancy test, to the day of his birth, I knew that deep in my soul we would be all right.

There are times when the love I feel for him cannot be described with words. Times I want to shout to the world, "This is my son, isn't he beautiful, isn't he smart?"

It hadn't been my first choice to raise my child alone, but it became my only choice. I don't think I realized how hard and lonely the journey labeled "single parenthood" would be at times. Two months after we had been on our own, my strength and ability as a single parent was put to a heart-stopping test. Kevin was ten months old and very bright and happy. He had a head of soft, curly brown hair, big brown eyes and a smile full of teeth that could blind you on a sunny day. It had been a typical day of playing, standing and trying to take those first steps. I put him down—against his pro-tests—for a late afternoon nap. When he awoke from the nap I was shocked to find him wet and dripping with sweat, whin-ing and moaning. I checked his temperature which was 103 degrees. I was reassured by those around me that children get high fevers. My churning stomach and racing heartbeat told me otherwise. Not wanting to be the "over-reacting" parent that all pediatricians dread, I chose to wait and see in the morning. We went to sleep.

Morning seemed to be an eternity away as I watched and dozed, cried and prayed. Dawn mercifully came and, to my horror, brought with it a new sky-rocketing temperature of 105 degrees. My bright-eyed healthy baby looked like a dif-ferent child. His curls were dripping with sweat, the bright brown eyes were now dull with the fever and dark circles had formed beneath them. The smile was gone. How could fifteen hours have changed my child into this inconsolable, sick baby?

As we headed for the doctor's office, I felt numb with a fear that I hadn't experienced since childhood, when mon-sters lived underneath my bed. Our doctor looked at Kevin, ordered a blood test and left the room. The nerve-shattering silence and the absence of the doctor told me more than any consultation I had ever been given. The wait was short and the results were shocking. Her exact words were, "Kevin is a very sick little boy and I would like you to go straight to Chil-dren's Hospital."

The ride to the hospital seemed endless as I cried without making a sound. To this day, I can't even recall how long it took or what the weather was like. I do remember taking a wrong turn in a neighborhood that I should have known like the back of my hand. Once there, the emergency room physician somberly and bluntly told me she suspected spinal meningitis. It was possible that the fluid surrounding the brain had been affected. After two hours of tests and X-rays (that will haunt my dreams forever), the staff informed me I would have to leave for the final test. They didn't want Kevin to associate my face with the final procedure that had to be done. I left that room sobbing uncontrollably. I hunted madly for a cigarette machine although I hadn't smoked for two years. I finally found a nurse smoking in an alley outside the entrance. I think I offered her five dollars for a cigarette. She took one look at my face, tear-stained and swollen, and offered the whole pack for free. Those were the longest and coldest fifteen minutes of my life. Enormous feelings of guilt, blame and failure tore through my aching heart.

When they let me back into the hospital room, I saw my child lying silently on a cold, stainless steel table, curled into a ball, wearing nothing but a diaper, sucking his thumb. He had never sucked his thumb before. I had failed him. I hadn't been there to comfort him. I picked up Kevin and looked into his big brown eyes, glazed over with the fever he could not break. At that moment the stone-faced doctor began explaining spinal meningitis to me and how long we would have to wait for the test results. I realized right then how much this tiny person really meant to me. I had always loved him, of course, but places deep inside me, places that I hadn't known existed, began to ache with fear. Dark places inside whispered softly the worst case scenario, while my heart and smiling face tried to show Kevin only the best and most positive. Then suddenly another feeling swept over me, like a light switching on inside me. YES! I loved this little boy more than anything on earth. When I focused on the warmth and sense of fulfillment he had already given me, my mouth automatically curved into a heartfelt smile. My tears instantly stopped flowing. Nothing in this white, sterile hospital around us would stop us from beating this.

Kevin was admitted and I didn't leave his side. From the

first antibiotic I.V., Kevin improved. The test results came back at midnight: negative. I smiled again. I knew Kevin and I were defeating this unknown monster.

We stayed in the hospital for three long days and I only left his side to shower while he slept. Something wonderful happened when we were there. Not only did we bond as an invincible team, we discovered a support system of family and friends that I hadn't noticed before. I learned we weren't alone. Kevin had a wonderful grandmother and an aunt and uncle that most kids can only wish for. I just hadn't been looking in the right places for these people who were waiting to help.

We never learned what evil monster we had defeated, and the events of those days still live in my nightmares. At times, when a high fever shows up, I'm scared the monster has returned. The beautiful little boy I have today, however, makes it all seem a lifetime ago.

After clearing this hurdle, I felt we could never be defeated. We were on our way to beginning a whole new life. It didn't take long to come down from that high, however. I soon learned no matter how hard I tried, I couldn't forget the past. I would often catch myself thinking back to the beginning and how it was supposed to be.

"It's a boy!" the doctor announced happily three years ago. At the time I thought this would be the outcome that would make everything turn out all right. My boyfriend of five years had not been happy about the pregnancy. I believed that a son would make the transition easier for him. This would definitely help us move on. We would be married as planned and our son would never have to know about his rocky and uncertain beginning.

Believing this with all of my heart, I chose to name him after his father, Kevin Charles Williams. Kevin was the name of his father. Our son would be the junior that all men desire. Charles was the name of his paternal grandfather. This would be the manly bond these three men would always have. Williams was the surname the three of us—mother, father and child—were going to share.

As time progressed, it became apparent that this would not come to pass. The wedding never happened and the manly bond between father and son never developed. I became a single parent. As I struggled alone to provide for my infant son, I began to have uncomfortable feelings about the differences in our names. Everyday happenings kept this difference in the foreground of our lives. Trips to the pharmacy with a sick baby burning with fever, waiting an eternity for the pharmacist to call my name.

"Mrs. Williams?"

"Mrs. Williams?" the pharmacist called again.

"Oh! You mean me," I said. "Ramsey, Ms. Ramsey, I'm sorry I didn't know you were calling for me." The anger and frustration would build up in me as I tried to smile at this complete stranger who couldn't care less what my name was. The pharmacist would always give me that look that said, "Oh great, another one of these."

There were also the endless annoying phone calls from telemarketing companies.

"Is Mr. or Mrs. Williams in?" the children's book salesman would ask.

"There is no Mr. or Mrs. Williams here," I would say in a tone dripping with hatred. The poor minimum-wage employees on the other end of the phone would often end up with the full weight of my frustration on their shoulders. Whatever they were selling, they never had a chance once the conversation began with "Mrs. Williams."

I began to think seriously about changing Kevin's last name to my own, Ramsey. I researched the process with phone calls to Superior Court and Municipal Court. I was originally told by an uninformed court clerk that there was no way to change the name of a minor without the signature of both parents. Kevin's father was among the growing population of absentee fathers, so I knew this possibility was out of the question. I put the idea in the back of my mind and went on with everyday life.

Kevin soon became active in preschool activities. The difference in our names began to surface again. Parents of his friends, who have always been acquaintances of mine, would invite "Kevin Ramsey" to birthday parties. "Kevin Ramsey" soon became the new kid in Sunday School.

"No, his last name is Williams," I would correct.

"Oh, are you divorced?" a nosy parent would always ask.

"No, his father and I were never married."

"Oh?" people responded with one raised eyebrow and eyes quickly lowering to the floor.

After these explanations I would be left alone to sit and wonder what right these people felt they had to question the most private and painful parts of my life. I always felt defensive and out of place with these "perfect" families surrounding me.

I decided I would contact an attorney about a name change. The attorney advised me that it was possible to petition the court since the father's whereabouts were unknown. She would be happy to handle the case for me for the mere charge of $900.00, no guarantees attached. I thanked her, lied, saying I would get back to her, and walked out feeling very discouraged. The plan was once again put in the back of my mind, soon to be forgotten.

At two and a half, Kevin began to have violent temper tantrums. Even worse than those of the average two-year-old. During these outbursts, he would often tell me he was different.

"I am brown and you are white. I am Williams and you are Ramsey, why?"

I knew that since Kevin was biracial, race and color were very big issues that I would have to address. I didn't, however, expect it to be so soon. We would talk about the differences and the reasons for our skin color as well as our names. He understood that there were black people, white people and lots of colors of brown in between. He thought it was pretty cool that he already had the tan that his Auntie Cheryl used to try so hard to acquire. When we got to the explanations for our names he would respond with, "that's dorky." The fear welled up inside me. My son was already feeling insecure and separated from me. I felt completely helpless.

Another month passed, and Kevin and I were going to spend the day at Discovery Zone, an indoor playground for kids. The friendly worker was taking our shoes and asked Kevin, "What's your name?"

"Kevin Charles Ramsey," he responded. I looked down at my son and saw him looking up at me, his face beaming from ear to ear with a huge smile. My son had decided on his own how to fix the "dorky" difference between us that I had fretted over for two years. I decided then and there that I would find a way to make this change legal.

I began to ask the people around me if they knew anything about the process. I found another single mother at my church who had been through the same thing. She had successfully gone to court on her own, without a high-priced attorney, and had her daughter's name changed to her own. She became my mentor. I received step-by-step instructions from her. "Just go for it! Everything will work out for the best," she reassured me.

Three months after the day Kevin announced he was Kevin Charles Ramsey, I found the way to make it legal. I prepared my own legal papers and went to court. The judge was very sympathetic to my desire for family unity. He told me he would, however, need proof of the absence of the father before the petition could be granted. I was disappointed but not defeated. I had an eight-day continuance to get some kind of proof. Now the only thing in my way was how to prove someone had vanished from the face of the earth. I left the courtroom and mailed a registered return receipt letter to his last known address. To my relief, it was returned to me five days later stamped, RETURN TO SENDER; MOVED LEFT NO FORWARDING ADDRESS. I had my proof, but would it be enough?

The day of my continuance, I arrived at the courthouse with thirty minutes to spare.

"All rise," the court clerk announced.

Oh no! It was a different judge. Before I had time to worry, she was announcing the first case.

"Kevin Williams," the woman with the black robe announced.

"Kevin is a minor. I'm his mother, Michelle Ramsey."

The judge didn't speak but looked down at the papers and began to read. The silence was deafening as I stood nervously in front of that high bench with a courtroom full of shoplifters, prostitutes and drunk drivers sitting behind me waiting their turn. It seemed like an eternity before she finally spoke.

"Has this matter already been heard?" the black robe asked.

"Yes, I was before Judge Chow last week and he asked me to provide some sort of proof before the petition could be granted," I said.

"Do you have the proof?" asked the black robe.

"Yes, I have a registered letter that was returned to me. It was sent to the father's last known address. I also contacted his last employer that was on file with the Washington State Office of Support Enforcement," I replied.

The robe reached for the letter and examined it. "Let the record show that a letter was returned with no forwarding address given," said the robe. "Petition granted. Please step forward and I will sign the order."

I was so ecstatic I could barely keep from bursting into laughter. I stepped forward to the clerk to receive the paperwork. As I reached for the papers, the judge leaned down and said with a smile, "Good luck to you."

"Thank you," I said with a smile. The black robe was actually a very nice woman who probably had her own kids at home. I looked at her again not wanting to forget this feeling, or the look on her face. She was already stern again, calling the next case. I never felt happier.

As I left the courtroom, I smiled at everyone. I felt as though a huge weight had been removed from my chest. Another chapter of the painful past had closed.

Kevin and I are healing and we're going to be just fine. I'll always remember Friday, February 19, 1993, as the first day of Kevin Charles Ramsey's life, as well as the last time I will ever have to explain who I am or who my son is. When I walked outside I saw my mother and my son waiting for me.

"Hi, Kevin Ramsey," I said.

"Thank goodness!" said my mother. As for Kevin Ramsey, he just gave me that huge smile.

Kevin will be four in April. He is the spark that makes my life wonderful. He is my motivation to go on. Tonight, as he was getting ready for bed, he stopped to sing me a song he improvised from one of our favorite storybooks.

I love you forever,
I like you for always,
As long as I'm being here,
My mommy you'll be!

As he went to sleep, I cried. I knew that somewhere, somehow, I had succeeded.

SHEILA RULE

Sheila & Sean

◆

I'd always wanted to be a mother when I grew up. Well, I finally grew up at about the age of forty. But by that time I was long-divorced and there was no man in sight looking toward "our" future or gleefully calculating that baby would make three. And I was living rather nomadically as a foreign correspondent, decidedly not a lifestyle conducive to maternity or other ventures grounded in stability.

But the yearning to be a mother fights long and dies hard. It was that yearning as much as anything else that threw me against a wall and blocked my exit until I examined my life. What I saw was a life made up of years of longing to be a mother, a good man's partner, a homemaker, a longing to be tied to routine, stability and responsibility for someone else's well-being.

I'd seemed headed in domesticity's direction in my youth, partly due to society's programming, no doubt, but I think overwhelmingly because of personal passion. Of course, I had another career in mind as well; virtually every black woman I knew worked outside the home as a matter of necessity. And, besides, my mother always drilled in her daughters the following: "Be able to take care of yourself." (Sometimes I think

I learned my lesson too well; I became intensely independent and rarely asked for help of any kind.) I decided early on that I would be a writer of some sort and from the age of nine or ten would spend St. Louis's humid, soporific summers writing what I passed off as novels, usually written on compact lined stationery. But invariably, those novels had as their centerpiece a very big, very happy, very loving family. In the eighth grade, home economics was my favorite subject. Even as a journalism major in college, I took a couple of home economics courses and enjoyed them far more than the biology, Italian and Journalism 101 that I was required to sit through.

After college, I married the boy next door; well, actually the boy who lived down the street. Now the fantasies would flower into reality, I figured. Wrong. After only a few years and countless emotional storms, the marriage seemed like just so much debris littering our lives. I moved to New York City—and later to Kenya and England and then back to New York—and lived the life of a single woman. I had somehow lost my way to that state of being called motherhood.

But at forty, in the throes of one hell of a midlife crisis (on second thought, maybe it was an unrelenting wake-up call), I found a compass inside myself and got my bearings. I had to face the fact that I had inadvertently stolen a part of me from myself and, in order to reclaim it, I had to become a mother. Sure of purpose, I decided to adopt a child.

As I write this, I am about nine months into motherhood and life with Sean. That's my son's name. He's four and a half and, you know, the usual: bright, adorable, funny, affectionate. What else can I say; he's a great kid who is a balm to my soul. I am truly blessed. But I think we were meant to be.

I first laid eyes on him in a photograph. I had taken my parents, who were visiting me in New York, to the Association of Black Social Workers' adoption services office to look through books filled with pictures and bios of children available for adoption. After I jotted down the ones who appealed to me—I was interested in a son between the ages of two and five—the adoption worker handed me a photo of a beaming little boy who had not yet been entered in the book. Something about him reminded me of my sister, Lynn, when she was little; maybe the way he was hamming it up for the camera. My parents and I agreed that he should be added to my list. As it turned out, the other little boys I'd picked had been featured in the books for some time and had a head start in finding homes. They were already spoken for. Sean was the only one still available.

We first met about a year ago at the adoption agency. I arrived, bearing gifts, after a sleepless night in which my anxiety conjured up a hodgepodge of nightmarish scenarios, including one in which he ran screaming from the room at the sight of me and another that had him staying in the room but standing cowering in a corner and refusing to play with me.

Of course, I didn't know then who I was dealing with. Sean, dressed in a suit and tie, came bearing joy, acceptance and curiosity. He is a gregarious meeter and greeter, a hi-what's-your-name-how-ya-doin-can-we-talk kind of guy. We hit it off, even though I don't think he initially had a real notion of just who I was and why I was there. I told him I was his new friend and that my name was Sheila; he decided to call me "lady" as in "hey, lady." Now Sean calls me "Mommy," a name often preceded by the words "I love you," especially when he thinks he's in hot water or when it's time for him to call it a night. This thing called motherhood is more wonderful than I ever imagined but at the same time unbelievably H-A-R-D and D-E-M-A-N-D-I-N-G, with lots of exclamation marks and absolutely nothing in lower case. Sometimes I feel inept and just want to cry out, "H-E-L-P!!!!" But then again, one of the best lessons I've learned in this journey is that I can put down some of my be-able-to-take-care-of-yourself spirit. While it's still not that easy to put aside my independence—or to fight my basic shyness—I know that when it comes to Sean, I need to do it. I am, after all, his advocate and when you get right down to it, I'm all that he's got. And so I pick up the phone and call a friend of a friend who's never heard of me but who I've heard has children who

benefited from lessons that helped prepare them for kindergarten. Or after trying for nearly an hour to remove a splinter
from Sean's finger, I take him to pre-school and ask one of his
teachers if she's any good at taking out splinters. I even talk to
strangers, reluctantly, at Sean's urging.

"Ask that man what that thing is he's carrying, Mommy."

"You ask him, Sean, if you want to know."

"No, you ask him Mommy."

"Oh, alright, okay.... Excuse me, but could you tell
us..." And I call on friends to help me out, to babysit, to
give me guidance, to lend me an ear or a shoulder.

All the while, I'm continually monitoring my behavior,
about as much as I monitor Sean's. At least it seems that way.
It feels kind of like standing outside myself and watching me
watching Sean. Did I come down too hard on him that time?
Could I have said that more softly? Good Lord, Sheila (also
known at times as Monster Mommy), where's that deep res-
ervoir of patience that you've always been admired for? Am I
letting him watch too much television? What's the big deal;
why not let him have pickles for breakfast? Do I really have
any idea of what I'm doing? Do I really like children? Would
it be easier if there was a daddy in our lives?

This last question is sometimes the hardest because it is
the one over which I have the least control. And also because
Sean is truly a man's man. He loves to mix it up with men,
truly lights up when one enters a room, seems to react to the
authority in their voices with greater haste than to the authority in mine. There are good men in our lives but no constant,
everyday presence who can be depended on to help guide
Sean in the rituals and ways of manhood. So we do the best
we can.

On Saturday afternoons, for example, I usually find myself sitting among other African-American mothers outside a
seen-better-days auditorium in Harlem. Inside the hall, our
sons and daughters are put through their paces as beginning
karate students. Sean doesn't particularly like going—too big
an emphasis on discipline for him, I think—but I think we've

got to give it a chance. The classes are taught by black men who are trying to cloak our sons in a rich coat of virtues, including love of self and others, respect and honor, strength and compassion.

In some ways, making our way to karate every Saturday is akin to standing watch over Sean in a society that places little value on the lives of black men, one that defines them in terms of pathology rather than promise. As a black parent, I must explore these and other ways of the world that white parents rarely consider.

For black children, it is a disheartening reality that even people who mean no harm will harm them with messages of inferiority or invisibility. It is also true that he will run up against children of his own race who may challenge his blackness, as they view his command of English or his interest in academics (if I'm lucky) as "acting white." The minefield of race and class will be everywhere, just waiting for him to take the wrong path or trip. I must help him cross this minefield without instilling in him paralyzing fear or anger. I must help him develop a strong racial identity and pride, while not alienating him from people of other races.

I wish I could stand guard over Sean everywhere and everyday of his precious life. But I know I cannot. For now, just as I check his little body for scrapes and bruises as a matter of course, I also look in his words, gestures or behavior for bruises of an emotional kind, even those I may have unintentionally inflicted.

As evening stakes its claim and I draw the shade in Sean's room, having honored our daily rituals and put him to bed, I sometimes pause to think about what my life was like before he entered it. I contemplate the hectic parade of humanity on the busy street outside his window and wonder where they are going, these people with blank stares, carefree smiles or knitted-brow scowls, and what awaits them at the end of their journey. I think of how, only a few months earlier, I was among them but am now locked into routine and responsibility that doesn't often allow me to be on the streets past dusk.

And then, the falling shade obscures my vision and I turn away. I dim the lights, look at my little boy sleeping, make sure he's still breathing (I can't help it) and walk softly out of his room. A sense of peace gently rocks my heart. I enjoy this child so.

BEVERLY DONOFRIO

Breaking Up Is Hard To Do

◆

When my son Jason left for college I wept for months. So what else is new, right? Except that back when I was seventeen and found out I was pregnant, I never in a million years thought I'd be sad when my kid left home. Even before he was born I looked forward to the day he would leave. I imagined it being like Bastille Day for the starving French masses.

Abortion wasn't legal and I didn't know how to get one illegally, so his father and I got married. Because I was carrying high, my mother and aunts said I was having a boy. No way would I believe them. There was no boy in my belly. It was a girl and she looked just like me. She had a round little baseball head covered with black hair. Her eyes were big and brown. She'd be my best friend and there'd be nothing in the world we wouldn't talk about. The minute she could string words into a sentence she'd say clitoris, orgasm, birth control. She would definitely go to college, and her name would be Nicole after a schizophrenic on my favorite soap opera. Just in case it was a boy, Stephen and I decided on Jason after Jason McCord, the Lawman.

I awoke from the anesthetic to a nurse holding out a wrinkly baby, saying, "Congratulations, Mrs. B., you have a healthy eight-and-a-half pound baby boy."

"Boy!" I screamed. His head was huge and shaped like a football. "What's the matter with his head? He has blond hair." The nurse turned white. I covered my face with my hands and cried my heart out. It was as though my daughter had died. The baby girl I'd been picturing and talking to for months had been a boy all along. What would I do with him? I didn't even like boys. He'd have army men and squirt guns and baseball cards and a PENIS. Later I took a walk to the nursery and looked at him, a little lump under a white blanket. If it weren't for his name on the bassinet, I thought, I wouldn't even know he was my child.

The first time Jason came to my room, I was scared of him. He was soft and warm and smelled sweet like baby, but he moved his head like a dinosaur in a Japanese movie. Then he got the hiccups after half an ounce of milk and started crying. The next time I was braver. I took off his undershirt and memorized how his diaper was pinned so I could duplicate it, then took it off too. I'd never seen an uncircumcised penis before. It looked like a tiny elephant's trunk. I kissed it. I nuzzled his stomach, his armpit, his neck. I licked his toes.

When I got home, I pontificated to my girlfriends: "It hurts like hell. That miracle shit is a bunch of propaganda. I'll never no matter what have another one as long as I live. I love him, but it's not what you imagine. It's more like you'd love an abandoned puppy you found on the street."

By the time Jase was a year-and-a-half old, my marriage had broken up, leaving me and Jase a couple. I went on welfare and began developing my child-rearing philosophy: If I'm unhappy, the kid will be unhappy. So, as much as I'm able, I'm doing exactly as I please, and Jase is welcome along for the ride. I took him hitchhiking, I took him on acid trips, I took him shoplifting. He was a beautiful hippie kid with long blond hair and big blue eyes; everyone thought he was a girl. I hadn't planned it that way, but he turned out to be a perfect lure for rides and a decoy for stealing—the ladies in the store followed him around instead of me.

Even so, it was a lot harder to do just about everything

with a kid in tow. I harbored a lot of resentment, and at times I was cruel. I'd repeat everything he said for ten minutes. I'd lather white soap on my face, then squinch it into a horrifying grimace and chase him screaming through the house. But he had his ways of getting back. Like the time he was three and we were eating breakfast. It killed me the way he was acting so big, holding a huge glass of orange juice teetering in one hand instead of two. I started talking to him in a pretend foreign language, and acting like he was crazy for not understanding every word. Then when he was about to cry, I reverted to real English. "What's the matter, Jase? I was just asking you what you want to be when you grow up, and you wouldn't answer."

"You were talking stupid."

"I know. I'm sorry. I couldn't help it. But, anyway, what do you want to be when you grow up?"

"A cop."

"A cop!" I choked on my juice. This was the worst thing in the world he could ever want to be as far as I was concerned and he probably knew it. "Why do you want to be a cop?"

"So I can shoot people."

"Shoot people?" This coming from a kid who'd never had a toy gun in his life. "Jason. If you become a cop I'll disown you."

"What does disown mean?"

"It means I'll never talk to you and you won't be allowed in my house ever again."

"Don't say that." His eyes were tearing up.

I decided to use reverse psychology. "Oh, forget it. If you want to be a cop go ahead. I don't care. Really."

I never got to hitchhike to California or live in Europe as I'd always dreamed, but I did get a scholarship to Wesleyan University, which probably never would have happened if I hadn't been an ex-teenage-mother and on welfare. I qualified as a "nontraditional" student. My presence diversified the student body.

Nearly every weekend of his childhood, Jase stayed at my

parents', so for two days a week I could pretend I was child-less and he could pretend he was a part of a whole family. He argued with my two sisters over TV shows, ate three square meals a day, and lived a routine repeated for decades: break-fast at eight, lunch at noon, dinner at five, TV, bath, bed. I spent a lot of time at my parents', too, and it got to be like not just Jase but the two of us were kids. When my mother freaked out about Jase being filthy dirty at the end of a day sloshing around down at the brook, we'd roll our eyes to each other behind her back. I smoked marijuana; Jase knew it was illegal and disapproved: "That stuff stinks. You smoke it too much. I'm telling Pop."

"Go ahead, you little rat. I'll tell Mim you ripped your new pants."

In contrast to my parents' house, ours was utter chaos. We never put anything away. We ate when we were hungry; he could keep as many frogs in jars in his room as he wanted; I let him draw on the walls with crayons. When my typewriter broke, I let him smash it to bits with a baseball bat.

Before I had Jase, my plan was to move to New York City, and as soon as I graduated, in 1978, that's what I did. I wrote poetry and fell in love with a couple of painters while I worked at various mindless and grueling jobs like word pro-cessing, cashiering at Persian rug auctions, and nude model-ing. . . . "Does that make you a call girl?" Jason said.

"What do you mean?"

"Well, men call you up and ask you to take your clothes off, right?"

This was when he was twelve and getting mighty curious about sex, which I'd told him all about when he was three and periodically thereafter, but he always forgot. "Hey, Ma," he said one day after school, "do you give blowjobs?"

That was one thing I hadn't told him about. I didn't skip a beat. "None of your business," I said.

"Come on, Ma. You could tell me. Do you give blow-jobs?"

"I told you it's none of your business."

"Ah, ha, you must or you would've said no. Ich! You

gave blowjobs to Michael?" (A boyfriend Jason particularly despised.) "What does it taste like, bitter?"

"Do you eat girls?"

"You can?"

The realization that Jason was actually very important to me, possibly my best friend, began to creep up on me when he was a teenager, taller than me, and increasingly separate—just when I was about to lose my place as the center of his life.

The summer he was fifteen, nearly sixteen, he had been going to a neighborhood bar on Avenue A, playing pool, then coming home at four in the morning when the bar closed. (When I was Jason's age my father had spied on me and given me punitive curfews like eleven o'clock, so I overcompensated a little.) Jason had a new friend named John, who was twenty-one years old and a carpenter; they played pool every night. Jase would come home excited. "I won seven straight. This guy, the worst pool player, had five balls left on the table and I scratch on the eight ball. I was so pissed, you don't know, Ma."

Once I woke up at five-thirty in the morning and noticed that the living room light was on. I got up to shut it off and saw that Jason's bed was empty. It was five-thirty in the fucking morning and my son wasn't home! I paced around the apartment remembering him earlier in the evening, standing in front of the mirror, turning this way and that, looking at his short T-shirt that left his belly button exposed. He'd asked if he looked okay. I'd told him yes.

I rushed down the avenue to the bar. It was gated and locked, but Tessie, the bartender, was still cleaning up. I rapped on the window. "Did you see Jason?"

She looked puzzled.

"He's tall. Skinny, brown hair, blue eyes. Comes here every night?"

"Oh, yes, yes. Young boy. Good. Don't drink. You his mother?"

I nodded, relieved.

"I see him. He come out with the kids, talk by the door with girls."

Jase, talking to girls outside a bar? I couldn't picture it so I dismissed it. I couldn't even remember the color of his pants to tell the cops. How long should I wait before calling? I remembered this feeling well. It was how I felt when his father told me he'd be home at a certain hour, then showed up half a day later. Was Jase becoming like his father?

I went home and lay on my bed trying to be calm. When Jason was eight years old he had been grazed by a car near the corner market. When I got there the woman behind the register was saying in a loud voice, "I tell these kids not to run across the street. You can't see when a car's coming around that curve." I was a terrible mother who let my kid run wild in the streets. Jason saw me and burst into tears. For the first time I could remember, I wished there was a father there to help me, and him. He got four stitches in his forehead and was forbidden to go to Cross Street again.

I heard the keys turn in the door and Jason sliding his feet as if he were ice skating through the kitchen. "Where were you?" I said, sitting up on my bed. He straightened up, startled, and switched to normal stride. "I didn't think you'd be awake. I didn't think you'd know," he said.

He'd been at John's apartment. We agreed that next time he should call. Once we were both in bed, I thought this over. "Do you think John's gay?" I said from my room.

"There were girls," he said.

Later that summer Jason fell in love with Sophia, a twenty-year-old high school dropout who ran away from home because her father beat her. She moved in with a rock star in England, who also knocked her around and then threw her out. Jason told me that Sophia considered him her friend, not her boyfriend. I went away one weekend and returned to find her sleeping in my bed. There was a note in my typewriter: "Dear Jason, Let us stroll down the street to the cafe and sip cappachino (is that how you spell it) on this lovely summer evening. This typewriter is great. You can erase your mistakes."

She'd been sitting in my chair, writing on my typewriter. She was sleeping in my bed. She even had golden locks. I tiptoed into my room to get something (I forgot now if I really needed whatever it was) and looked at her. She was beautiful. Her shoulder above the sheet was like alabaster, her lips pink and pouty and a little frightened. She was such a child. I wanted to protect her—and I wanted her out of my bed.

That night, as Jase and I ate at an outdoor café, at least ten people greeted him. Was he becoming a pool shark, a barfly, a gigolo? I batted a lemon around my soda and said, "You know, Jase, you're only innocent once in your life and when you lose it, it's gone. Gone forever. When I was young I couldn't wait to grow up. I rushed it. I wanted to know everything, do everything. I was attracted to the seamy side of life. I romanticized creepy people."

"That's you," Jason said. "It's not me. I'm not like that."

That was the truth and I knew it.

"Thank God," I said. We laughed.

For a time Jason had a girlfriend named Cara, from the West Village. She too was raised by a young mother—an artist who Jason said was a little crazy. Cara acted like she was forty. At dinner she gave me tips on how to roast a chicken to make sure it stays juicy. She took charge. She cleared the table and did the dishes. They made out all over the apartment. It grossed me out.

And so, as girls entered Jase's life, I took my last lover for a time, a twenty-one-year-old named Donald who confessed he was intimidated by my son. Jason towered over him and never laughed at his jokes. He all but snickered whenever Donald opened his mouth. The relationship lasted only a couple of months and then there was no other until Jason went off to college. The apartment would be too crowded, I rationalized. There was not enough room for two men in it. The image of the three of us getting up in the morning, drinking coffee, bumping into each other was a horror to me.

◆ ◆ ◆

Jason had planned on going to Wesleyan ever since we'd lived there. When it came time to apply to colleges, I told him he shouldn't limit his prospects. He should apply to other schools too. He was an A student at Stuyvesant with good board scores, but you couldn't be too careful. I urged him to at least choose a safety, CUNY or maybe Cornell.

"But you always told me if I got A's I could go to Wesleyan."

"That's true. But you just can't be sure."

"If I don't get in then I won't go to college."

"You're acting like a baby," I told him. The next day he called me at work to inform me that he was applying to the Air Force Academy. I broke into tears in the office. When I came home that night it was like he was three all over again, telling me he wanted to be a cop. "Jason, why on earth would you ever want to be in the military?"

"So I can fly a fighter jet."

"So, get rich and buy your own jet."

"You can't buy fighter jets. Besides, I want to wear a uniform. I want to carry a gun. I want to kill people." Just like that. Three bullets straight to my heart. So this is what parents mean when they say, "You're killing me."

I decided to use reverse psychology again. I called the Academy and asked for an application. Then I told Jase he would have to get up at dawn and run every day and do pushups. That would be really good for him; he was out of shape and a little wimpy. The only thing we'd have to figure out was how to get a senator to recommend him.

"Forget it," he said.

"Why?"

"I was mad at you. You said I'd get into Wesleyan. You better make sure I do."

This got me really mad. I'd just finished a master's degree, gone through all this college crap myself, and now I had to go through it all over again for him? With his attitude? I was stinked about every little thing. I'd raised a slob. A slob and a prince. He never did anything around the house, but his own dishes, and I had to remind him to do those.

One day I came home from work and Jase was lying on his bed reading.

"Jase, do you need money?" I asked.

"Why?" he said suspiciously.

"Well, I was thinking you could paint the kitchen."

"No thanks." He went back to reading.

"It's generous of me to offer money, considering it's your house, too."

"But I don't care if it's painted."

"Don't you think that after living in this dump for five years without a paint job, it needs one?"

"No. I told you, I don't care."

I thought, there must be some way I can make him do it. When he was little, I would do it with the tone of my voice. Then I thought, well, maybe I'll just kick the little jerk out if he refuses. But since I couldn't do that, I said, "I can't stand you."

"I can't stand *you*," he said.

"I can't stand you more," I said. He went back to reading his book and closed the door to his room with his foot.

I punched the door back open. Furious now. "Don't you ever slam the door in my face."

He looked at me like he was about to vomit. If I were either of my parents I would have slapped him, but because I'm me, I said, "You're an asshole and the biggest baby in the world. You don't even know how to paint. Big spoiled brat!" Then I slammed the door in his face.

By the time he had to fill out his Wesleyan application we were friends again. For his essay he had to write about the person who influenced his life the most. We decided he should write about the absence of his father.

Stephen volunteered for Vietnam after we broke up, and never returned to us. When Jason was eleven he started asking a lot of questions about his father, and I suggested he try to find him. We tracked him down through his grandmother. Jason talked to him for a few minutes on the phone and Stephen invited him to visit. He wrote about that visit in his essay. About how nervous he was alone on the bus ride.

About his great expectations: his father would be waiting for him on the platform when he arrived; would give him a big hug and ask him all about his life. Instead, Jason wrote, "He was standing across the street. We shook hands. He didn't ask me one question. He had bad teeth."

On Jason's last day home we got up early. The plan was to clean his room thoroughly, pack everything, then drive to Connecticut, sleep at my parents', and go to Wesleyan the next morning. I read a book while Jason cleaned his room, then thought, hell, I should help him. Ever since he was little we had an agreement that his room was his own property and he could do as he pleased in it. And except for three or four times a year, when I threw a fit, he never cleaned it. The last time I'd helped him clean was the day we moved in six years before. Now that he was leaving, I felt guilty. So I helped him sweep mounds of crinkled papers and cockroach-encrusted shirts, petrified pizza crusts, Monopoly money, baseball cards, his old Snoopy from under the bed.

Afraid I might blow up or launch into a this-is-disgusting lecture, he invoked my mother, the immaculate. "Could you imagine if Mim saw this?" he said.

"What would she say?"

"She'd be speechless. She'd have a heart attack."

"She'd jump out the window."

"She'd say, 'How can you live like this?' "

"Yeah, Jase, how can you?"

"I don't know."

When the room was spic and span he collapsed on his bed and said, "Now I don't want to leave. Let's go tomorrow."

"We can't. Your grandparents are expecting us."

"Are you going to let people sleep in my bed when I'm gone?"

"Yes."

"Come on, Ma."

"Jase, I'll be lonely."

"Oh. Okay."

It was seven o'clock when we finally left. Very dark and

pouring rain. Water swirled from the tops of trucks and splattered us from between tires as big as our borrowed Honda. Jase grabbed the dashboard and closed his eyes anytime we passed a truck, a habit of driving distrust developed during the times I used to whiz around corners and fly over bumps to get him screaming.

"So, Jase," I said, "what do you remember most about Wesleyan?"

"The kids. They taught me how to ride a two-wheeler a couple of days after we moved in, remember?"

"Those were wonderful years for both of us. I hope you still like it there."

"Me too. I'm gonna miss the city. Maybe I should've gone to Columbia."

"Connecticut's beautiful. It'll be good to live in the country for a time, smell the seasons change, have a slower pace. Everything's so hard here. Sometimes I wonder why I stay."

"Because people are stupid everywhere else."

"What an awful thing to say. They are not. Maybe they're not sarcastic, or quick, but they're not stupid."

"Yes they are."

"So you're saying if we never moved to New York and stayed in Connecticut all these years, you'd be stupid?"

"Yes."

"I never thought in a million years I'd raise a snob."

"I'm not a snob. It's the truth."

I looked at him then. Black jeans, black T-shirt, beat-up sneakers, an East Village kid.

His dorm room was a little mansion. A single all to himself. We stepped onto his balcony and oohed and aahed over the trees, the rolling green hills, the clear, sweet-smelling breeze on our faces. He had jammed his clothes into one suitcase. His wool sweaters were dusty and covered with cat fur. We shook them out over the balcony rail, folded them, and put them away. He started folding his shirts too. I explained that you hang shirts in a closet. He hadn't had a closet since we'd left Wesleyan.

I began to worry. What would it be like for him with all

these upper-middle-class kids? The one across the hall was setting up his room with his mother and father and older sister. He had a large and complex stereo system, a color TV, a message pad on his door, an Indian rug tacked to his wall. Jase had a Walkman and a clock radio. His sheets didn't match. If I'd been a real mother, I would have made sure his sweaters were dry-cleaned before he packed them. A real mother would have packed them for that matter. "Look at that kid's room," I said.

"Nice," he said.

"You know, a lot of the kids are going to be rich here. Most of them will have more than you."

"So?"

"Aren't you going to feel bad?"

"No."

"I mean, looking at that kid's room, don't you feel deprived?"

"Why?"

"His room is decorated so nice. He has a stereo, his sheets match." I didn't mention that he had a father and a sister in addition to a mother.

"I don't care if my sheets match. I don't care about that stuff, do you?"

"I guess not." I still don't know if he was just being nice to me.

After we exchanged I love you's and hugged at the car, I drove away thinking that I was supposed to be feeling happy.

I slept in his room so it wouldn't be empty. Every time I pictured his big foot sticking out of his sheets or thought of him groggy in the morning, running fingers through his hair, I'd start weeping all over again. It was not so long ago that Jase had held my hand wherever we went. No more.

But little by little, men started to look good to me again. When Jase came home on his first spring break, Gerard, a new boyfriend I really liked, gave me two tickets to the opening of a Broadway play he'd worked on. I hemmed and hawed about whether I wanted to take Jason, but I felt I had to. After all, he was my son, and so what if he didn't have the best track record with my boyfriends? The information was dated; he deserved a chance.

Gerard and I arranged to meet at the opening party at the Palladium afterward, but foolishly didn't specify where. Jase and I sat by the door. No Gerard. "Maybe he stood me up," I said.

"No," Jase assured me, then said, "Do you think so? Is he that type?"

"I don't think so, but I'm not the best judge of character when it comes to men." We chuckled, remembering some lulus from the past. "I'm probably just being paranoid."

"I get like that with girls, too."

After a while, I said, "This is ridiculous. Let's go enjoy ourselves."

"That's right, Ma," he said. "Let him find you."

"Is that what you think? Guys should do the pursuing?"

"No. That's bullshit."

"So, why did you say that?"

"Because you're my mother and I think guys should chase after you."

I was thinking I should take Jase out on dates more often.

When we walked up a couple of levels to get food where it wasn't so crowded, he said, "Everybody thinks you're my girlfriend, you know."

A passing woman looked at me, then Jason, and smiled. He was right and I knew it. After all, I'm a young-looking thirty-six and he's a mature-looking eighteen. It wasn't as though I'd never had that thought before. I just never admitted it, because it seemed too dangerous. But now that Jase had brought it out into the open it lost its potency. I was, simply, flattered.

When we got our food we walked to the outermost edge of the crowd and sat down in the bleachers. "Well, Jase," I said. "here we are as usual, on the edge, looking."

"I like to watch."

"But do you think it's good?" This wasn't a parenty

question. I genuinely wanted to know his opinion. I always had, even when he was little.

"Yeah," he said.

"Well, it's good if you're a writer," I said.

"Or a thinker."

"But it's good to be able to talk to people too."

"I have a technique for meeting girls now," he said.

"What?"

"I sit in a corner and look depressed and somebody always comes up and asks me what's the matter. Then we talk. It's easy if I'm a little drunk, but if I'm not I can't think of anything to say."

"Do you drink a lot?"

"Nah. Maybe once a week. Not even that. You know, Ma, I admire you just sitting here. If I were you I'd be going crazy inside thinking he stood me up. I'd be looking around."

We went looking for Gerard and found him at a bar, a tiny bit drunk. After I introduced Jase, Gerard said good-naturedly, "I can't believe it. He's so big. He came out of you?"

Jase and I laughed, and Gerard offered us drinks. "I don't know," I hesitated, "I've already had two."

Jase turned his back to Gerard and mumbled to me, "Go ahead, he wants you to catch up." We all drank, and after a while Gerard left to say goodbye to some people.

"I like him," Jase said. "Poor guy. He was probably standing here getting drunk thinking you didn't show. When he comes back I'll split so you can be alone."

Jason was interpreting this man for me. And he was being a gentleman. I felt relief and a tinge of regret: the kind of feeling when an ex-lover becomes your friend and is genuinely glad for you that you've found someone new.

◆

MAYUMI TSUTAKAWA

Good Karma: Starting Over with Patience and a Wit

◆

My definition of being a single mother is "providing it all, half the time." I am the mother of two children who spend half their time with me and half with their father. I choose to be unmarried but am involved in a committed relationship with a man who is a vital participant in our household.

I'm both defensive and weary of building those defenses against allegations that divorced-parent situations are inherently unhappy situations for the kids and are likely to inflict actual harm on them. Sometimes those prevailing attitudes about divorce and children succeed in making me worry that the kids will grow up nervous, disturbed victims who are unable to form good relationships. But most of the time I'm convinced that my two children, Kenzan, a fourteen-year-old boy, and Yayoi, an eight-year-old girl, are balanced and healthy, even though I feed them white sugar, white bread and white rice.

While in the Asian community the concept of "family" is strong and fundamental, usually it is based on the narrow assumption of a nuclear family of two married opposite-sex parents and their children, all connected to an extended family. But there are other realistic concepts of "family." For me, the combination of being a single mother with a caring partner and embracing the extended family as an everlasting, immutable concept is what makes my definition of single parenting viable. My new nuclear family must be basking in the good karma provided by other close families who lived before us.

In the fall of 1988 I decided to leave a marriage of fourteen years. My son was eight and my daughter two and a half. My decision to leave caused a quiet uproar in my close extended family. I had lived away from home and traveled abroad independently from the age of eighteen to twenty-five. I had been politically progressive and an active feminist for twenty years, but it seems my Japanese cultural heritage imbued in me the notion that I should never complain about the problems of my marriage to anybody. And so the family took my divorcing actions as capricious and, worse yet, potentially damaging to my children. My then-husband is Chinese American and the first son in his family—I *know* his family did not like my leaving, either.

I imagine my father and three brothers took it harder than their wives. It must have been frightening for them to imagine their wives leaving them. My dad is *Kibei*, born in America and raised in Japan. He left home in Japan at sixteen to become an artist and lived and worked with aunts, uncles and cousins in Seattle. He always has been philosophically broadminded and encouraged us four children to think for ourselves. We grew up with no particular religion, although eventually we became somewhat Buddhist.

Of my three brothers, the older one is an artist and the two younger ones are musicians—all have had long marriages and two have children. I think they were concerned for both me and my children. However, as with most Japanese-American families, we avoid talking directly about emotional subjects of a personal nature in the same way we avoid discussing finances with each other.

My mother, as traditionally Japanese as she seems, was the first to step forward for me. She is *Kibei*, too, and is the bonding agent which holds our close family together. Her own mother was married several times, and she was raised by relatives thousands of miles away from her own mother. She never knew the closeness of the traditional nuclear family, rather, it was the extended family that provided her lifeline. After discussion, my mother trusted that my pursuing a divorce was the best thing for my future happiness, given my situation. She sat with me throughout the divorce trial, with all its acrimony and financial wrangling.

Fortunately, I was able to move swiftly into another house my husband and I owned and had rented out. It is situated near the homes of my parents and two of my brothers and their families. On a weekend my husband took the kids on a trip out of town, my mother and close friends from work helped me move out of the old and into the new home. I wanted to set up the house for my children's comfort, given that they would be made to go back and forth, spending half the time with each parent. The logistics of setting up a new kitchen, gathering beds, linens, shelves for books and toys were one thing. But building a positive mental attitude that this house, more humble and in a poorer neighborhood than my previous one, was actually a better house, was part of settling in, too.

With my moving closer to my family and them seeing me more often, they all had to accept my resolve. I have been grateful for the closer proximity my kids gained to their grandparents, uncles, aunts and five cousins. Besides being able to walk the distance, the kids also are at those houses more these days because they enjoy playing with cousins, who are automatically closer than friends, and see their grandparents' home as a stable, secure and interesting environment. My parents have not only lots of good food, fascinating paintings and sculptures, but also cable TV, which I refuse to buy.

◆ ◆ ◆

At first my children expressed that they wanted their parents to get back together, but I never considered that a possibility. Perhaps they saw their father as lonely (although he has had a constant stream of foreign student roommates). Perhaps they were wary of the impending two-house lifestyle. Working as a government arts agency director left me with little spare energy and patience for dealing with the lost sweatshirts and lunch boxes, forgotten soccer shoes and notes from school that gave explicit instructions for how the student was to prepare for the next day. Both children are bright, motivated students most of the time and seem to survive well, given the flow of events. And my family members always have stepped in to provide instantaneous day care, give haircuts or play card games with the kids, as the situation required.

Kenzan is rather intelligent and hyper, given to reading quickly and thoroughly and then holding forth with copious opinions. He hates mundane assignments and loves science, geography, politics and being right. He likes to make fun of other people but is empathetic in a logical way. When he was five and I was pregnant and quite nauseated, he stated that being pregnant "is like having a big sliver—when it comes out you'll feel all better."

My daughter Yayoi, or Yaya, as we've always called her, is smart and has a talent for writing. (She wrote to, and received replies from, President Clinton and Seattle's Mayor Rice.) Typical teacher's pet material, she is cooperative and organized in her schoolwork and wants to become a doctor, that is, she says, "if I don't become a baseball player first." She has strong opinions but gets her feelings hurt easily. She carefully saves her money so she can buy birthday presents for others, a concept truly alien to her brother.

Although I doubted it could happen again, I find myself living with another male. At first I was dating some people and thinking "never again will I hook up permanently with one of these." But, through a close colleague in my office, I met her friend's friend, Michael, and, getting to know one another, we discovered a kind of spiritual connection. Some said our relationship could not possibly be serious because of our sixteen-year age gap, but my young partner and I have been (almost) perfectly happy for five years.

Michael is tall and quiet and white, although he is bilingual and bicultural, having grown up in Latin America. His parents are from Washington State, so he has roots here. He was born in Chicago and lived in Panama, Mexico and Peru from the ages of two to sixteen. He is a software programmer and a mathematician. Like me, he is deeply immersed in literature, and is eclectic and nonreligious. Our political values are compatible, and his sense of intellectual independence has allowed me to be myself and raise my kids the way I see fit. We have adequate patience with each other—he is patient with my bossiness and I am patient with his messiness. And we scrutinize every article we see that speaks of older women living with younger men.

Admittedly, the kids' schedule leaves me without the responsibility of taking care of them every other week (and a couple of weeks at a time during the summer). So Michael and I attend theater, films, art exhibits and literary readings. We've taken yoga classes and motorcycle trips together. I've learned a lot about computers and soccer and Neruda—he's learned about JA's (Japanese Americans), artists of color and kids' habits.

In retrospect, getting the children used to our sleeping together was pretty comical. At first I didn't think it was "good" for the children to know we were sleeping together, or at least they shouldn't see him staying all night. Why? Now I can't imagine what I was thinking. At first we took to sitting on the living room couch, "falling asleep" in our clothes and then telling the kids it was an accident he stayed all night. Finally, we gave up the ruse, and he began to stay all night quite often. By the time he moved into my house a year later, no one was asking questions.

After the initial suspicions the children had about Michael ("he's taking her attention away from us") versus his unspoken complaint ("they're taking her time away from me") our family grouping has turned out to be a good one. I've quit my government job and now have a more flexible schedule as an independent editor and curator. Michael is finishing his belated bachelor's degree at the university and works part time for a software company.

He and the children have bonded a lot more now. Probably by virtue of a common and vast interest in the world of high technology, Michael and Kenzan happily play video games together, read futuristic comic books and toss around scientific hypotheses (and try to one-up each other—both are Gemini).

Now that Yaya is eight, her minor tantrums to express tired/hungry feelings have abated. She reads well and has more to think and talk about. I see a mutual admiration growing between her and Michael—in fact, they're very cute together as Pictionary partners. The kids' positive relationship with Michael is aided by the fact that my parents and siblings' families like him and, in fact, think it's good for me to have someone quiet and trustworthy to live with. (Somehow "quiet" implies "respectful" and therefore "trustworthy" for some Japanese.) Also, I think my mother believes that I'm so involved with my work, I need help keeping all the logistics of life together.

The children are growing up with a continuing sense of their *tricultural* heritage (Japanese, Chinese and whatever American is). They are fourth generation Japanese American and third/fourth generation Chinese American (on their father's side, their grandfather was born in China and their grandmother in the U.S.). They're part of a growing number of mixed-heritage kids among nonwhite students in the schools today. They are aware of racism and how it has shaped the history of Asians and other people in America.

I can teach them pride in their *Asianness*, but in fact, I don't know what it feels like or what it means to be of mixed heritage. One year, I filled out a public school application that asked my son to "ONLY CHECK ONE:" and the choices included Japanese *or* Chinese. In my presence, he chose Japanese. Perhaps with his father, he would have checked the box "Chinese." Like many other children, they will face the choice of seeing their mixed ethnic heritage as either a confusing or an enriching opportunity. It is my aim to make it the latter.

My children eagerly visit their relatives on both sides of the family tree and have added an appreciation for my partner's family members, too. We choose to live in a racially diverse neighborhood. They know an entire spectrum of authentic ethnic foods and holidays. They celebrate both Japanese *and* Chinese New Year, participate in Chinese community banquets and Japanese *Obon* Festival dancing. They are learning to write their names in Chinese and Japanese and know a lot about Asia and their Asian ancestries. Michael's Latin American heritage, language and foods also are a positive addition to our lives.

The training I want to offer my children is the ability to think, to be original and to defend their actions and opinions. And I think our close proximity to the extended family, stepfamily, artistic friends and colleagues provides many role models for them. For all of my parents' attention to traditional Japanese culture and art, it is balanced with an interest in what is untraditional—in art or in people. My dad left home at sixteen because he wanted to become an artist, not a businessman as his family dictated. I can remember my parents encouraging me and my brothers to think on our own, to criticize and not necessarily to conform to the group. By the sixth grade, I quit being docile and was elected class president. By the time I finished college, I was tired of the hierarchy of professors telling me how to think and what to do.

Both the kids are fortunate enough to attend very small private schools. In these alternative-philosophy schools, many of the families are nontraditional—some children have single parents, some have two same-sex parents. The teachers try to instill self-esteem, responsibility and recognition for alternate roots in all the children.

Our dining room resounds with debate and discussion.

We try to keep a collective sense of humor. But I yell at the kids if they're wrong, they yell at me if I'm wrong. I want my children to grow up to be strong thinkers and responsible to their community. We attend the Gay Pride March and talk about AIDS and its effect on people, like friends of ours who are gay. We keep up with what's happening in Tibet, South Africa and the former Yugoslavia. With many relatives who are artists and musicians, they know what it means to try to make a living by pursuing a creative ideal.

Being responsible for a family does not have to be tedious or difficult, although it is hectic at times. We're all getting better at packing our own bags for trips. I find myself energized by having to keep up with what's new in young people's lives. I'm also finding it works better not to have a preconceived notion about what is bad and what is good. We all need to keep a sense of patience and wit to live in this fast-paced global life. And the faster the world, the more important the connection to family roots. Instead of conforming to other people's definition of what a family should be, we're living and loving by our own human definition and reaping the benefits of good family karma.

JULENE BAIR

Beacons

◆

I turned down another party invitation last week. I couldn't justify hiring a baby sitter. Not because of the cost, but because Jake had been in preschool all week, and then I had my two regular evening classes and my writing group meeting on Sunday night. Rose, one of the women who shares my house, told me I should get out more often. "Do something for yourself," she said. I told her that going to graduate school and developing my writing were for myself, that you have to make sacrifices when you're a parent.

"Besides," I said, "being with Jake is for me. We are a family, and if I can't take him to a party, I'm not interested in going."

One of Rose's eyebrows lifted, but she refrained from commenting.

"Where do you think most parents are on Saturday night?" I asked her.

Until about eleven o'clock last Saturday, I sat in bed, reading as Jake slept in the next room. Across town, my childless friends from graduate school were probably talking about the book I was reading, which had been assigned in one of my classes. Busy with Jake so much of the time, I don't get to read as broadly as my friends do. They would probably know more about the literary period, the author's other work, the critics' opinions. That night, I wished I could be at the party, learning. I remembered then, as I so often do, how it was when I was little, and there were card parties.

Eight families belonged to the club. Their houses were landmarks on the Kansas prairie. On summer nights, I could see their yard lights clearly from our front fence, where I used to cling, the toes of my cowboy boots wedged in the wire. The realms lit by those lonely beams were as inaccessible to me as the stars. Then, starting on the first Saturday night in November, we went visiting.

Dad's after-shave mingled with the scent of Mom's powder in the chill air inside our station wagon. I was the youngest, and sat like a bundled princess on the front seat between the majesties. We were five miles down the road before the engine was warm enough to turn on the heater fan. I put my Buster Browns under the dash and the warmth flowed up my white tights.

Snowflakes shimmered like rings of Saturn around our host's light pole. We stomped our feet and entered the overshoe-cluttered porch, the odor from work clothes threatening our well-soaped scent and sheen. We heard a muffled chorus of voices. I took off my coat and, shoving it at Mom, threw open the kitchen door, weaved through a forest of stockinged legs and high-heeled pumps, and ran up the stairs.

The hosts' children held court over their miniature John Deere tractors, Easy-Bake ovens, canisters of clay, slinkies, crayons and coloring books. Our parents interfered with us only when our screeches and thundering feet penetrated the din of their own games and gossip. My dad tells me he gave me a spanking once for being too rowdy at a card party and got chastised for it by Faye Blue, a teacher in the one-room school house my cousin attended.

"That oughta do some good," he said to Faye when I walked off, crying.

"Maybe it does *you* good," she spit back at him. Whatever damage he did me that night, I am none the wiser today.

My boisterous pleasure so outweighed the punishment that I don't remember it.

The fifties were hard times for farmers, with grain markets down and never enough moisture. Getting together after two weeks of little but work and worry heightened the color on the cheeks of even the poorest, most stoic farm people. Jokes traveled from card table to card table, sending waves of laughter around the modest living room. Shouts punctuated the steady chatter whenever someone succeeded in "shooting the moon." The men rubbed their wives' knees and bluffed their way through ten-point pitch as if it were five-card draw. The women leaned back in their chairs and let out enormous hoots, their faces shining through their powder.

Outside the snow would continue to fall, blanketing the miles of dark prairie that lay between our houses. The big kids helped the little ones into snow pants, and we burst from the house like popcorn jumping from a skillet, the snow cushioning our shouts as we ran through the drifts.

By the time we came back inside, the hostess was serving refreshments. The kids drank punch usually, but at some parties I was allowed to sip coffee from a delicate, transparent cup, just like a grown-up. I lifted the cup from its matching saucer proudly, even though it contained only enough coffee to tint the milk. As the adults handed out prizes for the highest scores and a booby prize to the worst player, I usually wandered off to the hosts' bedroom. I fished my mother's coat out of the tremendous pile and burrowed beneath it, letting its caress and faint scent usher me to sleep.

The few times I've taken Jake to parties, he's gotten tired and cranky, and I've wished he would simply nestle into a comfortable bedful of coats like I used do. But he's never been one to go to sleep easily. Used to be, even when we were at home, I had to lie down with him, pent-up in the dark, counting to myself. When I reached five hundred, I would begin *again*, as I waited for his fidgeting to stop and his breathing to tell me he was finally asleep. Then, after being so anxious for that moment to arrive, I would stay, his peace magnetic.

When he was two, I finally weaned us of that. As a single mother, I am mindful of the danger of spoiling Jake. We have some bad examples in my family—boys who were considered spoiled, the sons of widowed or divorced aunts. As if I weren't already sensitive about this, my parents nudge me with this aunt lore, encouraging me to get on the ball and find a man, to "give Jake a father."

I reassure them with statistics I read in magazines. Between 1970 and 1985, the number of single mothers in the United States doubled. Twenty percent of the families in this country are "maintained" (the Census Bureau's word) by women. And Jake and I are a lot luckier than most of them. With my parents' generous help and with my teaching assistant's salary, we don't have to depend on meager payments from rigid government agencies, on erratic support from a sullen ex-husband, or on the few pennies remaining of a menial wage after paying a baby sitter. Although I get nostalgic for those winter car rides when I nestled between two parents, my problems can hardly compare to the fatigue and hopelessness encountered by so many other women raising children alone.

In Gloria Naylor's 1982 novel, *The Women of Brewster Place*, I read about some of these others—African-American women who, like me, center their lives on their children. How unlike the heroines I am accustomed to in the "classics"! Madame Bovary and Anna Karenina sacrificed their children for men, then romance let them down. Naylor's women, members of a society where fifty-four percent of families are "maintained" by women, know better.

My man left me when I was two months pregnant. Like many of the men in Naylor's book, he got by on good looks and charm. Marrying him was the dumbest thing I did in all the years after leaving Kansas at eighteen. Today I tell myself I married him because I had reached thirty-five, the do or die age for potential mothers. But that first summer back on the farm after he left, you couldn't have told me that. I longed for the man, not the child.

Broke and humiliated by a marriage that had lasted only eight months, I did all I could to earn my keep, driving tractors throughout most of my pregnancy. Aaron's scent hung about me, despite the dust the farm implements stirred up and despite the stink of the tractors' near-boiling radiator water that record hot summer or the stench of the hydraulic oil I inevitably spilled trying to reach hidden spouts. I bounced across the fields in everything from my father's biggest, quietest, air-conditioned 4850 down to the thirty-year-old 4320. That tractor tore over the terrain, its engine screaming with fifties zeal. I cranked the radio on high and let the nasal laments of the country and western singers scour my emotions. I would bawl fervently, shouting and cussing Aaron over the noise, until I would see my father's pickup approaching. Then I'd clench down on myself and the steering wheel, trying to drive straight while reaching for my thermos. I splashed water on my face and wiped it with my sleeve. When Dad arrived, he would shout over the engine, "How's it goin'?"

"Fine," I'd yell back, never mentioning the cramping that could have resulted in a miscarriage. My son did not become real to me until he was born. On that day, I touched my nose to his scalp and inhaled a scent that surmounted and replaced the memory of his father.

I felt confident at first about raising Jake alone. I took heart from *Newsweek* stories about single women whose reproductive drives were so strong they had gone to sperm banks. "Who needs a man?" they said. Like those swaggering mothers, I told my family I shouldn't have much trouble. I was an outdoor person. I could rebuild a car engine and remodel houses. I could teach Jake all the things men taught their sons. My brother chortled condescendingly. I couldn't tell whether he laughed out of wisdom or whether it was a mere reflex of his sarcastic temperament, but by the time Jake reached six months, it seemed to me that the only thing worse than his not having a father would have been if his natural father had stayed.

The first hints were subtle, but haunting. My brother visited rarely, but Jake, at four months, would stare up from Bruce's knee, his eyes alight, as if he were seeing God. It could have been Bruce's beard that Jake found so fascinating. I hoped that was it. But the same thing happened when Morgan, a clean-shaven male friend, visited from San Francisco. Although Jake was very devoted to his grandfather, he seemed especially crazy about men who were the age of a likely father. Then his second word, after "hi," at nine months, was "da-da." I looked up the derivation and was appeased: "Dad: Middle English *dadd*, dadde; Irish *daid*, imitative of a child's cry." It seemed infants made the sound naturally, without attaching any meaning to it.

By twenty-four months, though, Jake was undeniably enthralled with dads. He would thumb through our photo album to look at the same picture over and over. My friend Leslie from Arizona had sent the snapshot of her daughter Sage's father holding Sage by her hands, her feet dangling over wet cement. Jake would land on the page and stare. "Sage's daddy?" he asked.

"Yes," I said, and wondered when the inevitable question, "Where's *my* daddy?" would come.

It wasn't just Jake's longing that troubled me. At two, he began hitting and biting other children and, more often, me. I struggled within a mesh of doubts. Did Jake need the love of a father to curb his aggression, a sparring partner to take it out on? As a woman, was I just ill-equipped to discipline him properly? Was my voice not authoritative enough, my love too unequivocal?

I felt as if Jake and I were free electrons seeking a nucleus. The balance just wasn't right. We were too often alone together, and the sense of isolation was tremendous. Oh, transcendent moments punctuated our days, as happened one afternoon on the farm when Jake was two. I was in the front yard pulling weeds after a rainstorm. Jake, as usual, straddled Allie, a duck on wheels.

"A-bow," he said. "A-bow."

When I looked up he was pointing at the darkened sky, where a rainbow glowed. It rose out of the wheat field north of the road and reached beyond the sheep barn into the south pasture.

Just then the yard light blinked on. Mercury vapor lights were the new technology on farms. They came on with the dark and extinguished themselves at dawn. The light they cast was icy blue, and I hated them. They obscured the stars and were installed without manual switches, so you were at their mercy. That afternoon our light mistook the storm clouds for dusk. "Foolish piece of crap," I mumbled.

"Pees-a-cra," Jake mimicked.

At night, alone on the farm, Jake and I stared off at the blue beacons of neighbors, and I felt as if my childhood were replaying itself but with a new, coldly eerie tinge. The card parties still occurred in the winter, and women's clubs, like the one my mother had belonged to before she and Dad moved to town, met in the summer, but I wasn't invited. I couldn't bridge the distance between beacons without a husband.

So, although I liked farming, I began laying plans to leave. I took correspondence courses toward the completion of my bachelor's degree. And now I am a graduate student at the University of Iowa. Jake and I go home to Kansas only during summers.

Our lives in Iowa City were compartmentalized and alienating at first. Jake cried every morning when I dropped him at the day care center. The director diverted him by holding him to the window to wave. I made faces at him, blinked my car lights and honked my horn—all in hypocritical glee, for I really felt just as torn and wounded as he. Then at night, with no one else to interact with, we were too fused. How many block towers could I build for him to desecrate, how many nursery rhymes could I read him, how many games of peek-a-boo could I play before going mad?

Meanwhile, his fascination with fathers crescendoed from "da-da" to "DADDY!" He clung to the men who worked at our day-care co-op, sometimes fighting with other children over their fathers. At two and a half, he asked it. "Where's my daddy?"

"Somewhere in California, I think, honey. I'm not sure where." Whenever he played airplane after that, he flew to California.

Indeed, it seemed as if all our hope resided in California. When our friend Morgan flew in from San Francisco for a visit, we were both exhilarated. Jake rode on Morgan's shoulders, and I was engrossed in watching the two of them. Jake seemed cuter than ever. I loved watching him do things with Morgan that had become tedious to do with him myself. Morgan's departure left a palpable emptiness. The following fall, on returning from a summer in Kansas, I couldn't face the isolation of our apartment. I took a financially unjustifiable risk and rented a house. Then I ran an ad, "Wanted, housemates."

The move disappointed me at first. Women called but lost interest when they heard the details. The neighborhood was uniform, with ranch-style houses and trim lawns. I hoped that some of its normality would rub off on us. But although the street teemed with kids, Jake didn't fit in as quickly as I thought he would. He was unaware of suburban property lines—the invisible yet indelible boundaries between lawns, between public sidewalks and private drives. Every afternoon upon coming home from the day care center, he grabbed Allie and rumbled down the sidewalk, looking for friends. I scampered after him, tugging Rex, a puppy I had gotten from the pound, thinking he might substitute as a sibling. Jake would abandon Allie (in sorrier shape than it had been in on the farm, since Rex had teethed on its nose), and I would catch up to him just in time to thwart his conquest of an idle fire engine or an army green mobile-strike-force tricycle. Other times, he ran excitedly into swarms of kids, who thundered down driveways in their kid mobiles. "Hey, you guys!" he shouted.

At best, the children ignored him. At worst, they said, "This is our house."

Nan arrived in the nick of time. She was a graduate student in art, looking for an inexpensive room to rent. "Do you like kids?" I asked. "I mean, Jake is no angel."

"I love kids," she said, giving Jake an impish grin. "You wanna do a flipping truck?"

I said, "What's a flipping truck?"

"I'll show you," Nan said. She positioned Jake, willing and curious, in front of her, grabbed his wrists from between his legs and flipped him over forwards.

Jake let loose a barrage of his squeaky-hinge giggles. "Again," he said.

We had two other housemates that first year, but it was Nan who did us the most good. Her warmth and tolerance, even of Jake's tantrums, helped me stop fretting about his aggressiveness. Finally, there was someone else around who loved him, not as much as I did, of course, but someone who was attached enough to him to refuse to see him as anything but normal. Nan told me not to worry, the aggressiveness was just a stage.

Looking back to that time, I realize that I longed for just such acceptance. Jake and I hadn't fit in Kansas because I was single and had become too worldly. Yet, in Iowa City, there weren't many events we could participate in either. Adults and children didn't mix socially. The church I went to for a while had a great nursery school, but seldom staged a social event at which children were welcome. The parties I was invited to were for adults, as were most restaurants.

Even dinners out with Nan proved challenging. One evening she prevailed on me to bring Jake and meet her at the new Japanese restaurant in town. Like a fool, I did.

Discreetly, I asked the waiter to sit us at a corner table. As soon as he left, Nan said, "So, Julene, I've been thinking. You know, you should really value your experience more. Just because your classmates have read more—"

"Mom."

"—books and seen more movies doesn't mean—"

"Mommy. I want a Shirley Temple."

"Okay honey, as soon as the waiter comes back."

"—doesn't—"

"But, Mom,"

"—mean that what you—"

"I want it."

"—were doing all those—"

"Now."

"—years wasn't just as—"

"Mom!"

"Yes, Jake. You don't have to shout."

"But Mom, I want a Shirley Temple."

"I know, Jake, and I'll order you one as soon as the waiter comes back. You can wait, can't you?"

Jake had to think a little bit. "Sure, I guess so," he said.

We flagged down the waiter and ordered Jake his Shirley Temple. Nan ordered some *sake*, and I got a beer.

The evening began to feel like an evening in a nice restaurant ought to. We were in our own luxurious little capsule, even if Jake bounced off the walls of it every so often—literally, since we were in the corner.

"He's tired," I told Nan, ashamed of evoking the refrain we mothers use to explain our children's bad behavior. It always sounds like a lame excuse even though it is usually accurate. But Nan understood.

When the sushi finally came, it was delicious. Jake didn't think much of it, but we got him a bowl of rice and since I let him put his own soy sauce on it, he was pleased. We had several laughs trying to show him how to use chopsticks. When he was done eating, he wandered over to a neighboring couple's table. He peeked over its edge, then fell to the floor in a fit of giggles when the woman, highly entertained, said "Boo!"

"Shh!" I said. "Come back here."

He said "Why?"

"You don't bother other people when you're in a restaurant."

"Why?"

I had to think about it. I didn't say, "Because it's not nice," because deep down I am still a product of farm culture. My own rare trips to restaurants as a child were always moments for gushing attention from strange adults, who were really neighbors. I settled finally on this: "It's the social custom."

"Oh," Jake said, and hopped back to our table, doing his frog imitation. The couple nodded at us, amused.

It took me a long time to eat, because I responded to Nan's advice with some complicated reservations and because I had to take Jake to the bathroom twice, even though the second time he was just bluffing—he really wanted to go by the dessert rack again. Toward the end, I had to hold him in my lap, trying to get him to settle down while we waited for the check. Finally I gave Nan some money for my part of the tab, and too soon for me but not soon enough for Jake, we were out of there.

Almost. Jake got excited about the water wheel at the door. A foot bridge spanned a little pond, which was littered with pennies. I didn't have any change, so I sent him back to the table to ask Nan for some. He dashed off on that mission, and I remained crouched on the foot bridge, a little tipsy and joyful, reflecting on my good fortune—a happy child, a good friend, a stomach full of good Japanese food.

A male voice said "Ma'am." I looked up. A portly man in a three-piece suit stood at the door, an overcoat draped over his arm.

Once certain he had my attention, he stated firmly, "Ma'am, if you can't control your child any better than that, you shouldn't take him out in public."

The only response I could muster was to stare. Where had they been sitting? I hadn't noticed them.

"I mean it," the man said. "You spend money for a nice dinner, and it's very disturbing."

I looked through the door he held open into the portico, where stood his dinner partner, probably his wife, for the couple had a settled air. She nodded and, backing her man, affirmed, "It really is."

Having said their peace, they made a dignified exit. I wanted to run after them and shout what sort of parents I imagined they would be, but instead I wandered, dazed, back to the corner where Nan sat searching her wallet for Jake's change.

I repeated the couple's remarks, and Nan said it was their problem. The bus girl, who had been clearing the table, shook her head and said, sincerely, "I'm sorry that happened." She and Jake had flirted off and on all evening.

Despite their assurances, I cried driving home that night. I sensed such disapproval frequently, even if it was seldom voiced. It unsettled me most because it conflicted with my own childhood. I still had the card party model rising in my mind, a glorious vision of the way things ought to be. Didn't children, like the adage said, belong to the world? Jake needed that world more than most, yet it seemed I had cast him, naturally outgoing and unsuspecting, into unwelcoming hands. Where were the Faye Blues, the adults who would speak up for Jake when *I* got angry at him? Why was I so often called upon to defend and explain him? I had grown up in what my memory insisted on reminding me was a nuclear family surrounded by an informal community of friends only to wind up as a single parent on the edge of a community that, as a rule, excluded children.

Naylor's women, though living in poverty and confronting different problems, had the wealth of spirit and good sense to find their solution in each other. This last year Jake and I chanced on similar, if temporary, respite. Two new housemates moved in, and along with Nan, the dynamic was right. We became a family. I had two evening classes. Nan took Jake to her studio on Mondays, where he was more than happy to "make art." On Tuesday nights, he frolicked with Laura, a twenty-two-year-old comparative literature student, who treated him like a younger brother. Our third housemate, Rose, a veteran day care worker, taught him songs and let him play dress-up in her room.

We had additional luck in Joe, the husband of a friend in my women's writing group, who offered to be Jake's buddy on the night of our weekly meeting. But over the past year, I discovered that I was as moved by seeing Jake ride on Nan's shoulders as I had been seeing him on Morgan's, that while Joe's attention was important should Jake want to do "guy stuff," he was actually less fascinated with him than with Laura, whom he now declares he intends to marry.

I would like to think this means that Jake's desire for a father is less intense, but I know better. Jake is four and a half now, and just a few months ago, I made the mistake of answering too candidly when he asked, "When is my daddy gonna come, Mommy?"

"Well, honey, it's almost as if you don't have a daddy. You've never met him, and he's never met you, and . . . "

Jake's eyes were instantly red and brimming. "I have a daddy!" he shouted. "I do too have a daddy!"

In the aftershock of such moments, I have contemplated writing something to warn off those *Newsweek* types. "You don't know what you'll be getting into. You may not need a husband, but your child will need a father." Naylor's women did not choose to mother their children alone. They simply made the best of the circumstances their disappearing men left them in. I try to imagine what it would have been like if Mom and I had been alone in that car back then. She would have been driving, instead of Dad. With all that empty space to fill, it would have been a lot harder waiting for the heater to get going.

But while there is no doubt Jake feels deprived in not having a father, I remind myself that my childhood wasn't perfect either. I clung to the front fence on many a night, watching yard lights blink off as kids, who were only rarely my playmates, went to bed. Remembering this is difficult, because I must ride up out of the groove the card party memory has worn in me. I must be a realist.

Jake has friends next door, an advantage I didn't have. And he has a family of women who love him. That love has helped us transcend our isolation and overcome Jake's aggression. It has been a miraculous year. The problem, of course, is that there is no commitment. Now that the school year is over, our family is disintegrating.

Last week Nan left to spend the summer in Seattle, and she isn't sure she'll be living with us again next fall.

"Nan is coming back, isn't she, Mom?"

"We're not sure yet, honey. She may need to live closer to her studio."

"Yeah, but she'll still baby-sit me, won't she?"

"Yes, I know she'll want to do that."

And Laura is packing up her things and putting them in storage. She plans to spend a year in France. "I wish Laura didn't have to go," Jake says.

"I wish she didn't either, honey, but it will be good for her. Just think of all the things she'll learn."

"Yeah, like how not to laugh when people cry." Laura loved to tease Jake whenever he whined.

That leaves only Rose. "You *are* going to watch our house for us this summer while we're in Kansas, right, Rosie?"

"Yes, I am going to watch your house for you this summer, Jake."

"But Rex is coming with us, right?"

"Right." Rose hasn't had the heart to tell Jake that in the fall she is considering going back to the man she came here to get away from.

Laura, Rose and I huddle in the living room and talk after Jake has gone to bed. We talk about Jake and his behavior, how he's grown. We exchange the addresses of our mothers and fathers, thinking if we ever lose track of each other we can contact parents, the only resolute ties. During the day, we are easily distracted, unable to concentrate on our work, on our preparations for departure.

I pack for the summer in Kansas and tell myself that Jake and I will always find others to love, to lose, to replace. The best we can do is to be open and take the risks. We are really no worse off, I tell myself, than most traditional families, which can be too insular. And how often are they a sham, their nucleus a television, casting a glow as eerie as mercury vapor over an empty farm yard? We will weather the losses, I tell myself. After all, Jake's first word was "hi."

JENNY MORRIS

Feeling Special

◆

My daughter, Rosa, was born in London nine years ago, the most important thing ever to happen in my life. Becoming a parent was everything and more than I ever expected. The experience grounded me emotionally, reconciled me to my own childhood and enabled me to love and be loved in a way which healed the scars of my own insecurity and neediness.

I cannot remember ever feeling loved when I was a child. I cannot remember my parents ever touching me with affection. My memories are of anger, of coldness and boredom. My memories are of desperate loneliness, of countless times when I wanted to kill myself. From the age of sixteen, I searched desperately for warmth, affection and love in a series of sexual relationships with men. Within these relationships I could not stop myself being destructive of love; I had no ability to sustain a comfortable intimacy, for my childhood had given me no opportunity to learn such skills.

Until I was thirty, I never thought seriously about having children. If I gave any consideration at all to the matter it was to assume that to have a child would be too restricting of my life. If an acquaintance told me she was pregnant I was quite unable to enter into any form of congratulation, let alone the joyful empathy which I observed in other women. But in 1980, I stopped taking the Pill and a desire to have a child hit me with an irresistible force. My menstrual cycle developed into a clear pattern of an overwhelming wish to become pregnant followed by a relief that I hadn't and a fear that I would never be able to cope if ever I did. I remember, during the weeks of desire for a child, working out in exact detail how I would organize my life to make parenthood possible, while the weeks when the desire had gone felt empty and flat.

Then, in the summer of 1981, my mother told me that she had discovered a lump in her breast and that she was going into hospital for a biopsy and possible mastectomy. I told myself that if she had cancer, then I would try to get pregnant immediately rather than wait until I had finished the teacher training course on which I was about to embark. At the time, I justified this decision in terms of a realisation of both my mother's and my own mortality. In retrospect, I recognize that any excuse would have done—I just wanted to have a child.

The relationship that I was in at the time was probably reaching the end of its natural life, but Mick also had a wish to be a parent. We had never lived together and did not intend to, but told each other that, even if our relationship did not last, we would still have a relationship as parents. I started to track my ovulation cycle and within three months I was pregnant.

I was very conscious throughout my pregnancy that I had no ambivalent feelings whatsoever about this child that I was welcoming into my life. I never panicked, never worried about how I would cope, never doubted that I had the capacity to mother. Which seems very strange, in view of my own emotional immaturity and neediness. Once I was pregnant, I felt completely fulfilled and self-sufficient. This, of course, resulted in the ending of my relationship with my daughter's father. I am not proud of the way that I used him, and many of my friends criticised me for not wanting to even see him during my pregnancy. However, I did keep my side of the bargain in that I was always very clear that he did have a role as a father and, from the beginning, I created space in which he could develop his relationship with his daughter.

Just before Rosa was born, I qualified as a teacher and completed the Ph.D. which I had started five years previously. I was living in a beautiful one-bedroom council flat which seemed perfect for a new-born baby. I decided to claim supplementary benefit for the first year as I wanted to stay at home and look after my baby before getting a teaching job. The summer of 1982 was hot and I spent many afternoons, both before and after the birth, walking on Hampstead Heath and eating cream teas in the Hampstead Tea Rooms with a friend whose baby was born six weeks after mine. I organised a rota of women friends to come round and do the housework and shopping for me in the week after Rosa was born. I felt very supported and part of a community. I went to few, very few, meetings—I had up until then been an active member of the Labour Party and a Labour Councillor—but a lot of that summer and the ensuing year were spent with other women and their babies and small children. Most of the time, however, I was on my own with my baby. I was never lonely, I never felt isolated or scared or any of the other things that mothers on their own are supposed to feel. I loved the home making which went with full-time mothering. I got such a pleasure out of turning second-hand clothes (both for me and her) into ours by washing and ironing them. The move into a two-bedroom maisonette—just across the road from my previous flat—was magical in the way that the space gave me the opportunity to create something that was mine and my child's.

The most magical part of that first year was what it meant to become a mother. I had always assumed that I would love this child, completely and utterly, but I was not prepared for the way that she would completely and utterly love me. It had never occurred to me to expect reciprocated love. I remember that a friend, who had two young children herself and who in many ways fulfilled the role that my own mother should have fulfilled for me at that time, made a remark which just astonished me. As I sat there, in her kitchen, comfortable in my unconditional love for my beautiful baby, she said, "Look at that, mutual adoration." And I realised that she was right—not only did I love this child, but she loved me back.

Rosa was one of those babies who are immediately in and of this world from the minute she was born. I felt that she came with a ready-made personality and, in spite of the fact that she looked the spitting image of myself as a baby, I never felt that she was me born again. She was, and is, too much her own person. Strong feelings were too dangerous in my childhood for me to feel passionately about things. Rosa's life, in contrast, is full of passion. She is passionate about animals, particularly horses and cats, passionate about her friends. She can express anger and sorrow at the drop of a hat, and the next minute be the sunniest, happiest child imaginable. I feel proud that I have created the space in which she can grow and I feel grateful that she has enabled me to come to terms with my own childhood.

A month after Rosa's first birthday, the day that I signed the contract for the full-time teaching post that I had just been offered, something happened to me which is every new mother's nightmare. While Rosa was fast asleep in her cot, I had an accident which permanently disabled me and took me away from her for five months.

When I had started taking Rosa to her dad's flat each weekend for him to look after her, at first for a few hours and then for a day, I used to be filled with fear that while I was away from her something would happen to me. That evening my fears were realised when I tried to rescue a child who had got stuck on a ledge over the railway line which ran at the bottom of my garden. I fell and broke my back. My legs are permanently paralysed and I now use a wheelchair.

On one level, my emotional self-defences very efficiently looked after me when this happened. While waiting for the ambulance I arranged that a neighbour would contact Mick and get him to come and look after Rosa. I never doubted that he would move into my flat and look after her competently and lovingly. Over the next weeks and months in hospital, I concentrated on getting myself physically into the positions so that I could look after her (for example, I did weight-training to learn to lift her on to my lap), getting a transfer to a wheelchair-accessible flat, and initiating legal action for compensation.

On another level, I was terrified and heart-broken. I was terrified that I would no longer be able to live on my own with my daughter, heart-broken at the severance of my relationship with her. During the early days in the hospital, I decided that it would be unfair on Rosa for her to grow up in a single-parent household now that I was disabled and Mick and I planned, therefore, to live together. In fact this would have been disastrous but everyone went along with it because we all assumed that a disabled woman would not be able to bring up a child on her own. Luckily, the council could not find us a three-bedroom flat which we insisted on if we were to live together and instead offered me a two-bedroom ground floor property and Mick a one-bedroom flat above it.

By the time I left Stoke Mandeville Hospital, it was clear that I could look after Rosa on my own. It was also clear that the only relationship Mick and I could have was as parents. He has continued to be a good father to Rosa. She spends twenty-four hours of every weekend with him, alternating Friday and Saturday nights, and one week every summer. He is a permanent and secure fixture in her life and she loves him very much. She has no concept of his being separated from her and her life.

In the first two days after the accident I did not want Mick to bring Rosa to the hospital to see me because I was in such pain and I would not be able to cuddle her in the way that I assumed she would want. However, when he did bring her to see me, the third day after the accident, she didn't seem to want anything to do with me. This remained the case throughout the time I was in hospital, even when I started coming out at weekends. I told myself that such a young baby was only interested in who was looking after her, and Mick had completely taken over my role in that way. If that was the explanation for Rosa's lack of response to me, then she was not suffering as a result of the break in our relationship and I found my own agonies of jealousy and grief easier to deal with than any recognition of the emotional pain that she might be suffering.

It wasn't until a year after I came out of the hospital that I was able to think about whether Rosa's lack of response to me might have been the result of feeling abandoned because I had suddenly disappeared and stopped looking after her. Having confronted that possibility and acknowledged the awfulness of that abandonment, however, I am still not sure whether she did actually feel abandoned. She was only thirteen months old and it really did feel at the time as if the replacement of one loving adult with another was not a problem for her. In many ways, it was my replacement of Mick when I came out of hospital when Rosa was eighteen months old which I think had more of an emotional impact on her.

It was very difficult to get back the "specialness" of my relationship with Rosa after I left hospital. It felt as if the bond with her had been completely severed. Physically, I was looking after her from the moment I moved into the new flat with her, but emotionally it took almost a year before I could truthfully say that it was as if I had never been away. During those five months that I had been in the hospital, Rosa had been closer to her father than she was to me, and—in retrospect—that time was a gift both to her and to Mick in that they now enjoy a closer relationship than they might otherwise have had. However, the closeness had been achieved at the expense of the severance of her bond with me and it was heart-breaking to recognise this.

My life was also difficult because I started work full-time four months after returning home. At the time, I was attempting to insist that nothing had changed as a result of my disability, that the structure of my life remained the same. The price of this was exhaustion, and if it had not been for the twenty-four hours each weekend when Mick had Rosa, I would never have survived. I used to sleep for ten hours then and spend the rest of the day catching up on preparation for the next week's teaching. And yet I was also engaged in local disability politics and started to do some research, in addition to my teaching job. I must have been mad.

My memories of those years are pretty blurred. I do remember that, until Rosa was about four or five, I used to get her into bed by seven most nights, then make my supper and collapse in front of the television for the rest of the evening. I watched all sorts of rubbish but it kept me going. I remember feeling guilty that I was so desperate to get Rosa to bed so that I could have time to myself. I would force myself to read her stories every night but most of the time I wasn't enjoying it. If I hadn't been confident that she was having a wonderful time during the day, with her childminder and at the nursery class she went to when she was three and a half years old, I would have been totally consumed with guilt.

The good times during those years were when I was grounded at home with Rosa for long stretches of time. I remember when we were snowed in one year and how wonderful it was not having to worry about time, about rushing to get to work, rushing to get back. I would never have been able to carry on working full-time were it not for college half-terms and holidays, when I could cease looking at the clock every other minute, and instead allow myself the luxury of slowing down and paying attention to Rosa.

Three years after my accident I received £350,000 in compensation. I immediately bought a three-storey Victorian house—just as the house price boom was about to take off—and converted it, installing a lift. Rosa and I now live in this huge house whose spaces we seem to fill quite adequately. A year after that I went part-time in my job and then, finally, last year I felt confident and motivated enough to earn my living as a freelance writer, consultant and researcher.

Gradually, after I started to work part-time and as Rosa got older, I have emerged from that desperate intensity of coping which characterised the years after my accident. There is so little stress in my life now that I cannot conceive of how I managed during those years. Ironically, however, I discovered while I was working very intensely at writing for three months last year, that I was again not paying attention to Rosa. My mind became so consumed with the ideas I was developing that it had little space for her. Maintaining a relationship with my daughter requires a concerted attempt to create emotional space for her, otherwise I become merely a "good enough" caretaker.

It both amuses me and fills me with anger that the stereotype of a disabled single parent means that many people will assume that Rosa is a deprived and disadvantaged child. Nothing could be further from the truth, but I am aware that I have to be careful to make sure that this stereotype does not dominate the way that people such as teachers react to my daughter. When it comes to choosing a secondary school for Rosa, for instance, I am uncertain as to whether I will play a full role in looking at schools. Quite apart from the problems of access, which I am not sure that I want to get into the way of deciding on a school, I am aware that strangers make all sorts of negative assumptions about us as a family and I don't want these to influence teachers' expectations of Rosa.

When Rosa first started at primary school, I and another parent, who is also a wheelchair-user, tried to persuade the school to take on the issue of disability in terms both of access for disabled parents and for disabled children. I became Chair of the governing body and helped to ensure that physical access into the ground floor of the school was improved. We started to discuss how the first and second floors would be made accessible and also tried to enthuse the teaching staff and the Parents' and Teachers' Association about the possibilities of the school welcoming children with physical disabilities. We failed in both these goals. Teachers and parents were too frightened of what they saw as the problems of having disabled children in the school and our needs as parents were seen as a special case which could not justify the expenditure. In contrast, the PTA has put enormous effort into raising £20,000 in order to install a play structure which is unsuitable for children with a mobility impairment and thus creates yet another barrier to such children attending the school. Their attitudes provoke such anger and frustration in me that I realised that I had to separate out my feelings about non-disabled people's prejudices against disabled people from my feelings about my daughter's education. On most other measures, the school is a good one and Rosa has always felt very, very positive about going there each day. In order to remain positive myself about the school, I have had to suppress my feelings about its discrimination against disabled parents and children, a discrimination which is found throughout the entire education system.

At the same time, I think it is important that Rosa recognises the prejudice and discrimination which face disabled people, in the same way that it is important that she recognises—and feels able to challenge—racism and sexism. I have to move carefully between my anger that this September she will have to move upstairs and I will no longer be able to visit her classroom; my despair that other children have harassed her because her class has been kept downstairs for two years longer than they would otherwise; Rosa's conflicting feelings about moving upstairs; and my wish that school should remain a positive experience for her.

Most of Rosa's activities outside our home occur in places which are physically inaccessible to me. The drama class which she goes to, the music club, most of her friends' houses—all these are places where I cannot enter. I have developed strategies for dealing with this. Most of her social life takes place at our house. While I was a college lecturer, I was able to organise my timetable so that I could pick Rosa up from nursery and then school at least twice a week. It was easy to start inviting her friends back for tea and now that I work entirely from home I am able to do this most days of the week. I bought a car telephone, so that even if I cannot go into the houses where she goes to parties or to play I can at least make contact and establish that I have brought her or come to pick her up.

Another legacy of my accident is my fearful realisation that life is very dangerous. I was always a cautious person but now I feel as if disaster is lurking in every daily activity. I can watch Rosa and her friends playing, or getting in and out of the car, or running down a country lane on holiday, and create a vivid picture in my mind of injury and death. I experienced absolute terror when Rosa started going horse riding. When I was first admitted to Stoke Mandeville Spinal Unit there were two girls in the beds opposite me who were both paralysed as the result of riding accidents—one of them had lost the use of both her arms and her legs. How could I possibly let my daughter engage in an activity which could have such devastating consequences? But I do.

Every Saturday Rosa spends half the day at a stables, riding, helping out and just being around the horses. I put up with my terror for her safety because her enjoyment of this activity increases the quality of her life so much. The separation of what riding means to me from what it means to her is part of her growing into an entirely separate person with her own passions and priorities.

People assume things about you if you don't have a sexual relationship. This isn't surprising. We are all so influenced by the idea that we need sex and that if we don't have it then there is something missing, even something wrong with us.

I have assumed for years that my desire for solitude, my need for solitude, is pathological, that it came from what was wrong about my childhood. Undoubtedly it did, but believing that the need for solitude in itself is wrong has prevented me from celebrating this aspect of myself.

More recently I have started to recognise my need for solitude as a part of my self that I value, perhaps above all else. While I've been a parent, I have tended to use Rosa as an excuse for not allowing another adult to become part of my life. I didn't want someone else to enter the life that she and I have, so my relationships have been conducted during the times when Rosa is at her father's. My "twenty-four hours a week relationship" as one man described them. This has caused difficulties, not least because when someone embarks on a relationship with me my disability makes it into a bigger thing than it may otherwise have been. Casualness has been completely missing from any sexual relationships I have had since being disabled. This is because, in our disablist society, people do not enter lightly into a physical relationship with someone who has a physical disability. How could they? There are so many barriers and inhibitions to be overcome.

The problem has been that the people with whom I have had sexual relationships since my accident thought that the physical disability was the barrier. But once this became neutralised they found that there was something else in the way. Days when I wake up on my own, in an empty house, when the hours stretch ahead with no one else to populate them but myself, these are my life-blood, and when my one day like this a week disappears into a relationship, I start to disintegrate. I can blame it on being a single parent—how necessary it is to have time for myself when my daughter is such an important part of my life the other six days of the week—but, if I'm honest, it was like this even before I had her. With each sexual relationship I've had in my life, after the first few months I would start gasping for solitude. During the later stages of my relationship with Rosa's father I would grab at "free" weekends; I became the "I want to be alone" stereotype, all the time feeling guilty, pathological.

It was when I—finally—had a relationship with a woman that she enabled me to confront the fact that a need for solitude is at the central core of my being. And that this need is a positive, not to mention productive, part of me. Above all, it is solitude which has turned me into a writer. Being a mother is not a substitute for a relationship; Rosa will grow up, leave home and lead her own life. It is my autonomy and solitude which are very superior substitutes and I cannot imagine wanting anything more.

The stereotypes which associate happy holidays and cosy Christmases with two-parent families and lots of children meant that I always felt I had to provide Rosa with a surrogate "family" at Christmas and holiday times. Up until two years ago we would either go to a friend's house for Christmas day or invite other people over to us. But "family" Christmases have disturbing emotional legacies for me. In my childhood they often ended with my mother retreating to her bedroom in anger and frustration and a cold disappointment settling over the house. So for the last two Christmases, Rosa and I agreed that we would spend Christmas Day on our own but would go over to a friend's house at tea-time. It feels as if our family of two is sufficient at a time when the social pressures telling us that single-parent families are inadequate are particularly strong.

As for holidays, Rosa *is* deprived in that she is the only child in her class who has never been on an aeroplane or a foreign holiday. This was initially because I have no desire to take such a holiday, although I think that I may well have forced myself to by now if it were not that Rosa is so happy with the kind of holidays which we go on. We have settled into a pattern of going to a village in Sussex where a friend has a bungalow. Up until recently I thought that I needed to invite other children to spend time with us there, otherwise, I assumed, Rosa would be very bored with only my company. In fact, all that Rosa wants to do when we go there is spend half the day with the woman opposite who has six cats and the rest of the time at the stables down the road. She enjoys having her friends to stay, but this year we are going to be there for most of the weeks entirely on our own. I think I may feel the lack of adult company, although I will find the experience interesting, but once again I feel very liberated from the social pressures which tell me that I cannot provide a proper family for my child.

When Rosa was younger, outings to the theatre, museums and so on, felt very special to me and in fact they still do. Establishing that somewhere was accessible and that she and I could enjoy something which other mothers perhaps take for granted, felt like a real achievement. In the early years after my accident such things took on a magical quality because while I was lying in hospital I could not imagine doing anything so ordinary as taking my daughter to a Saturday morning puppet show. Each time therefore that we did something like this it was an affirmation that life was still wonderful.

The specialness that I felt with the discovery of how I loved being a mother is now mixed up with the specialness that I feel because life has gone on and got better since my accident. I remember spending one Saturday afternoon, when Rosa was six, going with her on my electric three-wheeler scooter down to the local shops to buy books and paints for her and me, coming back along the canal looking for ducklings, Rosa chatting happily away all the time. Our companionship, her enthusiasm, my ability to buy whatever we wanted, our return to a wonderful house, felt very special. I didn't analyse why at the time, but thinking about it now, such things seem nothing short of miraculous when I consider the legacies of my childhood and the way in which my accident almost brutally destroyed our life together.

◆

KATHLEEN MOORE

Single Mother, Single Son

◆

My son is twenty now and has left home. I am alone again—just like before he was born. Twenty years of days that sometimes seemed endless are now just memories—those unsubstantial, did-it-really-happen, have-to-be-shared-to-be-real kinds of thoughts. But I am not the person I was before he was born. I am forever changed by having been his only parent and by him having been my only child.

March 28, 1969: I'm pregnant. It feels strange and scary. What do I know about babies? They're like something from another planet. And yet part of me is glad and really wants him. (I already know it's a boy.)

I made a scene in the doctor's office. As soon as he told me I was pregnant (he probably saw from my chart that I'm single), he said I should go to the business office and then he left the room. They told me I had to pay five hundred dollars down before I could see the doctor again. No one asked how I was, if I needed help—just, "How will you pay?" I caught the doctor in the hall and said loud enough for everyone to hear, "You're the most insensitive, money-grabbing, uncaring excuse for a doctor I've ever seen. I wouldn't come back here if you were the last obstetrician on earth." It gave me satisfaction. He didn't care.

My health insurance won't cover anything because I'm single. I don't even plan to tell Mom and Dad, or Jackie, so I can't borrow from them. I feel very alone and helpless.

April 13: Went to a social services office today. For four hundred dollars I can get all my doctor visits, the delivery and hospital bills paid. The social worker talked me into coming to some of their group discussions. I already know I want to keep my baby but I'll go. I know I *should* consider adoption. Maybe he would be better off if a couple took him, but I'll probably be married before he's old enough to realize he didn't have a father for those first few years.

April 30: I quit work. I'm showing and it's too embarrassing. I know they're wondering who the father is. I told him I wouldn't tell anyone and I haven't.

Barb invited me to share her apartment. I have the tiniest room imaginable, off the kitchen. Feels like the hired girl's room. Only good thing is it's next to the bathroom. Well, for fifty dollars a month I could live with Dracula. Feels like that sometimes, too.

May 14: Ann and Joe came over. She wants me to marry Joe, *her* boyfriend, before the baby is born so it will be "legitimate." I laughed—thought they were kidding. My best friend lending me her boyfriend to marry so my baby will have a father's name on the birth certificate! But she meant it. It's important to her. It isn't to me. I think the word illegitimate is stupid. *My* actions might have violated some law but a baby—a person—can't be illegal. I said no.

September 2: My friend Jack found me a job. A friend of his is directing a new educational program for social workers and needs a research assistant. She hired me! I can work as long as I want before the baby comes and take off as long as I want after he's born. I never realized before—never needed to know—how dependent I am, we all are. I thought I was a loner, a rebel. Ever since I was a little kid, I made my own decisions. I took care of myself and anyone else who happened to be around: my parents, my friends, my students. Now everyone's taking care of me. Even strangers. Gifts are abundant without my asking. Would people be this way if I wasn't pregnant? Is it the total neediness of an infant that inspires such generosity and joyful giving? Probably. But so what? If I wasn't pregnant, I wouldn't need all this help.

October 10: The Head Start parents gave me a surprise baby shower. All those gifts! They literally filled up my Volkswagen Beetle with everything including a bright red tricycle. These women live on the edge—not a nickel to spare, not even enough for necessities. Is giving to others a necessity of life? It must be because the fun and joy of that party was so real, so sincerely from their hearts. I felt accepted by them. They've endured poverty, racism, husbands leaving them, hard work.

And I was an outsider, a do-gooder who thought she could make things better for them. Now I'm one of them. My humanness, no, my womanness, has put me in their circle and they rejoiced at my coming in.

October 25: I've got a lot of shopping to do. The baby's due and I'm not ready to move into my own apartment. How do other single women manage? I don't know anyone to ask. Sometimes I feel so unique. Has any other twenty-five-year-old, unmarried woman gotten pregnant and kept her baby? If so, where is she so I can talk to her? I have so many questions. Not intimate ones like, "How has society treated you and your child?" It's things like, "Where do you do the laundry?" and "How do you find day care?"

(5:00 P.M.) I'm exhausted. I had no intention of spending so much time downtown. I wonder if I should write to that young girl in the bank? She told me she thinks she's pregnant and the fear in her eyes was so tangible. I wanted to tell her it's okay. She's probably only eighteen, never been away from home. She made me realize how old I am, how much experience I've had. I have been around the world and found the only thing that is fearful is my own feeling of uncertainty, doubt of my own capabilities. The world itself has proven to be a wonderful, safe, loving place. Everywhere, I have experienced kindness, helpfulness. Bringing a baby into this world is not at all a bad thing to do. But she doesn't know that. She's too young, too limited by the views of the world given to her by her parents, her church, her school, and the ten o'clock news. If I had only that to go on, I too would be afraid to have a baby, afraid to keep it, afraid for myself and for him.

October 28: At 5:36 A.M., October 26, Michael John was born: eight pounds, one ounce, twenty-one inches long. I kept saying, "Make him cry. He's not crying." I was terrified that he was dead. They told me he was fine, but I couldn't see him clearly through the haze of drugs I'd been given and he was so still, so silent. In all the movies the doctor slaps the baby's bottom and he cries and everyone is happy. I screamed at them, "Make him cry," until they did and then I felt bad that he'd been hurt.

I wish someone else besides Barb had taken me to the hospital and been there with me. I am grateful to her but I would have liked someone I love to be with me. I would have liked Michael's father to be with me.

October 29: The guys from work came to the hospital with champagne in crystal glasses, flowers for me and toys for Michael. We drank a toast to him and laughed and took Polaroid pictures. A wonderful celebration! A little odd perhaps to the other new mothers on the floor with their husbands and parents visiting them. Here I was with three married men, two divorced mothers, a bartender and a waitress, celebrating the birth of a child whose father they don't even know!

October 30: Dan picked Michael and me up at the hospital and took us home with him. He and Sally and their kids are so easy to be with. They treat me as part of their family, as if I were one of their sisters and this was the most normal, natural thing in the world. Sally says I'm doing everything right with Michael. But he still seems like a little stranger to me.

November 22: My mother came to spend a couple weeks with us. That was a surprise. She was so against my keeping him, I thought she'd never speak to me again. She hasn't told anyone she knows about Michael and doesn't plan to. How can I take him back to Detroit at Christmas if she doesn't want anyone to know? Will she make us stay in the basement? But I can see he has won her heart. I know Daddy will love him, and Jackie has already called and said how anxious she is to see him.

December 5: Feeding and changing Michael seem to take all my time. I just wash diapers, sterilize bottles, bathe him, and sleep! I've cried a few times over fear of his future. I feel inadequate and afraid he'll miss something important in life because I kept him. And I cry because I'm alone. I'm disappointed in Michael's father. I told him I wouldn't ask him for anything, didn't need anything. But I hoped that he would *want* to see Michael, would want to know him. He hasn't shown any interest at all. How will I tell this beautiful little boy that his father didn't care about him? Will I make up a lie? Will I tell him something that will make him feel good because I can't stand to see him suffer? Or will I let life be to him whatever it will be, with all its pain as well as its joy? How much pain can a parent keep from her child? And are we supposed to keep pain away? No one kept pain away from me, but then they didn't know I was hurting.

December 11: He smiled. I'm not imagining it, he really did!

December 12: He not only smiled, he almost laughed. Such a grin. I can't believe how cute he is. And how much I love him.

January 28, 1970: Michael has discovered the sound of his voice and it pleases him. He talks to Humpty Dumpty in his crib and plays peek-a-boo with his own face in the mirror. He finally got his thumb in his mouth but didn't know what to do with it.

June 18: Michael began to crawl! I was out of town, at a Head Start conference. He was sort of crawling and rolling over when I left but now he goes lickety-split across the floor. He pulls himself up on everything and tries to stand and walk.

July 20: Michael just took his first step—and then fell down, of course!

July 30: He got his first teeth, two together at the bottom and a little crooked. He bit my toe this morning and that's how I found out. I am overcome with an incredible sadness that there is no one to share these "firsts" with. I want someone else to know. I want someone else to *care* that this is happening to him. I can only call Ann so many times and tell her. She's gone through it all eight times, and it has lost its magic for her. Sharing it with Mom and Dad or Jackie isn't much satisfaction when I know they would rather I not even have him. This is the unbearable pain—of loving him so much and wanting to share the moments of wonder and joy and pride with someone and there's no one. Then I feel really alone. For something to be real—to *know* that it really happened—it must be shared, must be common knowledge with at least one other person. Everything that happens, everything I feel, needs the validation of another. I can get through the physical hardships alone. I can carry him and two cases of formula up the steps although it feels like my back will break. I can chase him all over the park so he doesn't get hurt. I can stay up until 2:00 A.M. washing diapers. That's hard but not impossible. What I can't do alone is rejoice in all the wonderful moments of growth, of fun, the amazing things he says and does, with just myself. And when I'm old and he's grown up and gone, who will remember with me? When something isn't remembered, someone said, it's as if it never happened. This is not what I thought the pain of single parenthood would be. No one told me about this.

October 26: One year old. I fear for the kind of world Michael will have. There are wars now in most of the countries I visited. Will he be able to go to Jordan and Israel and Egypt as I did, to meet and love the people? And there is that damned war in Vietnam, that took Rick. Rick who would have married me if he'd come back but whose body is scattered all over a field in Vietnam. Am I raising another winner of the Distinguished Service Cross, to be awarded posthumously? Will there be a war in Africa or South America when Michael is eighteen? Can I teach him to be a conscientious objector? Surely he will learn my values and refuse to go. But he needs to learn that from a man, someone like himself who faced the decision to go or not go, who can understand it from a boy's point of view.

June 14, 1974: I had Michael tested for early entrance to kindergarten. I've been working with some parents and teachers to start an "open" school. They assured me that kindergartners could stay all day if they were intellectually and physically ready. I *know* Michael is! He's been in day care since he was six months old. They can't stand him at the center any more. He wakes up the kids from their naps so he will have someone to play with! They ought to put him on staff.

August 2: Michael doesn't like to see me cry and asked why I was tonight. "Because Grandpa died so we won't see him anymore," I said, "and I miss him." "When I grow up I'm going to be your daddy so you don't have to cry." But I still cried and he asked what else made me sad. I told him I was lonely. He said, "You can't be lonely when I'm here," and he began to tickle me until I was laughing. How does he know so much? Where does that compassion come from?

August 12: *Now* they say kindergartners *cannot* stay all day! They say that five year olds aren't ready for that much structured activity. How dare they tell me about my child. *I'm* the one who's lived with him for almost five years, day and night. *I* know what my child is capable of. Parents know their children inside and out. No one helped us. We had to learn by being with them, by watching them, by trial and error, by listening to them, playing with them, punishing them, loving them, hating them—2,628,000 minutes of constant care, worry, observation, togetherness. And these teachers have never even met my child! Tomorrow I'm going to see the superintendent of schools and Michael is coming, too. This is one child who *is* going to go to school all day!

September 5: Michael's first day of school and I am deathly sick. All I can do is throw up and moan with pain. Thank God, Mom, Jackie and Shannon are here. Mom got

Michael up, Jackie made his breakfast, Shannon dressed him and combed his hair. Then Jackie and Shan took him to the bus stop and waited with him. Two adults and a teenager to get one little four year old off to school! Why am I so sick? Is this psychosomatic? I don't want my baby to grow up? Don't want him to become independent? Not need me any more? Don't trust the staff at school? Yes to all of the above!

December 2, 1975: One of the questions in Michael's workbook was "What does your father do?" Michael wrote, "I don't got a father." We talked about the story, but Michael never mentioned "father" so I didn't either. Does he care? Does he hurt—like I do—because he "don't got a father?"

October 26, 1978: Nine years old today. I never thought Michael would be growing up without a father. I always thought I'd marry and have more kids. I told Michael for his birthday I'd get him a puppy. I really wish I could give him a father and a family. It seems so lonely for him. I know I'm lonely. I wonder how he feels inside.

March 17, 1979: Got a call at work to come to school and get Michael because he was sick. Hurried to the doctor with him. He said Michael had to have his appendix out right away. I panicked. "Are you sure?" I kept asking. Finally, irritated with me, he got another doctor to come in and examine him and the second doctor confirmed it. "Right away," he emphasized. I was remembering when I was twelve and had appendicitis and no one knew and I almost died. I'd never had such pain. It was worse than labor. I can still remember it. They almost lost me on the operating table. All this was going through my mind while I alone had to decide whether Michael should have this surgery immediately. He wasn't in that much pain and how can they be sure? The thought of them cutting into this thin little body was so repulsive—yet if they were right? Would I dare repeat my experience, waiting until it was too late? I wanted someone, anyone, to help me make this decision. But there was no one, only me. Of course, I couldn't take the chance. He went right away.

(10:00 P.M.) It's over and he's back in his hospital room, his appendix in a jar on his bedside stand. They won't let me stay overnight, but I'll stop each morning on my way to work and then come after work. What would I do if I had other kids, or if the hospital wasn't so close? Or if I wasn't so strong and healthy?

May 10: Michael didn't come home from school today, and I spent three hours in sheer terror. When I finally found him, I had to figure out a punishment severe enough to make him understand he can't do that. But I hate to hurt him. I want so much to shower him with love and kisses and make his life one of total happiness. Of course, that's absurd. Then it wouldn't be his life. Perhaps these little panic times kids cause their parents are to prepare us for the big panic when they really leave.

April 15, 1980: Michael has been so difficult these last two years. I cry, worry, scream, and pray—and always feel that I've done the wrong thing. Whenever I get mad at him, he cries and says he's a bad person. I never know how to react, when to punish him, how to get him to do what's right. I get furious with him. It just happens before I can stop myself. If only there was someone else with us, another parent or child, someone who could say, "Stop it, Kathy. You're yelling at him for nothing. Calm down." Just the presence of another would make me stop before I went off into these rages. But there is no one to stop me. He doesn't deserve my inconsistent behavior. I wonder if I can ever explain that this is not how I wanted to be. I wanted to be perfect. Kind, loving, always knowing the right thing to say and do for him. Now I know that I've no idea how to raise a child. My parents only expressed one emotion—anger—and that seems to be my main feeling now, too. Can I change? Michael, I'm sorry for the wrong things I've done, for the things I haven't been, for the life that wasn't.

August 17, 1981: I applied to some private schools for scholarships, and if he gets one I'll send him. I never thought I'd give up on public education. I believe in it so much. But all year the teachers and principal called me about his behavior, yet they wouldn't try anything I suggested. The English teacher told me, after school ended, that he failed because he didn't do his research paper. Why didn't she tell me sooner so I could have done something?

September 3: He got a scholarship and now I wonder is this right? Education is so important to me. But will he be okay with these rich kids? Will they accept him? Will he make friends? He's mixed race *and* not rich. Does that matter to seventh graders?

July 6, 1983: Pat thinks Michael stole something from her house. I can't believe it. I haven't slept for three nights. Michael denies it and there is no proof, but the circumstances all point to him. I want to blame Pat. Why does she leave her door open? That dog is no protection. Anyone could have gone in there.

July 9: I found a little bag with some coins in it. That's what was taken from Pat's. Michael did steal from her! He's a thief and a liar. My son! Why? What am I supposed to do now?

July 10: Forced myself to call the police and turn him in. It was the hardest thing I've ever done. But I have to stop this behavior before it gets worse. He has to know this is completely unacceptable. They told me over four hundred dollars worth of things were stolen. I thought it was only the coins. Michael insists he didn't do it. I want to believe him. I think I do believe him, but he did take the coins. My heart is breaking for him and for myself. This is so hard for me. I need someone to help me through this but there is no one I can tell. Michael doesn't want anyone to know and neither do I. I feel as if *I* did something wrong, ashamed of myself more than of him.

August 27: Sitting outside the courtroom, waiting to go in. I feel like I want to throw up. Michael is scared. I know because he's so quiet. I wish we weren't alone. Just the two of us. I wish there was someone I could have brought to help me and someone he could have brought to help him. My worst fears for Michael were never like this.

October 15: Michael has been skipping classes. He says he doesn't have to do well in school because he'll get an athletic scholarship for college. I asked his coach why they let him stay on the team with his poor attendance and grades. "As long as they are making some progress toward graduation, they can play," he told me. I told him then I would have to take Michael off the team until his grades improve. The coach is very upset with me, tried to tell me how important sports are in a young boy's life. I'm really angry with them for making me the bad guy. Michael has to know he can't just "play" through life.

September 9, 1984: Michael really tried last year and improved a lot. I told him he could be on all the teams he wants this year as long as he does okay in school, too. He seems to care again. He goes to church now because he likes the teen group there. I hope he can find the male role models and companionship there that I've been unable to give him.

March 18, 1986: Michael has been skipping classes constantly. He may not pass any subjects. The school said they sent me a letter, but I never got it. Why didn't they call me? It's almost as if they don't want him to do better. Is it racial? Is it because he's on a scholarship? He doesn't respond to anything I've tried—reward, punishment, counseling, screaming. He lies to me all the time. Home feels like an armed camp. We have become hostile, enemies, foreigners. My desires for him and his future are not his desires. Am I such a product of the work ethic that I don't believe in any fun and rule-breaking? Is he such a product of the me-generation that he doesn't believe in work or delayed gratification? He's only sixteen, I tell myself; he'll change. It's just a teen-age phase.

June 3: He's been expelled. One more year and he would have graduated from this prestigious school and could have gotten a scholarship to almost anywhere. He would have been captain of his basketball team this year. I'm devastated, crying, broken-hearted. He is stone cold, says he doesn't care (but won't tell anyone). He shows no anger, grief, sadness, fear. I feel like he's a baby again, in need of my help. I want to hold him and tell him things will be okay, tell him what to do and he'll do it. But he's not a baby. He's six feet, four inches tall and puts his arm around me and tells me not to cry, that it's not so bad, and everything will be okay. It is more clear to me than ever before that the relationship between a single mother and her son is unique. Yes, he needed a father, but I needed a man in my life. I never asked him to be that man, but he must sense that need in me and feel somehow responsible to fill it. Perhaps unconsciously I am projecting that message to him, although, God knows, that is the last thing I want to do. Yet I know he knows it is there. There is something that is too grown-up about him, something that is not sixteen years old.

May 31, 1987: I didn't really believe Michael graduated until I saw his diploma. This year was a constant struggle. He started out on the honor roll, but then at every teacher conference I'd hear, "He could do so well if only he'd...." I stopped going to the conferences. It was too hard to hear that over and over, knowing nothing I could do would change it. And it was too hard to go alone, seeing other parents there in couples, hearing them talk together about their children.

June 5-6: The State Track Meet! It felt wonderful to be proud of Michael. He won every event he was in. I'd never seen him so concentrated, so determined, so willing to work hard until he dropped from exhaustion. I don't understand the thrill of physical prowess. I was not allowed to do anything as a child because I had asthma, and they thought I'd die if I so much as jumped rope. I was afraid when Michael was born that there'd be no one to teach him sports and give him the confidence I lacked.

So I took him to ice-skating lessons at age three, downhill skiing at five, swimming at six. He played baseball, soccer, basketball, football, and hockey in grade school and was good at almost everything. I got him the equipment even when we didn't have the money, went to all the games (although I had to sit next to another parent from his team so I'd know when to cheer and when to boo). Coaches, teammates, and girls loved him. The excitement of this weekend reminds me of when he was a baby, achieving all those "firsts": first step, first word, first tooth. The pride I felt and then the sorrow at being alone with it, no one else to share the joy. I thought I was used to it by now. It's been seventeen years. But I find lately that the aloneness is harder to bear, perhaps because he will soon be gone and I will really be alone, perhaps because I am worn out with the struggle of the last years.

July 25: I can't believe it but Michael was right about getting athletic scholarships. Based on his track victories, three colleges are willing to give him complete scholarships. I told him I was glad for him, but privately I was furious. I know other parents whose kids worked hard for good grades and are getting almost no assistance. I'm too embarrassed to tell them about Michael's good fortune and angry at the system that rewards physical but not academic skill. Now Michael knows he was right. He *can* get what he wants by playing; working is not necessary. How can he believe me when I am the only one telling him he needs to work and follow the rules, and the world he lives in tells him different?

November 2: I discovered that Michael stole a great deal of money from my account over the summer. I'm so angry and hurt by this I don't know how to cope with it. I don't want to report him to the police and have him arrested. I want to believe he will change, that he will pay me back when he can, that he will never do this again, that he will do well in college and graduate and get a good job and be someone I can be proud of.

February 5, 1988: It's been impossible to reach Michael at his dorm room. He never returns my calls. I'm very suspicious. Something is going on. Something not good. I have a terrible feeling I'm in for another big disappointment. I have this crazy urge to sell the house and leave town and not tell anyone where I'm going, not even myself.

March 15: Michael moved back home. He never went to classes, never did any school work, even dropped out of athletics. He spent all his school money on video equipment, throwing parties, clothes, his girlfriend, God only knows what. He wrote hundreds of dollars of bad checks. I'm letting him live here only if he works and brings home every paycheck, and I watch him write out the payments to the collection agencies. Then he has to start paying me back what he took. I suspect he has lost his driver's license, so I won't let him use my car.

May 7: Tomorrow is Mother's Day and Michael is in jail. Yesterday he was arrested for forging one of my checks. I find myself strangely unemotional about this. It's as if he isn't my son, as if a stranger had done this. I didn't have to press charges. They did it all. I don't know if I could have. Michael was never good about remembering special days. I always thought it was because there was no other parent to take him out shopping, to say, "What do you think we should get your mom for her birthday?" like my dad did with my sister and me, or Mom did when it was for Daddy. This is one Mother's Day *I'd* like to forget. I console myself with the kitten that he surprised me with last year. Of course, his girlfriend helped him with that. It was still fun to be surprised.

June 15: He's working and getting the debts paid off little by little. I often go and pick him up from work. It reminds me of when he was young, and I would pick him up from school after a game or practice. I feel very close to him then. He needs me again. There is something nice I can do for him and he appreciates it. We talk in the car about little, meaningless things and it feels good. It feels like I am in control of my life again because he is under control. I am not his victim during these times. I am his mother again, and I can love him again.

November 27: I don't like the new job Michael has. it doesn't make sense to me. It is a sales job but to me it sounds like a "con." He tells me about all the money he is going to make and how easy it is. I don't believe him. But he loves this kind of job—easy money—how that appeals to him! He has one excuse after another why he hasn't brought any of this "easy money" home yet to continue paying off his debts. He lies so much I never know whether to believe him or not. So I wait.

December 19: Still no money and he doesn't always get up in the morning to go to work. I've given him until January to start paying me or he has to leave. I hate to put him out. Where will he live? Yet I can't let him stay here without working and making an effort to pay me back.

January 11, 1989: One last effort to steal from me. This time I caught it before he could even try to cash the check. I still can't believe it. After being in jail for a week, knowing what would happen if he did this again, he still did it. And he knew I'd find out! When I ask him if he's on drugs, he laughs and says, "You know me better than that, Mom. I don't even smoke. I hate that stuff." And so I wonder, "What is it, then?"

January 15: Michael wasn't here when I came home, although it doesn't seem that anything of his is gone. I wonder if he will come back while I'm home or will he sneak in through the window as he so often has? I feel like I'm under siege. I should change the locks on the doors, should get bars for the windows. I park my car blocks from the house for fear he has a key and will take it during the night while I'm asleep. Is this my son? This person who steals from me, lies to me, breaks into my house, believes in none of my values, seems to be ruining his life? Is this my son? I don't know this person. I am afraid for this person, and I don't love this person. Perhaps sometime in the future I will find my son. Perhaps the day will come when I will have someone to love again. In the meantime, I am alone and my house is very quiet.

September 15, 1989: Michael has been in Kansas City for almost a year now. Living with Michael was hard but it's not easier living alone. At least there was someone else in the house, a live presence that was tangible even when he wasn't here. There were dirty clothes on the floor and dishes in the sink, the telephone ringing. He'd borrow a couple dollars or ask for the car and if he was in a good mood, he'd kiss me when he left the house with my money in his pocket and my car keys in his hand. Now when I come home after work, I say, "Hi, Michael, I'm home," in a loud voice when I'm unlocking the back door and it's dark outside. Just in case someone is watching, I tell myself. But it's really because it gives me the feeling for that brief moment that he is here and I'm not alone.

April 12, 1990: I have no address or phone number for Michael. I can't reach him or touch him. I have no idea when, or if, I'll hear from him again. Someone told me I'm experiencing the reality of life, the risk. One can never be sure of anything. Loving is a risk, the loved one might not always be there.

May 4, 1991: I heard that the Minnesota Legislature has a bill to make it legal for newspapers to print the birth notices of children of unmarried mothers. All these years such births were kept "secret." I never knew that! No wonder I have felt so guilty.

July 16, 1991: Michael called late last night and asked me to send him ninety dollars for a bus ticket home. He lost the business he and his girlfriend ran. He says it's all her fault but she's still there and doing okay. He's the one who doesn't have bus fare or a place to sleep.

Mother's Day, 1992: A letter from Michael was lying on the kitchen table this morning. He is explaining the money he stole from me last week to pay some debts back in Kansas City. ". . . . Love alone can not make up for years of pain or fear or sorrow or anguish but the truth is I love you."

I always blame myself when Michael does something wrong. I shouldn't have had a child outside of marriage. I should have given him up for adoption. If I kept him, I should have been a perfect parent. It's my fault he didn't have a father. But what if I had married, and the man wasn't a good father? Would I blame myself for that, too? Or what if I had given him up for adoption and he got a crummy family? Again, my fault? No matter what I did, there was an equal chance it would not have worked out perfectly. I couldn't know then and I can't know now. There never was any right decision. I did consider all the options, and I chose the one I had most control over and most faith in—myself.

My friends try to tell me I am not responsible for

Michael's life. He is not a book I have written; he composes himself.

October 4, 1993: Michael was supposed to meet me at the airport when I came home but he wasn't there and the house is empty. There's a note, scribbled in blue pencil saying: "The cat was well cared for. The house was kept quiet. Your car was stolen."

Thanksgiving, 1993: I got a card from Michael postmarked from California. It says only, "Forgive me?"

BARBARA KINGSOLVER

Quality Time

◆

Miriam's one and only daughter, Rennie, wants to go to Ice Cream Heaven. This is not some vision of the afterlife but a retail establishment here on earth, right in Barrimore Plaza, where they have to drive past it every day on the way to Rennie's day-care center. In Miriam's opinion, this opportunistic placement is an example of the free-enterprise system at its worst.

"Rennie, honey, we can't today. There just isn't time," Miriam says. She is long past trying to come up with fresh angles on this argument. This is the bland, simple truth, the issue is time, not cavities or nutrition. Rennie doesn't want ice cream. She wants an angel sticker for the Pearly Gates Game, for which one only has to walk through the door, no purchase necessary. When you've collected enough stickers you get a free banana split. Miriam has told Rennie over and over again that she will buy her a banana split, some Saturday when they have time to make an outing of it, but Rennie acts as if this has nothing to do with the matter at hand, as though she asked for a Cabbage Patch doll and Miriam is offering to buy her shoes.

"I could just run in and run out," Rennie says after a

while. "You could wait for me in the car." But she knows she has lost; the proposition is half-hearted.

"We don't even have time for that, Rennie. We're on a schedule today."

Rennie is quiet. The windshield wipers beat a deliberate, ingratiating rhythm, sounding as if they feel put-upon to be doing this job. All of Southern California seems dysfunctional in the rain: cars stall, drivers go vaguely brain-dead. Miriam watches Rennie look out at the drab scenery, and wonders if for her sake they ought to live someplace with ordinary seasons—piles of raked leaves in autumn, winters with frozen streams and carrot-nosed snowmen. Someday Rennie will read about those things in books, and think they're exotic.

They pass by a brand-new auto mall, still under construction, though some of the lots are already open and ready to get down to brass tacks with anyone who'll brave all that yellow machinery and mud. The front of the mall sports a long row of tall palm trees, newly transplanted, looking frankly mortified by their surroundings. The trees depress Miriam. They were probably yanked out of some beautiful South Sea island and set down here in front of all these Plymouths and Subarus. Life is full of bum deals.

Miriam can see that Rennie is not pouting, just thoughtful. She is an extremely obliging child, considering that she's just barely five. She understands what it means when Miriam says they are "on a schedule." Today they really don't have two minutes to spare. Their dance card, so to speak, is filled. When people remark to Miriam about how well-organized she is, she laughs and declares that organization is the religion of the single parent.

It sounds like a joke, but it isn't. Miriam is faithful about the business of getting each thing done in its turn, and could no more abandon her orderly plan than a priest could swig down the transubstantiated wine and toss out wafers like Frisbees over the heads of those waiting to be blessed. Miriam's motto is that life is way too complicated to leave to chance.

But in her heart she knows what a thin veil of comfort it

is that she's wrapped around herself and her child to cloak them from chaos. It all hangs on the presumption that everything has been accounted for. Most days, Miriam is a believer. The road ahead will present no serious potholes, no detour signs looming sudden and orange in the headlights, no burning barricades thrown together as reminders that the world's anguish doesn't remain mute—like the tree falling in the forest—just because no one is standing around waiting to hear it.

Miriam is preoccupied along this line of thought as she kisses Rennie goodbye and turns the steering wheel, arm over elbow, guiding her middle-aged Chevy out of the TenderCare parking lot and back into the slick street. Her faith has been shaken by coincidence.

On Saturday, her sister Janice called to ask if she would be the guardian of Janice and Paul's three children, if the two of them should die. "We're redoing the wills," Janice reported cheerfully over the din, while in the background Miriam could hear plainly the words "Give me that Rainbow Brite right now, dumb face."

"Just give it some thought," Janice had said calmly, but Miriam hadn't needed to think. "Will you help out with my memoirs if I'm someday the President?" her sister might as well have asked, or "What are your plans in the event of a nuclear war?" The question seemed to Miriam more mythical than practical. Janice was a careful person, not given to adventure, and in any case tended to stick to those kids like some kind of maternal adhesive. Any act of God that could pick off Janice without taking the lot would be a work of outstanding marksmanship.

Late on Sunday night, while Miriam was hemming a dress of Rennie's that had fallen into favor, she'd had a phone call from her ex-husband Lute. His first cousin and her boyfriend had just been killed on a San Diego freeway by a Purolator van. Over the phone, Lute seemed obsessed with getting the logistics of the accident right, as though the way the cars all obeyed the laws of physics could make this thing reasonable. The car that had the blowout was a Chrysler; the cousin and boyfriend were in her Saab; the van slammed into them from behind. "They never had a chance," Lute said, and the words chilled Miriam. Long after she went to bed she kept hearing him say "never had a chance," and imagining the pair as children. As if even in infancy their lives were already earmarked: these two will perish together in their thirties, in a Saab, wearing evening clothes, on their way to hear a friend play in the symphony orchestra. All that careful mothering and liberal-arts education gone to waste.

Lute's cousin had been a freelance cellist, often going on the road with the likes of Barry Manilow and Tony Bennett and, once, Madonna. It was probably all much tamer than it sounded. Miriam is surprised to find she has opinions about this woman, and a clear memory of her face. She only met her once, at her own wedding, when all of Lute's family had come crowding around like fog. But now this particular cousin has gained special prominence, her vague features crystallized in death, like a face on a postage stamp. Important. Someone you just can't picture doing the humdrum, silly things that life is made of—clipping her toenails or lying on the bed with her boyfriend watching *Dallas*—if you hold it clearly in your mind that she is gone.

Lute is probably crushed; he idolized her. His goal in life is to be his own boss. Freelance husbanding is just one of the things that hasn't worked out for Lute. Freelance fathering he can manage.

Miriam is thinking of Rennie while she waits through a yellow light she normally might have run. Rennie last week insisted on wearing only dresses to nursery school, and her pale, straight hair just so, with a ribbon; they'd seen *Snow White*. Rennie as a toddler standing in her crib, holding the rails, her mouth open wide with the simplest expectation you could imagine: a cookie, a game, or nothing at all, just that they would both go on being there together. Lute was already out of the picture by that time; he wouldn't have been part of Rennie's hopes. It is only lately, since she's learned to count, that Lute's absence matters to Rennie. On the Disney Channel parents come in even numbers.

Barbara Kingsolver   127

The light changes and there is a honking of horns; some-one has done something wrong, or too slowly, or in the wrong lane. Miriam missed it altogether, whatever it was. She remembers suddenly a conversation she had with her sister years ago when she was unexpectedly pregnant with Rennie, and Janice was already a wise old mother of two. Miriam was frantic—she'd wanted a baby but didn't feel ready yet. "I haven't really worked out what it is I want to pass on to a child," she'd said to Janice, who laughed. According to Janice, parenting was three percent conscious effort and ninety-seven percent automatic pilot. "It doesn't matter what you think you're going to tell them. What matters is they're right there watching you every minute, while you let the lady with just two items go ahead of you in line, or when you lay on the horn and swear at the guy that cuts you off in traffic. There's no sense kidding yourself, what you see is what you get."

Miriam had argued that people could consciously change themselves if they tried, though in truth she'd been thinking more of Lute than herself. She remembers saying a great many things about choices and value systems and so forth, a lot of first-pregnancy high-mindedness it seems to her now. Now she understands. Parenting is something that happens mostly while you're thinking of something else.

Miriam's job claims her time for very irregular hours at the downtown branch of the public library. She is grateful that the people at Rennie's day care don't seem to have opinions about what kind of mother would work mornings one day, evenings the next. When she was first promoted to this posi-tion Miriam had a spate of irrational fears: she imagined Miss Joyce at TenderCare giving her a lecture on homemade soup and the importance of routine in the formative years. But Miss Joyce, it seems, understands modern arrangements. "The important thing is quality time," she said once to Miriam, in a way that suggested bedtime stories read with a yogic purity of concentration, a mind temporarily wiped clean of things like brake shoes and MasterCharge bills.

Miriam does try especially hard to schedule time for the two of them around Rennie's bedtime, but it often seems pointless. Rennie is likely to be absorbed in her own games, organizing animated campaigns on her bed with her stuffed animals, and finally dropping off in the middle of them, limbs askew, as though felled by a sniper.

Today is one of Miriam's afternoon-shift days. After leaving Rennie she has forty minutes in which she must do several errands before going to work. One of them is eat lunch. This is an item Miriam would actually put on a list: water African violets; dry cleaner's; eat lunch. She turns in at the Burger Boy and looks at her watch, surprised to see that she has just enough time to go in and sit down. Sometimes she takes the drive-through option and wolfs down a fish sandwich in the parking lot, taking large bites, rattling the ice in her Coke, unmindful of appearances. It's efficient, although it puts Miriam in mind of eating disorders.

Once she is settled inside with her lunch, her ears stray for company to other tables, picking up scraps of other people's private talk. "More than four hundred years old," she hears, and "It was a little bit tight over the instep," and "They had to call the police to get him out of there." She thinks of her friend Bob, who is a relentless eavesdropper, though because he's a playwright he calls it having an ear for dialogue.

Gradually she realizes that at the table behind her a woman is explaining to her daughter that she and Daddy are getting a divorce. It comes to Miriam like a slow shock, building up in her nerve endings until her skin hurts. This conversation will happen only once in that little girl's life, and I have to overhear it, Miriam is thinking. It has to be *here*. The surroundings seem banal, so cheery and hygienic, so many wiped-clean plastic surfaces. But then Miriam doesn't know what setting would be better. Certainly not some unclean place, and not an expensive restaurant either—that would be worse. To be expecting a treat, only to be shocked with this news.

Miriam wants badly to turn around and look at the little girl. In her mind's eye she sees Rennie in her place; small and pale, sunk back into the puffy pink of her goosedown jacket like a loaf of risen dough that's been punched down.

The little girl keeps saying, "Okay," no matter what her mother tells her.

"Daddy will live in an apartment, and you can visit him. There's a swimming pool."

"Okay."

"Everything else will stay the same. We'll still keep Peppy with us. And you'll go to your same school."

"Okay."

"Daddy still loves you, you know."

"Okay."

Miriam is thinking that ordinarily this word would work; it has finality. When you say it, it closes the subject.

It's already dark by the time Miriam picks up Rennie at TenderCare after work. The headlights blaze accusingly against the glass doors as if it were very late, midnight even. But it's only six-thirty, and Miriam tries to cheer herself by thinking that if this were summer it would still be light. It's a trick of the seasons, not entirely her fault, that Rennie has been abandoned for the daylight hours.

She always feels more surely on course when her daughter comes back to her. Rennie bounces into the car with a sheaf of papers clutched in one fist. The paper they use at TenderCare is fibrous and slightly brown, and seems wholesome to Miriam. Like turbinado sugar, rather than refined.

"Hi, sweetie. I missed you today." Miriam leans over to kiss Rennie and buckle her in before pulling out of the parking lot. All day she has been shaky about driving, and now she dreads the trip home. All that steel and momentum. It doesn't seem possible that soft human flesh could travel through it and come out intact. Throughout the day Miriam's mind has been filled spontaneously with images of vulnerable things—baby mice, sunburned eyelids, sea creatures without their shells.

"What did you draw?" she asks Rennie, trying to anchor herself.

"This one is you and me and Lute," Rennie explains. Miriam is frowning into the river of moving headlights, waiting for a break in traffic, and feels overcome by sadness. There are so many things to pay attention to at once, and all of them so important.

"You and me and Lute," Miriam repeats.

"Uh-huh. And a dog, Pickles, and Leslie Copley and his mom. We're all going out for a walk."

A sports car slows down, letting Miriam into the street. She waves her thanks. "Would you like to go for a walk with Leslie Copley and his mom sometime?"

"No. It's just a picture."

"What would you like for supper?"

"Pot pies!" Rennie shouts. Frozen dinners are her favorite thing. Miriam rather likes them too, although this isn't something she'd admit to many people. Certainly not her mother, for instance, or to Bob, who associates processed foods with intellectual decline. She wonders, though, if her privacy is an illusion. Rennie may very well be revealing all the details of their home life to her nursery-school class, opening new chapters daily. What I had for dinner last night. What Mom does when we run out of socks. They probably play games along these lines at TenderCare, with entirely innocent intentions. And others, too, games with a social-worker bent: What things make you happy, or sad? What things make you feel scared?

Miriam smiles. Rennie is fearless. She does not know how it feels to be hurt, physically or otherwise, by someone she loves. The people at TenderCare probably hear a lot worse than pot pies.

"Mom," Rennie asks, "does God put things on the TV?"

"What do you mean?"

Rennie considers. "The cartoons, and the movies and

things. Does God put them there?"

"No. People do that. You know how Grandpa takes movies of you with his movie camera, and then we show them on the screen? Well, it's like that. People at the TV station make the programs, and then they send them out onto your TV screen."

"I thought so," Rennie says. "Do you make them sometimes, at the library?"

Miriam hears a siren, but can't tell where it's coming from. "Well, I organize programs for the library, you're right, but not TV programs. Things like storybook programs. You remember, you've come to some of those." Miriam hopes she doesn't sound irritated. She is trying to slow down and move into the right lane, because of the ambulance, but people keep passing her on both sides, paying no attention. It makes Miriam angry. Sure enough, the ambulance is coming their way. It has to jerk to a full stop in the intersection ahead of them because of all the people who refuse to yield to greater urgency.

"Mom, what happens when you die?"

Miriam is startled because she was thinking of Lute's poor cousin. Thinking of the condition of the body, to be exact. But Rennie doesn't know about this relative, won't hear her sad story for years to come.

"I'm not sure, Rennie. I think maybe what happens is that you think back over your life, about all the nice things you've done and the people who've been your friends, and then you close your eyes and ... it's quiet." She was going to say, "... and go to sleep," but she's read that sleep and death shouldn't be equated, that it can cause children to fear bedtime. "What do you think?"

"I think you put on your nicest dress, and then you get in this glass box and everybody cries and then the prince comes and kisses you. On the lips."

"That's what happened to Snow White, didn't it?"

"Uh-huh. I didn't like it when he kissed her on the lips. Why didn't he kiss her on the cheek?"

"Well, grownups kiss on the lips. When they like each other."

"But Snow White wasn't a grownup. She was a little girl."

This is a new one on Miriam. This whole conversation is like a toboggan ride, threatening at every moment to fly out of control in any direction. She's enjoying it, though, and regrets that they will have to stop soon for some errands. They are low on produce, canned goods, aluminum foil, and paper towels, completely out of vacuum-cleaner bags and milk.

"What I think," says Miriam, after giving it some consideration, "is that Snow White was a little girl at first, but then she grew up. Taking care of the seven dwarfs helped her learn responsibility." Responsibility is something she and Rennie have talks about from time to time. She hears another siren, but this one is definitely behind them, probably going to the same scene as the first. She imagines her sister Janice's three children bundling into her life in a whirlwind of wants and possessions. Miriam doesn't even have time for another house plant. But she realizes that having time is somehow beside the point.

"So when the prince kissed her, did she grow up?" Rennie asks.

"No, before that. She was already grown up when the prince came. And they liked each other, and they kissed, and afterward they went out for a date."

"Like you and Mr. Bob?"

"Like Bob and I do sometimes, right. You don't have to call him Mr. Bob, honey. He's your friend, you can call him just Bob, if you want to."

Instead of making the tricky left turn into the shopping center, Miriam's car has gone right, flowing with the tide of traffic. It happened almost before she knew it, but it wasn't an accident. She just isn't ready to get to the grocery store, where this conversation will be lost among the bright distractions of bubble gum and soda. Looping back around the block will give them another four or five minutes. They could sit and talk in the parking lot, out of the traffic, but Miriam is starting to get her driving nerves back. And besides, Rennie would think that peculiar. Her questions would run onto another track.

"And then what happened to the seven dwarfs?" Rennie wants to know.

"I think Snow White still took care of them, until they were all grown up and could do everything by themselves."

"And did the prince help too?"

"I think he did."

"But what if Snow White died. If she stayed dead, I mean, after the prince kissed her."

Miriam now understands that this is the angle on death that has concerned Rennie all along. She is relieved. For Miriam, practical questions are always the more easily answered.

"I'm sure the dwarfs would still be taken care of," she says. "The point is that Snow White really loved them, so she'd make sure somebody was going to look after them, no matter what, don't you think?"

"Uh-huh. Maybe the prince."

"Maybe." A motorcycle dodges in front of them, too close, weaving from lane to lane just to get a few yards ahead. At the next red light they will all be stopped together, the fast drivers and the slow, shooting looks at one another as if someone had planned it all this way.

"Rennie, if something happened to me, you'd still have somebody to take care of you. You know that, don't you?"

"Uh-huh. Lute."

"Is that what you'd like? To go and live with Lute?"

"Would I have to?"

"No, you wouldn't have to. You could live with Aunt Janice if you wanted to."

Rennie brightens. "Aunt Janice and Uncle Paul and Michael-and-Donna-and-Perry?" The way she says it makes Miriam think of their Christmas card.

"Right. Is that what you'd want?"

Rennie stares at the windshield wipers. The light through

the windshield is spotty, falling with an underwater strangeness on Rennie's serious face. "I'm not sure," she says. "I'll have to think it over."

Miriam feels betrayed. It depresses her that Rennie is even willing to take the question seriously. She wants her to deny the possibility, to give her a tearful hug and say she couldn't live with anyone but Mommy.

"It's not like I'm sending you away, Rennie. I'm not going to die while you're a little girl. We're just talking about what-if. You understand that, right?"

"Right," Rennie says. "It's a game. We play what-if at school." After another minute she says, "I think Aunt Janice."

They are repeating their route now, passing again by the Burger Boy where Miriam had lunch. The tables and chairs inside look neater than it's possible to keep things in real life, and miniature somehow, like doll furniture. It looks bright and safe, not the sort of place that could hold ghosts.

On an impulse Miriam decides to put off the errands until tomorrow. She feels reckless, knowing that tomorrow will already be busy enough without a backlog. But they can easily live another day without vacuum-cleaner bags, and she'll work out something about the milk.

"We could stop here and have a hamburger for dinner," Miriam says. "Or a fish sandwich. And afterward we could stop for a minute at Ice Cream Heaven. Would you like that?"

"No. Pot pies!"

"And not Ice Cream Heaven?"

"I don't need any more angel stickers. Leslie Copley gave me twelve."

"Well, that was nice of him."

"Yep. He hates bananas."

"Okay, we'll go straight home. But do you remember that pot pies take half an hour to cook in the oven? Will you be too hungry to wait, once we get home?"

"No, I'll be able to wait," Rennie says, sounding as if she really will. In the overtones of her voice and the way she pushes her blond hair over her shoulder there is a startling maturity, and Miriam is frozen for a moment with a vision of a much older Rennie. All the different Rennies—the teenager, the adult—are already contained in her hands and her voice, her confidence. From moments like these, parents can find the courage to believe in the resilience of their children's lives. They will barrel forward like engines, armored by their own momentum, more indestructible than love.

"Okay then, pot pies it is," Miriam says. "Okay."

JEANNINE ATKINS

Shelter

◆

I tap quietly on the door in case Beth, Jane's seven-year-old daughter, is sleeping, and let myself in. Beth calls hello from her bedroom. Until I became friends with Jane and Beth last spring, I hadn't spent much time around children; now Beth's high voice is enough to put me in a good mood. I call back hello, pull off my boots, unzip my down vest, and then decide to leave it on since the apartment is chilly. Jane comes from the bathroom with a bandanna crumpled in her hand. "What a day."

"Can I come hug Connie?" Beth calls.

"No." Jane looks at me while she speaks to her daughter. "Not now." She lowers her voice. "I just got her in."

"Mom, I want to kiss you again, too."

"Hurry." Jane's lips and eyebrows move in what could be either a smile or a frown. "I mean it. Fast."

Beth pauses in the doorway to look at her mother's face. She kisses Jane, then me, then Jane again. She returns to bed and I watch Jane pull the pink and pale green blankets securely over her. I envy Jane that gesture, though I know she earned it with a day I wouldn't have the patience for. But it's strange to think that Jane feels she's been kissed enough today. I can't imagine refusing an offer to be hugged.

"Leave it open, please."

Jane pushes the door to a measured angle.

"Thank you, Mom."

"She's so polite lately," Jane whispers. "Yesterday she even called me Ms. Harris, but it turned out she was playing school. She was calling me in for a parent-teacher conference." She bends over from the waist. Her long hair touches her knees. She straightens up and breathes deeply. "Everything's worse 'cause I'm tired. I spent the night making a dinner no one wanted and then chocolate chip cookies. I haven't made them in years. Help yourself."

The cookies sprawl into each other, still on the pan. I want to save them, scrape off the black bottoms, but instead I turn my back. The magnetic letters on the refrigerator door are stuck at random.

I follow Jane into the living room. Usually we sit in the kitchen, but Jane is probably afraid that our talking will keep Beth up. Beth calls "Good night!" and Jane answers firmly, "That's enough!" She leans against the sofa arm as if curling into her own exhaustion. I sit at the other end.

"I just want that part of my day to be over. We have a hard time getting back to normal after she's been at her father's. And I can't write my poems and type that professor's book at the same time. All day he's been calling me up with changes. How can I organize my life that way? If I wasn't so tired, I'd look for something else."

"Maybe this will lead to a better job. At least it's something to put on your résumé."

"What résumé? Applying for food stamps? A library card? I have those already."

I don't say anything. Jane thinks my newspaper job is glamorous, though I've told her I spend half my days in a dark closet, developing pictures, and that most of my conversations with colleagues are fights or complaints about whose work got on what page. Jane is impressed that my name appears each week in dark print over justified columns; I admire Jane's poems, and once told her that for all my columns, I have yet to write one true word. That was something I didn't know until I said it, and I credit our friendship for the insight.

"You inspire me," I told Jane, and began to wear red-and-violet, or saffron-and-pink, blouses and scarves like Jane's. But I'm secretly shocked that she's reached twenty-six, my own age, without ever having had a full-time job. I am careful to refer to time cautiously, as if it were the name of a disease. "Have you had any time for your poems?"

"I'll get back to them. The other day I put the professor's book aside and still got my hands over the typewriter for five minutes, thinking my own thoughts."

"And at least you have poems in the mail."

"The only time there's anything in my mailbox, it's poems coming back, envelopes addressed to me in my own handwriting. The mailman thinks I write letters to myself." Jane stands up. "I started tea brewing before you came. I forgot."

"Can I help?"

"It's ready," she says from the kitchen. "If you want it. I'm afraid it's a little cold and strong."

"That's fine." I look at the Rousseau reproduction of a naked woman lying among darkly outlined jungle flowers. A man in a white turban and cloak runs in the background. Scotch tape holds the four pieces of the poster together. I remember smoothing these pieces of glossy paper and picking up the four thumbtacks as Jane washed her face. I can't remember if we'd been talking about men, children or work when Jane jumped up, threw some books and ripped the poster.

She brings in two mugs of green tea and shuts the door. "She's heard enough already." Jane puts her tea on the floor. "I'm thinking of going back to Brian. I can't keep this up."

I think of all the time I've taken care of Beth while Jane and Brian tried to work things out. I think of talking on the phone to Jane in the middle of the night. I've invested in this separation, but I can't say, "Don't call your husband." It's like trying to help someone quit smoking or drinking: sooner or later whatever you say will be wrong.

"He's been sending Beth postcards every day. He sent me a mimeographed letter asking for donations for Guatemalan refugees. It wasn't signed, but I'm sure he sent it."

"Tell him you gave at the office." I know my voice sounds bored, but it isn't that. I am trying to keep emotion out of my voice as I wonder if I'm expected to support her as she reunites with her husband. I don't think I can afford to hear any more bad things about Brian.

"I just can't go back to looking at everything politically. Who am I to complain about my headaches when people are getting killed? He doesn't even have to say it anymore. I know he's thinking it."

I hear the tap on the door before Jane does. Beth opens the door a crack and says, "It's me. May I come in?" Her eyes dart around the room. "I just wanted to see if anyone else wanted some water." Beth looks at me, the only one who is smiling.

"No," Jane says. "Get back in bed."

Beth keeps her eyes on me until I say, "No, thanks." Beth takes a step toward me. I barely, tentatively, open out one arm. These times must be hard on her. Maybe she should sit with us a minute.

But the slight opening of my arm and Beth's second step toward me seem like a cue for Jane to stand and grab her daughter. She twists Beth's arm. She hits at the end of Beth's tailbone, hard on the bone. She pushes Beth toward the middle of the room, then restrains herself with what looks like more force than she's put into the blows.

I hear only my own blood rushing through my ears, as if my head were forced beneath a deep wave. The blows were not a controlled spanking or well-considered slaps. A smack with its ringing sound would have been a sign that the sting was already beginning to fade. My own skin feels terribly untouched. Beth whimpers, sits on the floor, clasps her knees, and keeps her back curved as if preparing to be hit again. Her neck is bare above her hunched shoulders, her blue-flowered nightgown pulled around her. She, like Jane, keeps her face down.

Now I understand the changes I've seen in Beth during the past few weeks: her voice too high or too soft, suddenly shrill as an old woman's; her sentences shorter instead of longer; the tightly held hands; her clinginess; her continual declarations of love. My heart opens and closes rapidly beneath my ribs. I feel solid and big. I imagine Beth unwrapping her arms, unbending her knees, standing solidly on the floor. Beth isn't just my friend's daughter, someone I care for as a favor to Jane. She is a complicated human, but she isn't an adult. She is seven years old.

I bend over her and rub Beth's back. I hold her head until she turns her face toward mine. Her eyes range again, as if they might never settle. They are like a crazy person's eyes. I feel like killing, but I only continue to stroke. Then Beth untwists her legs and stands. She moves toward Jane and says, "I'm going to bed."

Jane keeps her hands clasped beneath her breasts. She nods without really raising her head. She keeps her back turned as Beth leaves the room and as I get up to sit on the sofa. Her neck is bent to the ceiling as if she is silently praying or choking.

I think about leaving. We can talk later. But I can't stand. I am held listening to voices inside me that say: Don't say anything. You don't understand. This was a mistake. You're looking for trouble.

Jane unlocks her arms, sits on the chair across the room, and looks at the empty cushions next to me. "I've been so tense lately. She has this radar for when I mention Brian. I can't stand having her take his side."

I hardly listen. I steady myself to say what I know I have to say, while in my mind I hear the endless chatter: Don't interfere. Mind your own business. I have always believed Jane to be a good mother. Last week she drove to all the markets looking for really red strawberries for Valentine's Day. She spent a long time beating the whipped cream with her tiny hand mixer.

"She doesn't want me to even talk about him," Jane says. "She goes between me and him when I get mad, trying to make everything okay, asking sweetly, 'Is everything all right?' I can't stand to think of her watching. I can't stand that she wants Brian to come back."

Even in my mind, I can't make Beth's eyes settle. I rehearse my sentence and imagine Jane standing to her full height, stretching her long neck like an Egyptian goddess, pointing her arm and finger in a straight line toward the door. I don't want our friendship to end. Be patient. Wait this out. Don't jump to conclusions. Be careful.

I look at Jane. I don't care about her problems now. I haven't come to be a listener, a therapist or even her friend. "Jane." The words feel dangerous in my throat. I suddenly see that all night Jane has been more than nervous, tired, self-absorbed. She has also been afraid of herself.

"You can't do that again," I say. "Ever. You've got to call me if you feel like it. I'll come. But don't ever do that again." The words aren't the ones I considered. I meant to say please, to tell her that I understand, that I don't mean to interfere. But the air of the room allows no hedging.

Jane nods. It is unmistakable consent. The ringing stops in my ears as if my head were pulled from rushing dark water. This is why I am here. Jane needed to consent to the command that isn't just mine, but belongs to both of us, like the scarf and books swapped so often we've forgotten whose were originally whose. The words are like beads handed down for generations, belonging to more than one, and precious for that.

Jane lifts her head. "Yes, I will call you." I take her hand. This is a pact. Then Jane goes into the kitchen and brings back a pineapple, holding it by the leaves. "Want some?"

"Are you kidding?"

She shrugs.

"I mean, how are we going to eat it? It's all prickly."

"You eat the insides."

"Okay. Should we get Beth?" I want her with us. I feel as if I have a new right to ask for her company.

"Okay." Jane pulls out a leaf.

"Should I get her?"

"It's ripe." She yanks out another leaf. "You can tell by how easily the stalk pulls out of the top."

I feel hugely relieved to hear these words, as if that is another reason I'm here tonight. To learn how to tell when a pineapple is ripe.

"Yeah," Jane says. "You don't mind?"

Beth's bedroom door is shut. I knock and open it. She is bunched at the top of her bed. The blankets are at the bottom, though the room is slightly cold. I pull the blankets to just cover Beth's feet, then sit down. I stroke the back of her head over and over. Her face is hot. I leave one hand on her forehead, while she unwraps her legs, then her arms, and curls around me. I don't speak until her breath comes closer to my own slower rhythm. "We've got pineapple. Want to eat it with us?"

"With Mom?"

"She wants you to."

She leaves the room. I wait. All the games in the room are stacked in their boxes. The play clothes are folded, the stuffed animals are in a row. I look at each corner of the room and remember how I prayed as a girl, making long silent lists of things and people to be blessed, to be kept safe. I remember the long minutes, the urgent tone, then I go to the living room and switch on the overhead light. I don't like the glare, but I want a change.

"We're having pineapple," Beth announces, like an anxious hostess.

"You'll have to move, honey, while I cut it."

Beth and I watch as Jane holds the pineapple between her crossed legs and saws with a bread knife. The pineapple digs into the sofa cushion.

"I've never had one before. I always wanted to get one, but didn't know what to do with it," I say.

"Me too," Beth says.

"Me neither," Jane says. "I'm improvising."

"You're incredible." I take the slice Beth hands me. It

isn't as prickly as it looks.

"I hate those slimy, wheel-shaped things in cans," Jane says.

"You don't love tinny-tasting fruit? Yellow that glows in the dark?" We are talking for Beth, whose face softens as she listens to our two calm voices. It would be all right to talk about pineapple all night, to gnaw at the rind, to wipe the juice off our chins.

"Somebody get more napkins!"

"It's getting in my ears!"

But soon Beth will say she is tired or full. I watch Jane grip the rind and suck the juice. Beth holds the pointed ends gingerly. I put my piece down, with the feeling that I shouldn't be the first to leave a party. But despite the bunched and scattered napkins, the pale yellow fruit, the chatter, this is not a party. For now an emergency has passed, but I think we all know that there will be other emergencies. We sit too tentatively on the edges of furniture, like women with too little in common, waiting in a side room for the party to end. Waiting for the children.

♦

MARY PLAMONDON

Unwed Mother, 1970

♦

Before

My bedroom those nine months was very small and painted white, with a small double-paned window overlooking Broadway. I bought a mattress at the Salvation Army and put it on the floor up against the wall. There were about nine inches on either side of the mattress. In the space to my right, I put a small crook-necked lamp on a concrete block. To my left, I made two shelves with bricks and boards for my clock and books. I needed space only for those seven or eight books I got each week at the library. Underneath the window I put a three-drawer dresser that I bought secondhand and painted bright yellow. There was no closet, so I put my clothes in an alcove off the front room, hidden by a sheet hung on rings strung on a rod. There was nothing on the walls. I found an off-white burlap curtain for the window, so that the gas station sign didn't shine in my room. I often kept the curtain closed during the daytime, when I was reading or sleeping.

This was my hideout. Most days during those months I spent eighteen or more hours in there. I woke up after nine, after my roommates Bingham and Claudia had left for their jobs at the boot factory. I wasn't that hungry in the morning, even though I didn't have morning sickness. The first feeling when I awoke was a heavy, slow realization that I was pregnant. Alongside this feeling, I felt an urge to stretch and throw the covers back. Getting up to go to the bathroom seemed too much to do.

I got up, dressed in a pair of baggy gray pants and one of the two big shirts I had, one light and one dark blue. I had a boiled egg and toast. I tried to make the dozen eggs last two weeks and the loaf of bread one. Bingham teased me. I was embarrassed by how little food I could afford with the forty dollars a month of foodstamps.

After I ate, I went back into my room and lay down to read. I loved Russian novels. I could make something like *War and Peace* last a week. I loved the sliding into that other world. My own life faded, and I was lost among strangers more familiar to me than anyone in my own family.

Late morning, I walked for five or six miles. I was grateful for the distraction and the feel of my muscles moving vigorously. I often walked out a ways to a spacious, elegant cemetery. It was laid out like a park, with weeping willow and oak and small secluded ponds. I felt safe amidst the concrete monuments, leaning against one as I read or ate my crackers. I never spoke to anyone there and rarely saw another person.

I walked all over Cambridge, down through Harvard Yard, past the old buildings. They seemed small and run-down after my years at the University of Washington. I watched students play soccer, the first time I had ever seen it. I felt very remote. I walked the other direction down Broadway to M.I.T. The buildings were crisper, cooler. The professors wore suits and had very short hair. One night I snuck into the auditorium there to see the last half of the Laura Nyro concert. I loved her song "Eli's Coming." I was startled and pleased to see her brooding darkness absorb the dryness of the room and spill out passionate song. I was way in the back and could just barely see the sweep of her thick black hair over her eye.

I didn't feel afraid to walk anywhere by myself, even at night. The guys hanging out in front of the candy store by the housing project a block from my place didn't bother me. I figured getting pregnant the way I did, a year after Henry and I had officially broken up, was enough bad luck for me.

When I walked, I thought hard about what to do. I made lists in my head of the pros and cons of giving up this baby for adoption or keeping it. When I got home, I translated the lists to paper. Adoption—Pro: this will all be like it never happened; I can return to Seattle and just be another young woman; I can still be a good catch; the baby can have a mom *and* a dad. Adoption—Con: this will all be like it never happened; I won't ever know my baby; what if no one wants to adopt a mixed-race baby. Keeping the baby—Pro: I would be a good mother; I always wanted children; I love Henry and would enjoy raising his child. Keeping the Baby—Con: my parents will be mad; Henry will be mad; it'll be hard to deal with all the racism; I don't have any money; I don't have any way of earning a living; I don't want all the responsibility; I'm scared. The only list that made any sense to me was Keeping the Baby—Con. Whenever I reviewed the lists I thought, I have got to find a way out of being pregnant. The only way is to figure out how not to be pregnant. Sometimes I wished I had let myself get an abortion, no matter what I believed. Even if it wasn't legal in Massachusetts, I could have gone to New York. I could not bear thinking I would really have to choose.

I turned away from my lists back to *Anna Karenina*, grateful for that other absorbing world. I learned only to think about the pregnancy in small bursts, praying for revelation.

When I walked I sang songs, over and over. One song that comforted me was "Walk shepherdess, walk." I learned this at Camp Sweyolaken on Coeur d'Alene Lake when I was a girl. When I sang I felt blessed by the other Camp Fire girls, the half-grown counselors, the pine trees above us, the stillness. Their presence was a shadowy comfort under the ochre and red leaves of the New England fall. I sang the Beatles' song, "In My Life," imagining the deep voice of Richie Havens accompanying me. I sang to Henry and stroked my belly softly. I am too young to be this nostalgic, I chastised myself. But I continued to sing and to think of Henry. I wondered if he thought about this baby growing inside me. I wondered if he got the letter I sent explaining why I didn't want to get an abortion. Another song I sang often was "Let It Be." Maybe if I sang with enough faith, I could become the mother Mary of the song.

I made up a song for my baby and sang it very low. It ended, "Can you feel the sadness of my own childheart, as your loss looms everywhere?"

Once a week I walked the mile and half west on Broadway to the public library. It was an old elegant castle set back from the busy street by a big lawn and curving sidewalk. The rooms filled with rows of books were home to me. Each week I walked in with my arms straining with a big pile of books. I pored over the stacks, sometimes taking whole sections of an author I liked. I was hungry for anything good enough to draw me in. Fiction worked better than nonfiction.

I found one slim book on unwed mothers. When I turned to a section about how women who get pregnant have an unconscious desire to have a baby, in part to satisfy their own unconscious need to be loved and special, I quickly returned it to the shelf. I steered clear of anything like it.

My long walk or trip to the library could take me to early afternoon, if I stretched it out. When I got home, I was hungry. I fixed myself peanut butter and honey on bread or made a salad. I tried to bring reality into the phrase "eating for two," but it seemed impossibly abstract.

After I ate, I lay down and read. The afternoons were long, and I moved between reading and dozing. I occasionally forced myself to get up to go to the bathroom. I could not seem to get enough sleep.

Claudia and Bingham came home about six, tired and grumpy from their long day at the factory. Bingham envied me my long, lazy day and teased me about it. Once he said, "You know, I think you probably got pregnant on purpose just so you could get on welfare and sit around like you do all day."

I wanted to say something, but I kept it inside. That day I

had lost five dollars on my walk and cried most of the way home. I wanted to say, "Yeah, what a great deal! $140 a month and $110 goes for my share of this place and $15 for the phone and my calls home. Yeah, wow, it's a great deal." I felt bitter. I also felt guilty that I did so little all day.

On Sunday mornings, Bingham called out to me from his bedroom, "Hey, Mary, why don't you run get us a Sunday paper?" I wanted to yell back, "Get your own damn paper!" Instead I dragged myself out of bed and walked down the three flights and across the gas station lot over to the little grocery store that doubled as a bookie joint. The paper cost seventy-five cents. I wanted to ask Bingham to pay me back. But I knew he'd get mad, and I wanted to avoid that even more. We already fought over the dishes. He had a clear position: "Look, I washed dishes the whole time I was growing up. I swore I'd never wash another dish!" I felt like being sarcastic, "Look, Bingham, everyone washed dishes when they were kids. That's ridiculous reasoning." But I said, "Well, there are three of us here, and I'll do my share, which is one third." I had just joined a women's liberation group and felt strongly about the need to share tasks with men. The trouble was that I would do my share, but Claudia would do both hers and Bingham's. Instead of righteous fairness I felt guilty toward Claudia. And mad.

One time Bingham's friend, Ned, was there playing chess with Bingham, and I asked them if they wanted a glass of wine. As I walked back from the kitchen carrying the two glasses, I felt a surge of pride and pleasure at serving them, then a quick flush of shame. In my group that week a woman had said, "Oh God, I feel so ashamed. I shouldn't have done it, but I baked him a birthday cake!" The other women hooted and laughed, "Oh, Nancy, you're hopeless!" "You'll never change!" I kept quiet, feeling confused and backward.

Those were the best evenings, when Bingham's friends came over to play chess. No one talked, but I could sit at the table and watch Ned or Milo or Bingham pore over the next move for long minutes.

One night, Ned and I moved together into my room,

stroking each other's hands and smiling shyly. His hair was reddish-brown and fell straight to below his shoulders. His body was sturdy and tall, fitting his broad and open face. We spoke little. I tried to make my pooch of a tummy stay in, hoping he wouldn't notice. He knew I was pregnant. But knowing that is different than feeling the strange hard sensation up against your groin. My mind was wild, *Oh, dear God, maybe he'll want to marry me, then I won't have to give the baby up. I'm sure he'd make a great dad. Look at that open, sweet face. There's still months before the baby's due, plenty of time to fall in love. Dear God, please give me a chance.*

All the time, he was touching me—quiet soothing big hands all over my body. I was lost, enraptured, kissing, touching, pleading. When I came I saw stars: first a hot, encompassing blackness and then stars of light shooting off in all directions from the region of my forehead. I thought, *Oh God, this is amazing.* I didn't know this kind of thing was real. I was swept, grateful, rosy, soft, soft.

He propped himself on one elbow. He looked at me with some amusement and a little shying away and said, "Boy, you really get into it, don't you?" I was embarrassed, startled back to my little room and this guy I barely knew. I wanted to apologize to him, but what could I say? "I'm sorry. I didn't mean to feel so much when I hardly know you. I got carried away. I'm sorry, don't worry, I won't take it to heart." I didn't say anything like that. I chuckled and said, "Yeah." I hoped I could sneak my way out of being too exposed. It worked pretty well. He didn't want to make love with me again, but he was friendly and only a little distant around me.

After

My parents welcomed me and Elena. My dad was big, kind and reserved. In the picture I took at Elena's baptism a week after I flew in from Cambridge to Yakima to visit them, he is holding her gently. The smile on his face is slow and sweet. She is tiny in his strong arms.

My mother was nervous around me. She said, "I'm sorry for this tragedy in your life. You're so young." Both she and Dad had independently told their neighbors that I was coming home with a new mixed-race baby. (Dad saying, "But don't tell Catherine I told you, I don't think she'd be comfortable with that." Mom saying, "Martin wants to keep this private, but I'd rather you knew instead of trying to figure out what is going on.") That first week I was home, the neighborhood women and children came, even the traditional Mormon family across the street, two or three each day, with baby gifts, big smiles and curious eyes.

I didn't mind. I was pleased to be welcomed. Their curiosity was just what I would have felt if I had been in their shoes. I was ashamed, but the cocoon of love protected me.

Two weeks later, my baby and I flew on a small commuter plane from Yakima to Seattle. I waved out the narrow window as my parents, one big and one small, waved back. I could see my mother trying not to cry, my father's arms around her shoulders.

We found a small and fairly clean bottom-half of a house on John Street. It was a short walk from the Broadway Theatre and Dick's Drive In. I bought a mattress for myself and a bassinet for Elena at St. Vincent's thrift store and began to settle in. The woman who lived upstairs gave me her old stroller.

I don't know how Henry heard we had arrived in town. I didn't call him. I was too afraid of his reaction. I hadn't heard from him since I'd written and told him I was pregnant, the week after I left Seattle to live in Cambridge. He wrote that he wanted me to have an abortion. I wrote him a second letter and told him I felt too Catholic to get an abortion. I told him even if I wasn't Catholic it was illegal in Massachusetts, and I didn't have enough money to go to New York. I didn't say how much it scared me. I didn't write him again until right after Elena was born. I told him she was born and that I had decided to keep her and that her name was Elena. I didn't know what else to say.

I answered the phone and his gruff voice said, "Mary,

this is Henry. I want to come over and meet her. I don't even know for sure if she's mine, but I want to see for myself." I was not prepared for the bright burst of hope in my chest.

"Hi, Henry, I'm glad you called. Sure, I'd love to have you meet her. When do you want to come by?" I didn't want any hint of the longing and hope I felt to leak out.

"How about later this afternoon, after I play a little tennis?"

"Okay," I said. I hung up the phone. I looked over at Elena asleep in her white wicker bassinet and felt the thrill of sharing her sweet life with someone who might care for her as much as I did. I pushed into the corner of my mind the other thrill I felt. I needed to find a way to be an old friend and not a woman dying to touch and be touched by him.

I woke Elena up and dressed her carefully in her yellow stretch suit. It was still a little big. I checked her diapers every ten minutes. I wanted her to smell good when he got there. I put on a yellow and green shirt I tie-dyed myself. I felt young and pretty in it. I shaved my legs one more time.

The sound of knocking startled me. I had been straining to hear it all afternoon. Henry stood at the door, smiling a little sheepishly. He was flanked by his old friend Joe and his brother Andrew. The three men filled my small living room. When they sat down, Henry and Joe's long legs stretched way across the rug. I felt shy and delighted. I wondered how soon to take Henry into my bedroom to meet Elena. She was asleep again in her bassinet.

I felt awkward with Joe and Andrew, even though I'd known them for three years, ever since I was eighteen. I knew they knew there was a month-old baby asleep in the bedroom. I knew they were wondering whether this really was Henry's baby. They were the jury.

I stood up and said to Henry, "Well, do you want to go in and meet her? She's still asleep but I'm sure she'll wake up soon." I turned to Joe and Andrew and said, "How about if you guys hang out here and when she wakes up, we'll bring her out."

I wanted to have a moment in which the three of us were

in one room together, alone, like a little family.

He walked in behind me, moved to the side of the bassinet and looked down. He was tall enough to tower over it. He bent down closer and said, "Oh, shit."

I knew he'd know as soon as he saw her. She had a petite version of his broad nose, his tiny ears, his elegantly-shaped head. The first time I saw her, right after she was born, I said, "Oh, shit, she looks just like Henry." I was happy, but also worried that he would be mad.

He knelt down and reached his long-fingered hand in and found her little hand. She began to stir. Her little hand curled around one of his fingers. His voice was very low, "Hi, little lover. Hi, little love."

Inside I was cheering. I was not the only parent. She woke up just then and looked up at him. Her little brown eyes looked straight into his big brown eyes. I was entirely peripheral. He stood up a minute later, turned to look at me and said, "Well, what do you know, we've got ourselves a little girl! Let's bring Joe and Andrew in to meet her."

I opened the door and called them in. I wished for more time with just the three of us. The three men crowded around the bassinet, laughing and jostling. Joe pointed and said, "Hey, Henry, look at that, she's got your big old nose." Elena started to cry.

I said, "Come on, Joe, you're hurting her feelings. She may be little, but she can already tell when someone's making fun of her." He kept laughing, but I meant it. I didn't want anyone making fun of my baby. Even if it was part of the jury giving a yes verdict.

Henry said, "Well, we gotta hit the highway. I'll try to stop by again before I leave for Alaska. I'm fishing the rest of the summer."

"Wait, just a minute, I want to take your picture before you leave, " I said. Henry looked uncomfortable. I moved quickly. I picked Elena up and thrust her in his arms, grabbed my camera and took their picture. He said, "Okay, one's enough. I've gotta split."

When I got the picture developed later that week, there

they were. He looked suspicious and handsome. She looked round-eyed and alert. She looked like a cheery tiny light-brown version of him. I had something that could show she did too have a daddy.

JULIA A. BOYD

The Art of Parenting

◆

In preparing to write this essay I asked my twenty-year-old son if he had any thoughts or feelings about being raised by a single parent. Giving me one of his what's-she-writing-about-now looks, he responded in his typical laid-back fashion.

"As opposed to what?"

"Come on, Michael, work with me here. Do you ever wish you had two parents, you know, like some of your friends." I pushed for a response, and then braced myself for a dose of parental guilt.

"To be perfectly honest you've probably thought about it more than I have. You're the only parent I've ever known. We understand and love each other. As for my friends with both parents, I really don't think their lives have been any better than mine."

Is this kid good, or what? But being the recovering Catholic that I am, it stands to reason that I will not only look a gift horse in the mouth, I'll also check for cavities, so I pushed a little more.

"Hasn't there ever been a time when you wished for a father?"

"Well, maybe during football or baseball season but

other than that, no. What's this father thing about anyway?" he questioned as he cocked his head to the side and raised one bushy eyebrow in my direction.

"If you're fishing for compliments...," he said, reaching across the table for his car keys as he planted a firm, juicy kiss on my cheek, "you're a great mom and I love you. I'm outta here."

Oh well, so much for my research. Hearing Michael tell me that I'm a good mother helped to relieve my overworked conscience a bit. It's not that I don't believe that I've done a good job as a single parent, but there have been times when I've wondered. Like the time when Michael returned from his annual summer vacation with my parents in California and informed me, as I fixed his favorite dinner of fishsticks and Spaghettios, that he knew what real fish looked and tasted like 'cause his grandmom cooked him real fish. Or the time that he informed me that you could make French fries from real potatoes as I reached into the freezer for the plastic bag of Ore-Ida fries to fix his snack. "Who told you that?" I asked, with just a tad bit of panic in my voice. "I saw Grandmom make me some," he calmly replied with a sly smile.

Every time I look at my son, the surge of pride I feel curls my toes and makes my hair stand on end. Maybe other parents feel this way about their children, but for selfish reasons, I alone feel akin to the Blessed Virgin (a little Catholic relapse) whenever I think about how truly blessed I am to have Michael in my life. When I think of all the things that could have gone wrong in his life and mine like drugs, alcohol, crime and violence—but didn't—I give thanks to my God. Michael's hand never touches the doorknob without a silent prayer escaping my lips "Lord, watch over my child" and "Thank you God for bringing him home safely."

These prayers are more of a natural spiritual reflex, because my parenting practices have been more intuitive art then traditional method.

I once read that an artist only creates one true masterpiece in a lifetime. That masterpiece embodies the life, breath and soul of the artist. Michael is my masterpiece, my creation, my gift to the world for all eternity. While I don't believe that Michael is perfect, I do believe that he's priceless.

Actually my parents, my five sisters and I have always been at odds about the art of parenting. My three brothers really didn't say much on the subject. In fact, my childrearing methods are still an issue of heated debate at family gatherings. How they think I should parent versus how I choose to parent is one conversation that's guaranteed to go from heated to hot to nasty in three to five minutes tops: "You better start feeding that boy right" or "You're spoil'n that boy giv'n to him all the time" or "You better break that boy outta talk'n back—he's go'n make you cry one of these days, just you mark my words." With statements like these, my family gave me what they believed to be helpful childrearing advice.

Being raised in a solidly Catholic home (with a liberal dose of good old fashioned Southern Baptist values tossed in for good measure) meant that God was worshipped, the belt was law and children were seen but seldom heard. In the segregated South of my childhood, an unruly or missing child could mean a dead child. Because of this harsh reality, my parents laid down a fairly rigid set of parental guidelines. For my parents, as for many Black parents of their generation, loving your child was equated with survival, and the rules for survival—"always believe in the Lord," "don't talk back" and "mind your manners"—were limiting and unyielding. And the threat of quick harsh punishment for disobedience of the family survival rules often rendered children invisible.

Michael can never be invisible; he's too much a part of my life. Family members and friends would smile sympathetically and exchange disheartened looks whenever I calmly stated that Michael is my sun, moon and stars and that no man would come before him. "Girl, you better keep that boy in line or he'll rule you one day, just you mark my words," was often the response to my comments. "But Michael is my world, don't you get it!" I always wanted to shout, but couldn't, thanks to my own rigid upbringing.

A couple of family members and more than a few friends even suggested that I ought to find a man and settle down, 'cause after all, that boy needed a good strong male role model, unless, heaven forbid, I wanted him to turn out to be gay or hate women. I wasn't shocked by these comments, but I must admit the ignorance of the statements cut my heart like a razor. How could loving, nurturing and accepting my son unconditionally make him hate anybody? As for who Michael chose to love or care about in his lifetime, so what? In my mind Michael's decision to love another man or woman only meant that he had learned from me how to love and how to share that love with another human being.

As for male role models, I've never felt it was my duty as a parent to supply Michael with an endless stream of suitable men so that he could pick and choose who he wanted to be when he grew up. Michael has always been pretty good at selecting his own role models. My brothers have shown him the art of male pride, my father has shown him the value of working hard and the ease of laughter, and my male friends have shown him the art of compassion. With just a twinge of pride, I can honestly say he's done a great job in his selection process.

While I understood and respected my parents' values regarding childrearing, I wanted and needed a different set of rules for raising my son. Being the single parent of a Black man-child increased the family pressure on me to "raise that child right." My family, like many in the Black community, viewed my son as a member of an endangered species: if he didn't follow the rules (survival code), he would end up in jail or dead. After all, they reasoned, he was a Black male, and we all know what happens to Black men in White America if Black women don't protect them. . . . Clearly my family saw my role as not only parent but as protector of the race.

As a parent, I saw Michael as a child first, not as a man, and while I didn't know if he was a member of an endangered species, I certainly knew that he was precious not only to the Black race, but also to me, his mother.

I wanted more than anything to be a good parent to Michael, but I've never been good at following rules, survival or otherwise; I have always tested the limits, and I wanted to raise my child to do the same. I wanted Michael to know the freedom of questioning things he didn't understand, and I wanted him to know the power of making choices that would affect his life. But these were skills I didn't learn until I became an adult. I worried that I didn't know how to parent and was often scared to the point of tears.

I can remember when I first discovered I was pregnant at the tender age of twenty-three. I approached the situation like I approached most things at that time—I went with my best friend Loretta to the local Taco Bell and cried like a baby while wolfing down six tacos. In the midst of heavy sniveling and chewing, I explained my dilemma, "I (sniff, sniff) don't know (chomp, chomp) the first thing, pass me the hot sauce, about (sniff) being a parent."

Loretta, being the source of strength and wisdom that she continues to be today, gave me my first bit of parental wisdom by saying, "I don't know a whole lot about the subject either, but it makes sense to trust your instinct and not your impulse. Just love your child the way you want to be loved. Pass the hot sauce."

I didn't truly understand the impact of Loretta's words at the time, but when I look at my life as a single parent I recognize that her words have been a guiding force. I didn't always know what I was doing but I took it one day at a time. I remember the time Michael told me he needed a sports cup for his upcoming Little League baseball game and I, thinking that he wanted a drinking container when he was on the field, innocently offered to buy him a water bottle instead. I had a lot to learn, and my instincts weren't always right on the money, but I loved my child as I wanted to be loved—unconditionally and with respect.

I believed that honesty was important so I was honest with him, "Michael, I've never raised a child so you're going to have to help me figure out some things, okay?"

"Okay Mommy, I'll tell you what's normal for me." And Michael was as true to his word as I was to mine. "Mommy, I'm ten, it's normal for me to want to spend the night with my friends." When neither one of us knew what was what, we consulted with other parents, sometimes even my own, and then made a decision.

True, I wasn't always sure of my direction as a parent, but I've always been clear about the direction I didn't want to take. I didn't want my son to fear or distrust me, because I knew that fear and distrust breed separation, not love.

My instincts coupled with the daily news of Black-on-Black violence told me that hitting was wrong, so I didn't resort to physical punishment but chose to use time-outs, and restriction of privileges as alternative forms of discipline. My instincts told me that hearing Michael's point of view on various subjects and being open to disagreement would help him to build a strong sense of character. Discipline versus punishment and verbal disagreement versus "talking back," as it's commonly called in my family, have been the biggest bones of contention between me and my family. But over the years they've come to see my notion of parenting as another one of my strange and different ideas about life.

In the thirteen years since my divorce, Michael and I have been a team; I can't say that our union as mother and son has been perfect. Let's face it, I've come to understand that parenting holds no guarantees. But I do know that following my instincts and loving my son with respect and integrity has made me feel good about being the best parent I know how to be. I'm proud of my son, and now that he's a man, I can proudly say that I've given my masterpiece to the world. And, recovering Catholic guilt aside, I'm pretty proud of myself, too.

◆

BARBARA WALKER

A Woman's Right To Choose

◆

My great-grandfather was a blacksmith's labourer and supported his wife and twelve children in a shared house in Hoxton, in London's East End. The Carmichael family downstairs also had twelve children. For my grandmother, escaping from the East End was a great dream and she admonished her only daughter with "Any idiot can have babies, you get an education." The war interrupted my mother's education and soon she was struggling with a sick husband, two young children and the poverty trap. In the pre-pill days, when I grew up, teenage sex was taboo and I was moulded in the work and education ethic so when I eventually did start work and became unintentionally pregnant, I had no qualms in choosing an abortion once I realised the father had bolted in horror.

I spent my twenties building a successful career and was a deputy head teacher within six years. I had experimented enough sexually to decide that relationships with women were more enjoyable than those with men and settled with my first lesbian lover. Our relationship was to last for ten years. We enjoyed a fairly affluent lifestyle, traveled, became involved in the new-wave lesbian politics and pretended not to be jealous when non-monogamy became the fashion. When we split up, we divided the household amicably and bought two flats next door to each other. Around that time other things were happening which led to further stress in my life: my father died and was buried while we were on holiday in Greece; I started a new job, and my sister, already a single parent, had severe postnatal depression after the birth of her second child. I stayed with her for a short while to help out with housework and her three-year-old son and the joy I experienced looking after the baby took me by surprise. Over the next month, as she found it impossible to cope, she asked if I would consider fostering my little niece, Jessie, and for the first time I imagined that life with a child would be exciting.

I realised that the demands of child-raising could be met from my own resources and offered to bring Jessie up if negotiations with her father were fruitless and if my sister really wanted it. Painfully for us all, the baby died a few weeks later, but I shall always be grateful to her for bringing such a lot of good into my life. Although it wasn't too late to have my own child I realised that my emotional development had become stuck and I couldn't see forward, so I went to the Women's Therapy Centre. After a few courses there my confusion increased so I applied to the Tavistock Institute of Human Relations in the hope of being offered maybe one free session a week.

Instead, to my surprise, they diagnosed that I had a depressive illness and referred me to the Cassel Hospital, a psychotherapeutic community run without drugs on the NHS [National Health Service]. Death and separation were only two of the issues I was to deal with and I arrived in a very crumpled state in my father's old car, with my niece's carrycot and clothes in the boot. I emerged a year later on a black and silver motorbike, full of energy for life. I was thirty-five.

Bringing up a child was something I realised I would probably enjoy and do quite well. My former materialistic lifestyle seemed to be pointing to a dead end. I had sampled travel, sports, study, ambition at work, and sexual relationships. A future of doing more of the same felt vaguely undemanding. Ninety percent of women have children and I believe the inherent drive to reproduce is a powerful one. As I could see my child-bearing years slipping away I became anxious that fate would deal a cruel blow and send me an early menopause. I was aware that a wrong decision now would mean years of regret later.

Deciding how to become pregnant was the next step. The horror of the possibility of myself and the baby contracting AIDS immediately led me to rule out the option of a one-night stand. My hope was to give and care for life, not the opposite. Besides, I felt that women's rights to, for example, abortion had been won by bringing our needs out of the back streets. Open and honest negotiation with a man therefore seemed the most positive way forward.

The first option I seriously, although only briefly, considered was to seek a long-term relationship with a suitable man. I didn't, however, want to confuse the search for a father for my child with the search for a live-in partner which in itself could be a lengthy process—and I didn't even know if I was still fertile. The second option, asking around gay and straight friends for a sperm-donor, proved fruitless. The third possibility was to use the anonymous donor network set up with a local anti-sexist men's group which believed in supporting a woman's right to choose how she becomes pregnant. A close friend in a long-term lesbian relationship had successfully used this network, although it had taken her two years to become pregnant, and she had spent many tense moments in traffic jams holding the precious donations close to her, warming the jar that contained them with a woolly sock. This arrangement of mutual anonymity was a direct result of judges ruling lesbians to be unfit mothers in custody cases in the seventies, as it seemed a sensible safeguard against possible unlooked-for future interference by the donor.

I did, however, want to leave open the possibility of my child knowing her/his father, so, eventually, I settled for the fourth option of a known donor and placed two differently worded advertisements in *City Limits*. Within weeks I was gratefully sifting through thirty-eight replies. Discarding the offers from America and Scotland and one about sexy suspenders, I worked my way through meetings with four unsuitable donors until I met John, a highly intelligent and sensitive man of my own age, who, as a market analyst, would appreciate the importance of delivery dates. We compared medical family histories and talked of possible ways of sharing the future. I had charted my mucus and temperature cycles and could, to my surprise and delight, pinpoint ovulation day with total accuracy.

The year I became pregnant there were 10,000 artificial insemination by donor births in the U.S.A. alone and I reasoned that, although my journey to pregnancy would appear out of the ordinary to some people, by the time my child grew up, the irrepressible tide of women's initiatives towards fulfillment would have widened the availability of choices around conception and motherhood still further.

One of my great heroines when I was deciding to have a baby was Dervla Murphy, who trekked 1,300 miles through the High Andes with her nine-year-old daughter and a donkey. Her achievements (or was it my image of her achievements?) kept me going for months.

Pregnancy was no problem physically until the tiredness set in near the end, when I pushed myself to keep working right up to the day Tom was born, so I could keep the maternity allowance to enjoy being at home with him afterwards. During the first months of pregnancy, I canoed down the River Wye, competed in the National Shearwater Sailing Races and backpacked alone around Mont Blanc (125 miles, 48,000 feet ascent and descent). On the negative side, however, was an unpleasant feeling of going in and out of an emotional hall of mirrors.

I shall always be grateful to my old school friend, Wendy, who offered to be my birth partner. We were an odd pair at the National Childbirth Trust class, especially when she had to join the men's group for some discussions. I think we may even have been mistakenly identified as a lesbian couple. My first lesbian lover, Teresa, agreed to be the other birth partner and when we eventually all ended up in the operating theatre for an epidural, episiotomy *and* emergency caesarian, it was like a party. There was consultant Wendy Savage and her henchwoman duty doctor snipping and pulling at one end, and a woman anaesthetist and my two birth partners at the other, with a midwife and gay male nurse thrown in for good measure—and there was Tom held up in the lights for the first time. He was perfect. It was love at first sight.

Becoming a mother has meant experiencing a different area of the human struggle, so I have new concerns and different priorities. As a young childless teacher living and working in an area of urban decay, I was politically active around issues like violence to women, abortion, gay rights and equal opportunities. The shift in my personal world towards homebuilding, love for my own child and increased investment in the next generation finds me supporting organisations campaigning against homelessness, child abuse, international famine and disease and the destruction of the environment. Before, I would turn out at five in the morning, in the dark, in thick snow, to picket for the miners, whereas now I am not proud of the fact that I even neglected my own union membership this year and the support I do give to causes is mostly in sending cheques for small amounts from the comfort of my armchair.

Partly this change of concern is due to the emergence of new urgent issues in the last few years. Wages for housework pales into insignificance when faced with pictures of twenty million people short of food in the Horn of Africa. Partly the change illustrates for me how clearly politics is linked to organizing around self-interest and neatly debunks any sanctimonious occupation of moral high ground by activists. Partly getting to any meeting is so difficult now, having to take into consideration my tiredness, finding a babysitter, and whether Tom should be left. It is frustrating to be thought of as a complacent oldster by young, childless teachers leading the kind of life that I used to lead.

As a single woman, the wars of the 1980s left me fairly uninvolved but, as the mother of a male child in the context of the Gulf War, I was deeply horrified by the anguish of mothers and their children in Iraq and Kuwait and appalled at the suffering that families endure when adult men go to war. Yet I can now envisage supporting physical violence in defence of what is so precious to me, and a further paradox is that I would not want *my* son to go to war.

One unexpected positive result of motherhood, with all its contradictions, is that I do feel generally more rooted in that I can now relate to a larger number of women and men who also carry the burden of child-rearing responsibilities. From those early days when I was feted with gifts and congratulations in the maternity ward, I realised that I was entering into a new relationship with the community. As I was waved down the hospital steps surrounded by friends and whisked away in a high-status car to a champagne homecoming, I remember thinking that this is what it must be like to get married.

From being a single, childless lesbian in a position systematically marginalised by society, it seemed that I was suddenly being received everywhere by warm smiling faces. As a sportswoman or motorcyclist, a lesbian, teacher or single woman, I can remember receiving verbal abuse, ridicule, criticism and discouragement from all sorts of hecklers and members of the general public. Now that I am a mother such harassers have gone strangely quiet. Instead, a supermarket trip with Tom as a small baby became a jolly social outing as complete strangers lined the aisles to talk to me, eager to share and relive memories of their own early motherhood. Older women told me what I shouldn't be letting my child touch on the shelves, and offered various other forms of advice. All this was a surprise and reminded me in part of the time I went in fancy dress as a clown to the children's Christmas dinner at the school where I was teaching. To be greeted with universal affection is very uplifting but of course is only a change in outward appearance. I was now enjoying the sanctified image of mother and child, totally safe and totally under control.

Tom is four now and I am forty-four. We live together with an aging and much loved Samoyed dog, Jezzie, in our own small terraced house on the edge of Walthamstow Marshes by the River Lea in East London. This unploughed wild marshland is a ninety-acre site of special scientific interest and teems with wildlife, so we can watch the foxes run along the railway line at the bottom of our garden at night, watch for the return of the cuckoo, swifts and frog spawn in spring, search for adders and tongue fern among the sedges and fill our lungs with breathable air in the evening while watching bats and flights of geese return from feeding on the Thames mudflats. I am very pleased that I have been able to make a secure home for us here and that there will be plenty of educational, cultural and sporting opportunities around as Tom grows up.

The cost of this security is having to live more of a monocultural life based around working longer hours than I would prefer. Fortunately I enjoy my work as a specialist music teacher in schools five miles away and it has been easy to shape my working week around Tom's changing needs. For the first six months I was at home with him just working on Saturday mornings and when the maternity benefit and the 1,000 pound "Baby Fund" that I had saved dried up, I found a babyminder so that I could do two days work a week. Overhead costs on our tiny flat were low and I was lucky to have a low interest, fixed-rate mortgage, a good network of friends, offers to baby-sit and time to enjoy being together. I even enjoyed rehearsing and performing at local community events with a women's steel band which was personally very satisfying, especially when Tom was there too, bobbing about on my back in the baby carrier.

Although in selling my flat at the end of the house price boom in 1988 I released another 1,000 pounds, the increase in bills at the new house, inflation and the 200 pound per month babyminding fees, soon meant that my working week had to extend into the evenings and weekends with private teaching. For the next two years during termtime I was often numb with exhaustion and became more isolated as the work timetable cut though the usual hours when people get together.

I bought equipment second-hand, ate a lot of cheese sandwiches, and gratefully received large sacks of toddler clothes from friends. During the holidays it was a relief to grow back together again. We visited friends and I could spend some time just enjoying being with Tom and watching all those precious toddler activities like putting pebbles in puddles.

Holidays didn't equal relaxation, however, as I always used part of them to tackle as many exterior and interior house and car repairs as I could, as it is much cheaper to do them myself, so I often found that I was returning to work having had little respite.

Now that Tom has started in the nursery at the school where I teach, I can see a lot more physical and economic freedom in the coming year and I plan to reduce my workload and overdraft accordingly, so life should become less stressed for both of us. Tom learns fast, is confident, helpful, consider-ate, intelligent and well liked and I am confident too that I am a good provider and a "good enough" mother.

The circle of people I come into contact with are usually en-couraging and complimentary and, of course, some are single parents themselves or were brought up by single parents. It wasn't until recently when I started to focus on the broader public response to single parents that I realised there were so many hostile criticisms being made of us. My first observa-tion about this response must be that any generalisations about single parents are difficult to make because we are pres-ent in so many conditions of society and for some it is just a transitory lifestyle. We have also arrived at the position from many different directions. If there are negative images in people's minds in general, they probably stem partly from the fact that almost half of single parent families live on the poverty line compared with six percent of married couples with children. If asked about what it means to be a single parent, a superficial response might mention wailing children, exhausted young women and piles of dirty washing. This, of course, is a good description of most of my married friends trying to bring up their children, pay the mortgage and work outside the home.

It is not only poverty in itself, however, that some people seem to object to but the two-fold social "crime" of being a drain on the national economy and of being unhealthily dependent on handouts by accepting social security payments. I have found this a fairly complex area to unravel. Very few people make these criticisms directly to me and a comment like, "Did you know my father thinks single parents are the cause of all the problems in society?" casually made on a Sunday afternoon walk, leaves me boxing the shadows. Was this just scapegoating or does this father fear his own dependency feelings? Is it the fast pace of post-industrial change that makes him feel he is losing control and leaves him wanting to revert to the security of past conditions and does he feel rejected by images of women looking to the state for baseline security and avoiding more male-centred lives? He may well feel his past struggles and achievements for his own family are devalued by other people "getting it easier" and I suspect that his work and social life will have bypassed any real contact with either single parents or people who struggle with downward spirals of poverty. With 164,000 decrees absolute given in the U.K. in 1989, and given that two thirds of divorced husbands subsequently lose all contact with their children, it seems to me that anyone who censures the single parent who *does* fulfil a commitment to the children must be either thoughtless, perverse or a bigoted misogynist.

Although the broad front of criticism against single parents does not sway my personal beliefs or decision-making directly, there are ways in which my life is affected. Critics use their political vote to put in power a party which does not advance my lifestyle in its philosophy or policies. For example, the political right does not want to promote single parenthood or working mothers and will pay for and report on research which "proves" that children who have been cared for by babyminders will find making sustained relationships in adult life impossible. It has brought in new anti-gay legislations, and newspapers aligned to the right sell copies by headlining stories of women loving each other. It discusses issues like surrogacy in terms of "prostitution of fertility" rather than delighting in the joy children can bring to those who long for them. It has brought in legislation resulting in a situation where single women are now afraid that the new regulations applied to infertility clinics will make it difficult for them to gain access to artificial insemination by donor. The alarm of a Scottish baroness in the House of Lords that an anonymous donor creeping into a family pedigree would give rise to a fake clan chief epitomises for me the establishment's concern about property and inheritance in the context of the traditional family.

All this means that when I meet someone for the first time I can never be sure whether their initial friendly response will evaporate or, worse still, turn to disgust when they discover that I am a lesbian single parent and that Tom was conceived as a result of advertising for a sperm donor in *City Limits*. I begrudge the energy it has taken from my life to work against this flow and feel frustrated that I can do so little at the moment to fight for what I believe in. Prejudice is integral to an unjust and unequal society and I feel angry that the refusal to share wealth has played its part in a steady increase in crimes of hate in the home and on the street. Last winter, when Tom and I came face to face with an old woman—a heap of filthy skin and bones—lying on the hard pavement in a snow storm outside London's multi-million pound Broad Street development, I felt deeply ashamed of the society in which I live and didn't know what to say to my bewildered little boy.

When politicians and others talk of single parents as

young unmarried mothers scrounging on the state they are proliferating stereotypes. Such distortions seem to be used most when there is a lack of any real knowledge about a social group and some are so persistent that proliferators must have an interest in maintaining them. I have been confused by such distortions in searching over the years for my real self and have half believed in some of them, despite daily seeing the evidence disproving them under my nose.

Some of the hardest stereotypes to supplant are those I was indoctrinated with as a child and they are associated with taboo, prejudice and a closed mind, so I am mindful about this as Tom grows.

In trying to break the moulds in my own mind, I have also had to throw out a lot of ideas which were built around fantasies of group identity which had seemed at the time to offer a welcome security. For example, the way I thought about the lesbian community after the first national lesbian conference in 1976 was confused because it didn't look the way I hoped it would. Many women were shouting and few listening. In the hurry to change people's minds, the truth was foreshortened and yet the lesbian cause demanded loyalty which I was happy to give. I would say now that loyalty is hard to maintain without reciprocal support. When a lesbian at a party recently called Tom a mutant, behind my back of course, and my part of the lesbian baby boom is seen by some writings in the gay press as taking care and support away from lesbians, my "female energy being sucked into caretaking more boys," I feel I don't fit in with this ideal community I have partly invented, and partly been fed in stereotypical form, by the need to appear unified in order to campaign successfully.

These days the people Tom and I spend time and enjoy being with are those whose diverse lifestyles and interests are yet compatible enough to make worthwhile the effort to arrange to meet. Whether we are Black, bisexual, single, or part of a couple doesn't seem to matter as much as whether we would enjoy some company at the swimming pool or a park, or after a busy week, catching up with each other's news over a cup of tea or gin and tonic. More objectively, our friends are usually liberal-minded, value education and struggle to make ends meet, although most are employed.

One outing in particular stands out from last year as illustrating our positive experiences of companionship. Four of us, single mothers, had traveled down from London to Horstead Keynes in Sussex with our five children, for a bluebell picnic and ride on the preserved steam railway. As we relaxed after sharing each other's food and the children played happily in the nearby stream, I watched an unpleasant scene developing in a Mini in the car park where driver dad was haranguing map-reading mum and both ended up shouting at their two children in the back seat. This brought back so many memories of claustrophobic nuclear family rows for me that, in contrast, the space and light between the members of our party positively seemed to glow. *We* could all drive and map read at the same time. Living alone with our children, the adults in our party had sought out each other's company freely and the day's activities unfolded with common consent and respect. The number of social interactions possible with nine people made for an interesting day and a group can probably cope better with any individual mood swings. It wasn't until a long while after that I realised what a wide variety of experiences we and our children had brought with us that day—gay and straight, divorced and unmarried, different ethnic and social backgrounds—and our children are growing up boys and girls in a society radically different from the one experienced by each of their parents. As a group we certainly don't live in each other's pockets, but we generally get together to enjoy the year's cycle of holidays and celebrations.

As for my family, my mother has been a steady support to Tom and he loves her dearly. My father died fifteen years ago and Mother's second husband was a very loving grandfather, generously sharing his passion for steam trains and model making for a short while before he too died when Tom was three.

Relationships within my original family were never easy

and my mother and I had practically severed ours before Tom was born. My mother's feeling about the birth was of being excluded and mine was that it was too stressful to involve her. Since then we have gradually constructed a stable truce based on a shared love for Tom. We visit for short periods and Tom loves staying with her for an occasional weekend in Norfolk. She enjoys watching him grow. We also enjoy visits with my elderly aunt and her daughter's family in London. That is our total family involvement, which is very different from the tribe of grandparents, great aunts and uncles and cousins and their children who used to come and go during my early years.

During the early meetings with Tom's father, John, we discussed possibilities for a creatively shared future. These evaporated when he disappeared the day after Tom was born. Since then he has resurfaced and disappeared three times in four years and has proved to have a more immature personality than I originally allowed for. For my part, I was naive to allow myself to fantasise on the basis of early conversations and the external trappings of education, accent, high I.Q., briefcase and high-powered job. Under all that he was just another man looking for a mother/wife for himself and not any of the adult experiences of fatherhood. Some of my friends who are involved in stressful conflicts with the fathers of their children envy the idea of such an absence. It wasn't what I had hoped or planned for, but I can adapt to reality once the facts become clear and I hope Tom will have that ability too.

After years of trying to re-establish contact I did eventually arrange a meeting in Devon for the three of us. I did this partly because of all the published work which points to the importance of children finding and experiencing their roots and partly to find out the reality of John's situation.

It is obviously important to remain aware and open to the question of roots and identity. Too much anxiety on my part could create a self-fulfilling problem, just as too little concern could be a pitfall. I am very aware of the current philosophy in this culture to "sell" the father's essential goodness to the child so that it becomes incorporated in a positive self-image. Books and experts can be very wrong but a few weeks before the meeting Tom made a passing remark as the clouds were gathering and darkening one night when we were walking the dog. He referred to a dark monster in the park being his daddy.

Since the meeting with John a few things have been clearer. The first surprising result was that I felt a new freedom to take the credit for successfully bringing up Tom alone. John's life seems less "together" than mine at the moment and he has begun therapy, looking at abuse in his own childhood. Far from sitting on a fortune while we have been struggling, he has managed on a student grant and then a salary half that of mine. I am sure we haven't seen the last of him and would welcome further contact. Although I now don't feel the perplexed sadness, the bitter disappointment or the anger I felt when he first disappeared, I still get emotionally involved when discussing the performance of fathers in general in society. The second result of the meeting is that the dark monster has never been seen again. We did see a little dog one afternoon, however, in the middle of a big field, which was "A daddy all on its ownly."

With few relatives on one side and almost none on the other, fortunately we are free to choose friends who are very important to us, and, to a lesser extent, neighbors who are a friendly and positive part of our lives.

It took me many years to realise that lesbians are everywhere and can be titled or tattooed, soldiers, midwives, criminals or doctors. On the whole I have stopped assuming from people's outward appearances either what their contribution to society is likely to be or how at ease they feel about their identity. It is these last factors which I believe to be the key issues governing Tom's future happiness. I enjoy encouraging and providing opportunities for his emotional, physical, spiritual and intellectual growth as best I can. He goes to dance class, swims regularly with friends, enjoys gymnastics and cycling

and we always spend several weeks each year at our old cara-
van on the sand dunes in a remote part of the Norfolk coast,
communing with nature and friends who come to visit with
their tents. We enjoy sledging, flying kites, gardening and
blackberrying as the seasons come and go and, of course, he
attends an excellent school. I tell him often how proud I am of
him, how happy he makes me and how I will always love him.

Despite all I can do, it is inevitable that one day he will
meet up with some of society's censorious attitudes to homo-
sexuality. Our local council decided last year to encourage
gay men and lesbians to come forward as possible foster parents but met with minority vociferous opposition. One Tory
Councillor declared, "I am not prepared to deliver the children of this borough into the hands of filthy perverts." I hope
that Tom will not be hurt or divided by such attitudes. So far,
the issue of having a lesbian mum is a latent one as I have not
had a lover since I was pregnant so neither he nor I have had
to deal with my adult sexuality in its new context. He stays
regularly with his beloved "Aunt Treesie" and her lover, Barbara, and it is part of his natural world that they sometimes
sleep together, not an "unnatural passion" at all.

Most people living worthwhile, fulfilled lives are happy
to get on with them and for others to do the same, but I am
very familiar with situations at school where the seeds of conflict are continuously sown by a few children who feel bad
about themselves and want to project their negative feelings
on to other children. Fortunately the school that Tom attends
and where I teach, has up-to-date policies and confronts issues like bullying, racism and dealing with conflict, so that
these things do not get in the way of learning as much as they
might. Moreover, although there are of course occasional
problems which disturb the calm, there are enough supportive, kind children, who are often very considerate to each
other, to make it a very pleasant place to be.

There were times soon after Tom was born when I would
have liked to share my joy at every little thing he did with

someone equally indulgent, but being a single parent also means having the luxury of complete freedom to explore being the kind of mother I want to be.

My two greatest hopes are for Tom's happiness and that we will stay the best of friends for many years to come. I hope he will have a personality with a secure core, with less guilt, and therefore less resentment, and more happiness in his growing years than I had; less forbidden enquiry, less isolation and less fear of expressing his feelings.

A young male psychiatrist once told me that a child needs two parents. He seemed to have an irrationally fixed idea about the quantity rather than the quality of parenting. If I believed that the traditional family of mum, dad and 1.8 children was the only guaranteed recipe for success, then I would have to admit that I had been selfish in deciding to have a child on my own. But this so obviously is not the truth that there is no case to answer. Who are the people who call single women who choose to parent selfish? Certainly none of my friends, colleagues, or acquaintances, all of whom say admiringly that they don't think they could take on the hard work involved. It was partly because I felt that my life had become too self-centred that I could wholeheartedly throw myself into motherhood. Having found myself, explored myself and enjoyed myself when I was younger, I could put self aside and enjoy providing for someone else's dependency.

Many philosophies accept that it is a human condition to avoid pain and choose pleasure. If being selfish is choosing what will give us most pleasure, then most humans are selfish and I am no more or less selfish than any other mother whose child gives her great pleasure. I believe emotional bonding between mother and child is above words like selfish and that every woman has a right to reproduce if she can and chooses to. I hope that women will increasingly be able to exercise the kind of choices which I have made.

BECKY BIRTHA

Route 23: 10th and Bigler to Bethlehem Pike

$\blacklozenge$

Ain't no reason for you to be gaping at me. I pay my taxes, just like everybody else. And it just don't make no sense. The mayor and all them city council men sitting up in all them little offices over in City Hall, ain't never been cold in they life. And me and my little ones freezing to death up on Thirteenth Street.

Last time I was down to City Hall to try and talk to one of them men, heat just pouring out the radiator in that office. I had to yell at Kamitra and Junie not to touch it, scared they was gonna burn thyself. Man I'm talking to done took off his jacket and drape it over the back of his chair. Wiping his forehead off with his hanky, talking bout, "No, Miz Moses, we can't do nothing for you. Not a thing. Not as long as you living in a privately-own residence and you not in the public housing...."

I'm thinking how they only use them offices in the day time. Ain't nobody in em at night. And my babies is sleeping in the kitchen, ever since the oil run out two weeks ago and they ain't deliver no more. Landlord claim he outta town.

Hasan, my baby here, he don't hardly even know what warm is. He so little he can't remember last summer. All the

Becky Birtha   177

others done had colds all winter. Noses ain't stopped running since last October. And Kleenex just one more thing I can't afford to buy em. Scuse me a minute.

—I know, Junie. I see it. Yeah, I see the swings. Can't get off and play today. Too cold out there. Maybe so, honey. Maybe tomorrow, if the sun come out. Lamont, let your sister have a turn to sit by the window now.—

Don't you be thinking I'm homeless, cause I ain't. You ever see a bag lady with all these kids? These here sleeping bags is just a temporary measure. Like I said, I live up on Thirteenth Street. Seventeen hundred block. North. Top floor. You don't believe me you go look. My name on the mailbox: Leona Mae Moses. And all the rest of the stuff belong to us right where we left it. The kids is got other clothes, and we got beds and dishes and all the same stuff you got in your house. We ain't planning to make this no permanent way of life. Just till this cold spell break.

—Cherise, honey, would you get the baby bottle out that bag you got up there? Right next to that box of Pampers. And you and Lamont gonna have to get off and get some more milk. Next time we come up to the A & P. Junie, get your hands away from that buzzer. We ain't there yet. We got to go all the way up to Chestnut Hill, and then turn around and come back down. Anyway, it's Kamitra turn to ring the bell this time.—

Ain't nobody got no call to stare at me like I'm some kinda freak. My kids got the same rights as other people kids. They got a right to spend the night someplace warm and dry. Got a right to get some sleep at night. Last night, along about eleven o'clock, when the man on the radio say the temperature gone down to fifteen below, he didn't have to tell me nothing. The pipes is froze, and the wind lifting the curtains right up at the windows in my kitchen. And my little girl crying, "Mama, I'm cold." Air so icy I can see a little cloud come out her mouth, every time she cry.

—Kamitra, sugar, don't sing so loud. Mama trying to talk. Anyway, other people on here besides us. They don't want to be bother listen to all that racket.—

You got kids? Well, think a minute what you would do if you was in my place. Last night I'm trying so hard to think what to do, feel like my head gonna split wide open. Nobody in my building ain't got no more heat than we do. I don't know no neighbors got space for all of us. They be sleep anyway. All my people still down south.

Kamitra crying done waked up the others, too. Then all of em crying they cold. I ain't crazy yet, but I like to went crazy last night trying to think what I'm gonna do. I just kept thinking theys got to be some place in this great big city that I can carry these children to, where it's warm, where it stay warm, even in the middle of the night. And then it come to me.

"Mama, where we going?" the kids is all asking. I just tell em to hush and go get they blankets and towels and sweaters and stuff. Comb everybody hair and dress real warm. Start packing up some food to last us for a couple of days. "Mama, what we gonna do? Where we taking all this stuff?" And Junie, he tickle me. Say, "Mama, we can't go no place. It's dark outside."

I just hush em all up and hustle em down to the corner. Little ones start crying again, cause even with all them layers on, they ain't warm enough for no fifteen below. Lamont done lost his gloves last week, and Cherise just got one a my scarf wrap around her head, cause it ain't enough hats to go round. Ain't a one of em got boots. Cherise still asking me where we going, while we standing at the corner, waiting. I tell em, "Mama got a surprise for you all. We taking a trip. We going on a nice, long ride."

—Get outta that bag, Kamitra. You can't have no more crackers. Mama gonna fix you some tuna fish for supper, pretty soon. What's the matter Junie? You gotta pee? You sure? Well then, sit still. Lamont, next time we come to our corner, I want you to take him in to the bathroom, anyway. It don't hurt to try.—

I guess that explain how come we here. We intend to stay, too, right where we at, up till the weather break. Or the oil come. Whatever happen first. It ain't no law against it. I pay my taxes to keep these things running, just like everybody else. And I done paid our fare. The ones under six ride for free, just like the sign say. I got enough quarters here to last us a long time.

My kids is clean—all got washed up at the library just this morning. And look how nice and well-behave they is. I ain't got nothing to be ashamed of.

I hope your curiosity satisfied, cause I really ain't got no more to say. This car big enough for all of us. You better find something else to gawk at. Better look on out the window, make sure you ain't miss your stop.

—Cherise, sugar, we at the end of the line again. Go up there and put these quarters in the man box. No, Junie. This trolley gonna keep running all night long. Time just come for the man to turn the thing around. We ain't getting off. This trip ain't over yet.

BONNIE TAVARES

Welcoming the Solitude

◆

As I lay in my bed my first night as a single mother, I was struck by the silence—the wonderful silence. The silence that wasn't interrupted until the sounds of morning began. The silence brought wonderful solace—a sense of peace and long-overdue calm. It was not the calm before the storm—it was not the quiet before the next round of screaming and accusations, but rather a true calm. This calm was almost tangible in its depth.

That night, I suddenly realized what gave me strength to end the marriage. Ultimately it was not the horrible, emotionally depraved atmosphere of my life or the constant posturing to avoid conflict or the total lack of understanding of who I am, but instead it was the realization that I no longer liked who I had become. I never laughed anymore. I was a shrew who focused on the negative without any leeway for the positive. I had grown hateful. I had no respect for myself, and it was from that knowledge that I stopped the carousel and stretched for the gold ring in the hope of touching my innermost self again.

All of the "creative financing" that has become necessary is small payment in exchange for the calm. Coming home from work starving and yet telling the children I just wasn't hungry because there were only two hamburgers—and not three—left in the freezer, is a small price to pay for the calm. The confrontations with the children who test me to see who is really boss in this house is again a small price to pay in exchange for the calm.

As the days and nights pass and gather in number, I begin to gather my strength from the calm. I am amazed to suddenly hear myself laugh. I cry in the shower not from desperation but from relief and exhaustion.

I'm beginning to put myself back together—one day at a time and one moment of peace at a time. The children and I now sing in the car to the tunes of Whitney Houston and enjoy ourselves by piecing together the dollars to drive to Plymouth, feed the ducks and go out for a modest lunch.

I now live alone—without a partner—with the peace and solitude that brings me back to myself again and again.

LINDA HOGAN

New Shoes

◆

Even shaking the folds out of the sheet, Sullie formed questions in her head about the shoes. She looked as if she might divine answers from the whiteness of afternoon light in the fine weavings of cotton. The way an old woman might read the future inside a porcelain teacup.

Manny came in quietly, leaving her cart out on the balcony walkway of the motel. "Up where I come from, people read the newspapers instead of the sheets," Manny said, and then she went out the door, her legs two shadows inside her thin skirt.

Sullie tucked the sheets beneath the mattress and smoothed the worn green bedspread across them. It was the color of algae, mossy and faded. New motel guests would arrive soon to sleep between the sheets and the cotton was fragrant with the odor of laundry soap and the smell of scorch from the big mangle. Sullie's short hands tightened a wrinkle away. She watched herself in the dresser mirror as she folded a blanket. Some hair had fallen down the back of her neck. She pinned it up. Her dry and darkened elbows bent toward the ceiling and the pale blue smock rose up away from her hips. She watched the reflection of herself push the soiled bed-clothes deep into the canvas bag that hung on the side of the metal cart. In the loneliness of the room, in the mirror with its distortion right at Sullie's forehead and another at her thighs, she saw herself the way others probably saw her—too serious, dark-eyed, her shoulders too heavy, but alive and moving, filling up the room that had never known a permanent tenant.

In the storeroom the black hands of the clock on the wall said three o'clock. Already too late for the bus and Donna would be home ahead of her, sitting on the sofa listening for the sound of her mother's shoes, lazily turning the pages of an old magazine. Or perhaps she would have opened the metal wardrobe and stepped into one of Sullie's outdated dresses and stood before the mirror, turning herself this way and that, sticking her chest out a little too far, piling her own dark hair upon her head. With the one tube of dime-store lipstick Sullie bought and once treasured, Donna would paint little smudges on her cheekbones and smooth them out, darken her full lips that were still rosy from childhood. And she would step, barefooted, into the new shoes and stand at the full-length mirror inside the door of the wardrobe and look at the narrow lines of her hips curving out beneath the small of her back.

Sullie unsnapped the blue smock and hung it on the coathook. On its pocket in red thread were embroidered the words "The Pines Motel." The words hung there in the sky-blue cloth like writing from an airplane.

"There's only one pine in this entire vicinity," Manny said, "and it's that half-dead straggler over there across the street. Behind the white house."

Manny had already replaced her unused sheets on the shelves, had dropped the canvas bag of soiled linens into the corner for the laundry. "You going to walk?" she asked Sullie. "You ought to take the bus. How much money you fig-ure you save walking those two miles?"

"I only walk in the morning."

"When your feet are still good?" She removed the safety pin from between her teeth and pinned her shirt from the underside. "Does it show?" Manny smiled and the rich gold of her eyes warmed Sullie. Manny with skin the color of earth, black hair straightened only enough to look smooth on the surfaces, like water where the undercurrents twist and pull beneath a seamless and laden skin. Manny's voice was slow, not full of fast chatter like the other maids, not talking about boyfriends and children, about whether to go dancing or save money for a car.

Manny made thirty-five cents an hour more than Sullie because she was colored instead of Indian. When Sullie got the nerve to ask the manager about money, he said, "Don't gossip. I don't keep people on when they gossip. And take that chip off your shoulder."

The house with the pine stood alone and surrounded by a few shrubs, a small area of lawn, a remnant of farmland cut through with new streets and clouds of exhaust rising up from buses. In front of the house was a diner and Sullie's bus stop. It was all visible from the second-floor balcony of the motel. The dying tree bent by an invisible wind, shaped like a tired old woman reaching down to touch children.

Sullie seated herself on the bench that advertised used cars. Manny gestured with her head toward the diner. "Want some coffee?" But Sullie shook her head. "Suit yourself," said Manny and she walked toward the diner, slowly as if she were wearing green silk and gold bracelets instead of the thin printed shirt and skirt. She went into the diner, a converted house trailer that had an extra room built on the back side of it. The windows were slightly yellow from the grease of cooking. Behind them Sullie could see Manny sliding down into a seat behind the brown oilcloth and the little mustard jar vases with plastic flowers.

Sullie sat outside in the whirl of traffic, thinking of home, of large and slow-moving turtles migrating by the hundreds across the dirt roads, of silent nights when frogs leapt into water and the world came alive with the sounds of their swelling throats.

The wind began to blow off the street. With her hand Sullie covered her face from the dust and grit. Other women held down their skirts, their red and gold hair flying across their faces. A motion caught Sullie's eye. Up in the sky, something white was flying like a large bird. In spite of the blowing sand, she looked up, but as she squinted at the sky, the bird lengthened and exposed itself as only a sheet of plastic churning and twisting in the wind. It stretched out like a long white snake and then lost its air current and began falling.

On the bus two elderly women sat in front of her. They were both speaking and neither one listened to the other. They carried on two different conversations the way people did in the city, without silences, without listening. Trying to get it all said before it was too late, before they were interrupted by thoughts. One of the women had steel-blue hair. The other one fanned herself with a paper as if it were hot and humid, talking to her own face in the window about her children, one in San Diego in the Navy, one in Nevada running a gas station. She put the paper down on her lap and powdered her nose, squinting into the little circle of mirror that was caked pink with powder.

A man with dark hair in front of the women puffed hard on his cigarette. The powdered woman fanned away the smoke. Sullie watched it rise, nearly blue, into the light of the windows, drifting like a cloud in the air currents, touching the hair oil spot on the glass. It was like mist rising off a lake in the early morning. Steam from a kettle of boiling vegetables, squash, tomato, onion. It smelled good, the sweet odor of burning tobacco.

Buildings blurred past the window. The early shift men carried lunch pails to their cars and buses, all gliding past the window as if Sullie were sitting still and watching a movie, a large fast-moving film of people disappearing into the south. Even those people walking north were swept into it, pulled finally backwards across the window and gone.

Sullie stood and pulled the narrow rope. She felt exposed, the people behind her looking at her tied-back hair with its first strands of white, at her cotton dress wrinkled from sitting on the plastic seat, at the heaviness of her arm, bare and vulnerable reaching upward to ring the bell. She stepped out the door and it hissed shut behind her.

Donna was not there. Her notebook was on the table and there was a dirty glass sitting beside the shiny new dish drainer Sullie had bought with her last paycheck. Sullie rinsed the glass and placed it, upside down, in the orange plastic drainer, then wiped the glass and the drainer both with a towel. Her shoes creaked the gray linoleum where it was bulging.

Donna's sweater was on the floor beside the sofa bed. Sullie picked it up and then, once again, she reached beneath the sofa and pulled out one of the sleek black shoes. New shoes. They were shiny, unworn. Patent leather with narrow pointed heels and a softly sculptured hole in each toe. Sullie brushed the dust from them with her skirt. She saw her face reflected in the shiny leather, her wide forehead in the round-ness of leather. Her heart jumped in her chest again as it had when she first found the shoes.

They were prettier than the shoes Anna May had worn that summer when she came from Tulsa on the back of a man's motorcycle. And Anna May had worn them, dust-ridden, red leather, all the way from the city down the dirt roads, over the big gullies that washed into the soil. She wore them home, wearing also a red and blue dress flying out on the back of a motorcycle.

What a big to-do the family made, admiring the bright dress and shoes even before they welcomed Anna May and her thin-faced boyfriend. Sullie had polished the buckles of her sister's shoes, walked around the floor in red shoes that were too big and wobbly, her dry and dirty legs rising out of them like old sticks and her ankles turning.

Sullie put Donna's new shoes back under the sofa. She lined them up and put them where they couldn't be seen from the table.

It was dark when Donna returned. Sullie's eyes wandered

from Donna's face down the small shoulders held too high, the large hands that were always out of place, looking right down at her feet in her run-over saddle shoes. She glanced again at Donna's light-skinned face. "I've been worried," she said.

"I was at a friend's," Donna said.

"Hungry?"

"We ate."

Sullie opened the refrigerator and stood in the light. Steam rolled out the door and surrounded her. She took out the bologna and, sitting at the table, made herself a sandwich.

Donna looked at the window, watching their reflections in the glass. A woman and a girl like themselves sitting in the dark square of glass.

"What did you eat?"

"Meatloaf and potatoes." With her finger Donna traced the pattern of the black matrix in the gold-colored plastic table. "Look, this one is shaped like a hawk. See? There's its wing. See its beak? It's saying, the train is about to come by."

"I haven't had meatloaf in a hundred years," Sullie said. She reached across the table to touch Donna's arm. Donna pulled away, got up and filled the glass with water from the faucet. The water clouded and cleared.

"What do you really think a hawk would say, Mom?"

Sullie was quiet. She stood up and went over to fold the quilt Rena had made. She was careful with the quilt, removing it from the sofa back. Each patch was embroidered with stories of Sullie's life. If Rena had lived long enough, there would have been more stories to stitch, Sullie's life with Donna's father. That one would have contained a car and a man smoking cigarettes. There would have been a patch for the birth of Donna, the little light-skinned Indian who would someday wear black patent leather pumps on her bony feet. There would be a square containing the Pines Motel with Sullie standing on the balcony looking out at the yellowing pine tree that had lost most of its needles and looked like an old woman weeping. What else? A small coffin containing her dead son. Sullie taking the bus to Denver with little Donna crying and snuffling next to her. It was all like the great stained glass window, the quilt colors with light behind them. There was a picture for every special event of Sullie's childhood, a picture of Sullie's birth, the swarm of bees, little circles of gold, flying across the pale blue cotton, the old people all standing on the front porch of the old house. One of them, an old woman named Lemon, was wearing a yellow dress and holding the dark infant up to the sun. Her legs were red. There were indigo clouds.

The last patch had never been finished. Rena was working on it the summer she died. On it was the lake with golden fish stitched down across the quilted waves. And there were the two glorious red mules whose backs were outlined in ink. Nothing solid to them. Nothing filled in or completed. They were like shadows with white centers.

Sullie folded the quilt and put it on the table beside the couch. "Help me pull out this sofa, will you, honey?" She looked at Donna. "You know, I really think the hawk would say, it shall come to pass that all the world will be laid bare by the doings of men."

Donna looked at the quilt. "Can we sleep under it?"

"I'm saving it," Sullie told her once again.

"What for? When you get old and die?"

"No, honey, I just want to keep it nice. When you grow up, I'll give it to you."

Donna lay down between the sheets. Sullie sat next to her and ran her fingers down a loose strand of Donna's hair.

Saving things for old age. The very idea. Sullie reprimanded herself. Saving things when the girl wanted something pretty to hold now and to touch. No good. A mother and daughter alone in the city, no good. It was what happened when you married a man who drove up in the heat of summer after being gone two years and you had to tell him about the death of his son and then you wept and went away with the man, going anywhere just to get out of that desolate place and the heat. Just to get out of that place where your uncle had come home drunk and shot his wife, the place where your cousin sold off everything you owned one day just to buy a bottle and then tried to kiss your neck. Not that it was much to look at, but he sold it off to a young couple in a pickup truck that looked like they came from back east. And you went away with the white man and he went into the Army. So the hawk would say.

It was better with him gone, with her husband gone. Even trying to earn a living. To mend socks and underwear for only two people. To not have to listen to that man bragging about what he used to be when he sang in bars or when he played baseball with some big team or other. Better to not even get any more of his letters or the snapshots, the shiny snapshots he sent of himself and his Army friends sitting it out in bars with pretty oriental women smiling behind him. Still, Donna was growing up different. Like a stranger. She was going to be a white girl. Sullie could already see it in her. In her way of holding tension, of shaking her foot. In the hair she kept cutting. She was growing up with the noise of buses and cars, the GIs and red-dressed women laughing outside the window at night. She wasn't growing in the heat of woodstoves that burned hot even in the summer and the fireflies with their own little lanterns going on and off. Well, she wouldn't be picking cotton for the Woodruffs either like Sullie had done, feeling mad because Mrs. Woodruff was half Indian herself and spending that cotton money on silk dresses and luncheons at fancy places while Sullie was out there picking it from the dusty fields with her eyes watering. And she wouldn't be growing up laying down with men on the road at night like Anna May had done.

It must have been the quilt that moved her to dream of walking in the big lake at home. The water was warm against her legs. Silent except for the sound of water dripping off her, touching up against the shores in a slow rhythm like maybe it loved the land. And suddenly she was standing in the street by the diner, cars bearing down on her and she was paralyzed, unable to save herself.

Sullie woke up. It was cold. She covered Donna with her own half of the blanket and got up. The sky was growing lighter outside the window, beginning to light up the white cotton curtains with the rose colors of sunrise. Traffic picked up. Standing in her pale gown, her long hair loose and down around her waist, Sullie opened the curtains while the coffee water boiled. She called softly into the other room. And then she went over to pull back the covers. "Time to get up."

Outside, Donna stood at the end of the bench, waiting for the bus. Two young GIs slouched down on the bench. They wore olive drab, one with his military hat pulled down as if he were sleeping, one leg crossed over the other. His hands were folded loosely in his lap. Donna stood almost at attention.

A train passed over. It clattered and thundered along the trestle and it seemed to blow open Donna's tightly held sweater. It blew her hair in a blur of heat and exhaust, the heat waving up like a mirage, a summer field or highway. The soldier who sat straight up waved at an invisible conductor leaning off the platform between cars, and then he glanced at Donna. His eyes took in her thin body and chest. Under his gaze, she was stiff and unmoving. She stared straight ahead, but her body tightened inside her blue-gray sweater.

The train hurried past, carrying coal in the sweating black cars and speeding east on the vibrating track.

Donna was still. In the center of all the motion, the automobiles filled with people, the gold and red plastic streamers that waved and twisted about the used car lot, she was still, and then the train was gone.

Indoors, Sullie wiped the black shoes with a dish towel. She set them down on the table, on the speaking hawk laminated into plastic. She dried the dish drainer. It was pretty, the color of wildflowers at home. Bright orange like children's new toys and painted Mexican salt shakers, city swing sets. In the morning light, the entire kitchen shone, each item clear and full of its own beauty. The cereal bowls were dragonfly blue. The coffee cup was deep rich brown. It sat on the table beside the black shoes.

The shoes were small. Donna's size. Inside, the place where Donna's delicate arch would touch and rise when she walked, were the words "Montgomery Ward." Monkey

Wards, as Sullie's cousins called the large white department store on Broadway, the store with the wires going through the ceiling, across the desks, the little tubes of money sliding through the air and stopping.

Sullie's own shoes were flat and worn, scuffed. The soles were worn down at the heels. Last week a nail had pushed into the heel of her foot.

Suppose Donna had stolen them, she wondered, standing back and looking at the new shoes. She sipped her coffee. Suppose Donna had stolen these woman shoes? Or stolen Sullie's money. Sullie picked up her handbag and unzipped her money compartment. Eighteen dollars and twenty-nine cents. It was all there.

Sullie imagined the fancy shoes on Donna's little horse legs. With the pink toes and jagged toenails protruding through the sculptured holes. Donna's thin calf muscles flexed above the high heels. Destitute and impoverished thin legs the color of cream and with fine and scraggly hairs and big knees all looking so much worse above the shining black shoes. And there were those young soldiers already looking at the little breasts and at the red-black hair moving unevenly across her shoulder blades. What would they think when they saw the girl walking at a slant, wearing them? Surely they wouldn't want to touch those pitiful small legs and thighs or cup their big hands over the bulges of her breasts.

Someone must have given them to her. The meatloaf friend.

Donna could not count money and she was shy with sales clerks, holding her handful of pennies too close to her own body and waiting for the clerks to reach over and count out what they needed from the moist palm. Donna's school-teacher, Miss Fiedler, had herself told Sullie that Donna couldn't count money. She had visited their place and all the while Miss Fiedler spoke, her blue eyes darted around the room, never resting on Sullie, who believed the woman was looking for bugs and dust. Those cornflower blue eyes looking at the nail holes in the bare walls, at Donna's drawings taped on the kitchen wall next to the window, at the quilt with its needlework pictures of Sullie and her own mother standing surrounded by a field of green corn with a red turtle floating in the sky like a great sun and a yellow frog and curled scorpion in each corner.

"What's that?" Miss Fiedler pointed at the turtle and the scorpion. "Oh, a red turtle. It looks like it's swimming."

"The sky turtle. From an old story my father used to tell."

Miss Fiedler kept her feet square on the floor and her knees together. Sullie was aware of her own green blouse. It was ironed but growing thin beneath the arms. Sullie remembered to lean forward as she had seen other women do, to look at the teacher's face and occasionally at the pale yellow sweater and its softness and at the blonde curled hair. The teacher sat like a gold light in the center of the sofa that day, like a madonna in a church surrounded by a quilt of stained glass pictures.

Finally Miss Fiedler looked right at Sullie. "I was passing by and thought I might as well stop in. I thought it would be better than a letter."

"Oh?"

"Donna isn't ready to go on to seventh grade. It's out of the question. She doesn't even count money." She added, "She doesn't get along with the other girls."

And in the long silence following the words, the room brightened as the red turtle sun came out from behind a cloud. The teacher's hair lit up like brass. She expected Sullie to say something. Sullie watched the woman's face brighten. Then she said to the teacher, "She'd good at art though, don't you think?" And Sullie went over to open the drawer and remove the collection of pictures she kept there. "See here? This is Lucy Vine. It looks just like her." And there was old Lucy wearing some plants in a sling of cloth on her back. She was bent, nearly white-headed, leaning over a fire. Behind her was a metal tub for washing and some men's shirts hanging along a fence like scarecrows and a raven flying overhead, its blue-black wings spread wide.

"Nice. That is nice."

Sullie looked up at the teacher and repeated, "She's good at art," and the teacher looked back at Sullie and said nothing.

Even remembering this Sullie felt ashamed and her face grew warm. She removed her apron and hung it on the doorknob that was heavy and crystal. The color of larva, with light pouring through it. Sullie lifted the apron and looked again at the doorknob, the room reflected in it a hundred times, herself standing upside down and looking at the tiny replicas of the motel apartment. She left it uncovered. She put the apron over the back of the kitchen chair. The doorknob was the nicest thing in the room besides the quilt and Donna's pictures. The pictures were lovely. There was one Donna had sketched of Sullie from the back, her shoulders soft and round-looking, the hair unkempt, the heavy face just visible in profile. And there was a picture of women dancing in a row. They wore gathered skirts over their heavy hips, dresses with sewn patterns, the Diamondback design, the Trail of Tears, the Hand of God. They were joined hand to elbow. Their white aprons were tied in neat bows at the back. "Funny dresses," Donna commented when she completed the picture.

Pretty as a picture postcard, Mrs. Meers was standing at the door with her arms folded, the red and gold streamers flying behind her in the car lot. There were flags on the antennae of a used Chevy that said $250 in white soap on the windshield. Mrs. Meers, the manager, fidgeted with her hair, one arm still crossed in front of her stomach. Sullie opened the door.

"You got a phone call from the motel. They say you're mighty late coming in today."

"The Pines? I'm not going in." Sullie didn't look surprised at the message.

"You don't look sick to me." Mrs. Meers dropped both hands to her hips. They were slim in white pants.

"I didn't say I was sick. Just tell them I'll be there tomorrow."

Mrs. Meers looked more seriously at Sullie. Like a doctor might do when he discovered you were not just entertaining yourself by sitting in his examining room. She squinted and sucked in her cheeks. "I don't mean to step into your business, but to tell the truth I'm not good at lying. You tell them. And tell them to quit calling me. Tell them you'll get your own phone."

Sullie shrugged. "It's not lying." Only the hint of a shrug, so slight that Mrs. Meers did not notice. And she continued talking, more softly now. "What's so important that you can't go in? What's worth losing your job over?"

"Look there!" Sullie was pointing toward the street. "Look there. Is that your little cat?"

Mrs. Meers looked impatient. "You know I don't keep cats."

"It'll get run down."

Mrs. Meers tucked in her red shirt. "Look, I know I ain't supposed to be looking out for you tenants."

"Shows through," Sullie said.

"What?"

"Your shirt. It shows through your pants."

The landlady waved her hand in exasperation. "Listen to that. You worry about my shirt."

Sullie half-listened. She nodded. She was still watching the kitten stumble away from the wheels of one car and toward another.

"Okay. Okay, I'll tell them." Mrs. Meers went off grumbling, saying how was it these people could buy fancy black shoes like those there on the table and not ever go to work. Must be government dole or something. She herself could not afford shoes like those and she was running this place. She waved her arm as if to clear her mind, to get rid of Sullie and that sneaky quiet kid of hers. Deserved to lose her job, she mumbled. And all the while Sullie was out in the street calling to the kitten, a scrawny little cat with greasy fur. "No pets!" Mrs. Meers yelled at Sullie. "No pets allowed. We don't even let goldfish in."

After the cat coiled up on the sofa, Sullie washed her

hands and returned her attention to the shoes. If they were stolen, they would have to be taken back. That would be the right thing to do, to hand the shoes to the sales clerk. She might be one of those older, efficient types who wore maroon suits and shirts that tied in bows at the neck. Pearl earrings. Or one of the tall ones in the thin dresses. If she were a young clerk, she would be nervous and call the manager. The managers were tight about the rules. They stuck with the rules. They might call in the police.

Sullie had never stolen anything. Just the thought of it sent her heart racing and made her knees weak. She had no courage against teachers, clerks, police, managers, and even now the fear came flying into her.

She put the shoes back where she found them.

It was a quiet day. Early afternoons were quiet. The traffic died down. The red and gold streamers were lifeless. A good day just for walking.

Sullie stepped across the railroad ties that smelled of creosote and the penny smell of oiled metal. She went across the vacant lot filled with weeds and a few spears of green that were irises. Behind the rows of houses, there was a lake, a few elm trees. She heard the doves in the mornings from her kitchen and she was hungry to look at the water, the blue sky lying down on its surface.

Two ducks swam there. The bright-colored male was showing off. He shook himself, ruffled his feathers, and paddled his orange feet. The female ignored him, diving under water with her backside exposed. Dipping and surfacing. A plane flew over and Sullie caught its light on the water.

An old man with a cane tipped his dark hat. He wore a heavy coat as if it were still winter and he had not noticed the change of seasons, the warm sun and the green dusty leaves on the few elms. A woman sat on a swing, her two children pushing at one another. The woman stared at the ducks. Her face looked bored and vacant, the look of mothers with young children. She would have spoken to Sullie if Sullie were thinner and looked different. If Sullie had worn a pair of slacks and a flowered blouse. The woman wanted to speak to someone. She greeted the old man.

When Sullie headed back, she had to wait at the tracks for a train to pass. It was a passenger train and the faces in the windows rushed past. One small boy waved at her. The wheels clattered, metal on metal. A man and woman stood on the platform, the wind in their hair and faces. His arm around her waist. The sounds roared in Sullie's ears and the earth beneath her feet rumbled and shook and then the train grew smaller in the distance, growing lighter, and she picked her way over the tracks and through the weeds of the field, out of the heat and cement and into the fresh smell of the grocery store. Cool. The banana odor, the laundry soap fragrance. There were cartons of eggs on the rack, tan and perfectly smooth and oval, red meats with their own fleshy odor. "How much?" she asked, pointing at the ground beef. The man in the white cap gestured to the marker. Sullie ordered a pound and he scooped it out and wrapped it in white butcher paper, wrote .31 on the top with black crayon.

Sullie left the store, walking slowly, her arms full of the large bag, her face to one side of it watching for cracks and settling in the sidewalk. Carrying milk and a small bag of flour, a half dozen eggs, an apple for Donna, two potatoes. And there was a small container of cinnamon inside the bag. A gold and green shaker holding in the sweet red odor of other countries, of islands with their own slow women carrying curled brown bark in baskets. The metal box was the color of their dresses, water green and sunlight color.

Sullie would make bread pudding out of it and fill the apartment up with the odors of islands and Mexico, warmth and spice and people dancing in bright colors and with looseness in their hips, at least as far as she imagined.

When Sullie arrived, there was another smell in the apartment, the wax and perfume smell of the lipstick Donna was wearing. The rouged cheeks and red lips made her look younger, against the girl's intentions. Her big dark eyes were innocent in contrast with the crimson lips. The lipstick paled her skin. All of her facial weaknesses were revealed by the rosy cheeks and the painted lips, as if her plainness normally strengthened her, camouflaged the self-consciousness of her expression and the awkwardness of her movements, the pensive bend of her shoulders. She looked away when people spoke to her and she did not look up into Sullie's eyes now while Sullie stood, her arms full of the brown paper bag. She stood one moment before putting the groceries down on the table, and Sullie said, "So." Nothing more or less, simply, "So."

The kitten slept in the child's lap. Its paws were twitching slightly. Down in the quick of it, beneath the smell of transmission fluid, the kitten was dreaming of something pleasant. Cream, perhaps. Or of stalking brilliant green flies. Lord, Lord, Sullie breathed, what things we put in our heads. All of us. Filling ourselves up with hopes. Looking out for an extra dollar or good job. Putting on these faces. Even the cats. And here it was, the kitten, all comfortable while Mrs. Meers over there was plotting how to get rid of it. No pets. All these dreams and hopes, and nothing out there but rules and laws. Even in the churchyards. Even in the big homes, the ones that smell like paint and god-fearing Sunday dinners. Even in the motel rooms, a sign on the door saying when to move on. A bible full of do and don't. A boss clocking you in. Red lights. And there was a girl with red lips whose eyes do not meet yours and her head filled up with pretty things and men who would someday love her right out of her loneliness for a few hours. Her head filled up with pearls, silk dresses, shining hair. Even in Paris perfume in the pretty blue bottles. All those thoughts flying around in there like crows circling over something down on the road.

Sullie was quiet as she put away the groceries. She removed her shoes and walked on the gray linoleum, her feet with a soft animal sound against the floor. She struck a match against the stove. The odor of sulphur and then of gas as she held it to the little hole inside the dark oven. All at once, as the fire took, there was the sound of burning, of the box-like oven opening up. She was going to cook meatloaf. Donna, holding the kitten, stood by the table and traced the black marbled patterns with her finger. "It's a monkey."

"Does it talk?"

"It says you got fired for missing work today."

Sullie put down a fork. "Who says that?"

"The monkey says Mrs. Meers told him."

"Monkeys lie. Besides, what's he doing hanging around women with black roots in their hair?"

"Did you ever hear of television? It's new. It's like a radio, only with pictures. And they move like in a movie." She was filled with amazement and the magic of it. Her eyes darkened. "I saw one."

"How do they get the pictures?"

"They come in the air."

"Pictures? You mean they are in the air?"

"Even in here and if we could turn on a button they'd show up. Yes, they would." And Donna saw the apartment peopled with men and women, animals, new places, all around her the black and white pictures of the rest of the world.

"I'll be. They think of everything, don't they? They just sit back up there in Washington with old Eisenhower and they think of everything." Sullie rubbed on the soap bar while she spoke and the bubbles foamed up in the dishwater. She smiled down at Donna. She dried her hands. "Sit there. Stay there." She went over to the couch. "Don't move." Donna remained at the table while her mother bent and reached underneath the couch for the shoes. Donna's hands tightened.

"Child," Sullie said, standing up. "I don't know where they come from but they are about your size."

Donna was still. The light from the ceiling was on her hair and behind her, the small lamp burned an outline about her, like a small fire, like a burning match. Her delicate face was soft-looking even with red lips.

"I found these. Here, put them on."

Donna stood and balanced herself by holding on to Sullie and then to the chair back. She put one small foot inside a shoe and then the other. She stood taller and thinner than before. She looked frail. The leg muscles tightened. She wobbled.

Sullie went to the wardrobe cabinet and opened the door to reveal the picture inside. "Look," she said and she was almost breathless. "Look. You're pretty."

Donna looked herself up and down. She looked into the depths of the mirror for the moving pictures of men who were flying through ordinary air, for the women selling Halo shampoo on the television. She heard their voices. She looked at the black patent leather shoes. She lifted one foot and polished the shoe against the back of her leg. She stood, turning herself in front of the mirror. Her skin looked moist, childlike in its warmth and lack of pores.

Sullie stood, her bare feet quiet, rocking a little, swaying in place. Donna could see her mother in the back of the mirror behind her, a dark woman, plain and dark and standing way back in the distance with her hair tied, her feet bare, a heaviness in the way she stood there in that air, that very air all the perfect white kitchens floated through, all the starched blonde women drifted into like ghosts. Sullie moved more fully into the mirror, her darkness like a lovely shadow beside the pale girl, her hand on the girl's narrow shoulder. "Pretty," she said, "You sure look pretty."

◆

WENDY DUTTON

Life as a Writing Mom

◆

The point, or part of it, is that babies eat manuscripts. The poem not written because the baby cried, the novel put aside because of a pregnancy, and so on. Babies eat books. But they spit out wads of them that can be taped back together; and they are babies only for a couple of years, while writers live for decades; and it is terrible, but not very terrible.

—*Ursula K. Le Guin*

Before my daughter Molly was born, I had this picture in my mind of a baby cooing happily in her swing while I tapped away at my computer. We lived side by side, tickling and singing to each other now and then. I am embarrassed to write that now. It is so far from the truth.

Now, four years and two babies later, everything comes in pieces. I used to write during my daughters' naps. Now I wait until they are asleep late at night. Either way it averages about an hour a day. Slim pickings, you might think, but not really. An hour a day actually produces quite a lot of stuff. I have no time for something as luxurious as writer's block. When the house falls silent, I dash to my desk. It's like I'm leading a double life. While we were taking our walk and building towers and doing dishes and collecting acorns and reading *Is Your Mama a Llama?* I was secretly plotting and scheming for this precious hour of writing time.

Also, I am divorced. This means it is all me when I am with the kids. Though Molly and Jesse, ages two and four now, officially "go down" by eight o'clock, they creep out of their room for the next two hours, wanting to pee, wanting milk, wanting their daddy. By ten o'clock I am a wreck. I am tired from my teaching and freelance work, but more I am frazzled from the almost physical pull between my children and my writing. To wait until deep night just to be alone! For a solitude junkie like myself, it's a shock.

Of course, the logical route would be to give up the writing for a while and return to it when things settle down. After all, I make no money from it. In fact, if I calculated the hours I have spent over the years writing, I would be minus millions of dollars in unpaid work. Talk about labor of love. It's a lot like mothering.

Nevertheless I seem to be riding on some kind of artistic high. I envy my children's energy, wallow in it for long stretches of time, and yet I want to separate, want to have an intellectual life of my own while they sleep. I know to my core that if I give up the writing, especially now, I will seal my fate. (You'll just have to put up with my melodrama. Remember I live with a two year old who, when we're all out of olives, throws herself on the kitchen floor, sobbing.)

This is the story of my struggle to keep writing while I was raising small children. And it's also the story of other women who survived this frenetic lifestyle; for early-on in my experience as a writing mother, I began somewhat frantically to look for role models. I felt adrift, cut off, not just from the work-a-day world, but from the literary world. My image of a real writer was someone who wrote in utter solitude, surrounded by books, not stacks of laundry. But after a great deal of soul searching, and also just plain searching, I have a whole new vision of what a writer is, and what I am too. My quest began by reviewing the lives of my favorite writers. I found frighteningly few had children. When I did come across a writing mom, I clipped her picture, typed up her words, and tacked these treasures to my bulletin board. It is as if I was telling myself, "See here. Evidence. Writing Mothers. They exist!"

Take for example Harriet Beecher Stowe. She was one of the few writing mothers to come out of the nineteenth century. She wrote in her diary in 1841:

All last winter I felt the need of some place where I could go and be quiet and satisfied. I could not there [the dining room table], for there was all the setting of tables, and clearing up of tables, and dressing and washing of children, and everything else going on, and the continual falling of soot and coal dust on everything in the room was a constant annoyance to me.

Stowe had seven children. She finished *Uncle Tom's Cabin*, her first novel, when she was thirty-nine, much of it written on that same dining room table.

All Harriet Beecher Stowe wanted was a room of her own. That's what Virginia Woolf said every woman writer needed—that and a steady sum of money. Woolf paints a cozy vision, but usually it's unattainable for the writing mother, even more of an impossibility if she's single. Virginia Woolf! Sometimes I hate her.

In her groundbreaking book, *Silences* (1972), Tillie Olsen documents the major gaps in the writing careers of women (and also of men). One writer told me how Olsen's book gave her writer's block for years because the prognosis was so bleak. Olsen writes:

In the last century, of the women whose achievements endure for us in one way or another, nearly all never married (Jane Austin, Emily Brontë, Christina Rossetti, Emily Dickinson, Louisa May Alcott, Sarah Orne Jewett) or married late in their thirties (George Eliot, Elizabeth Barrett Browning, Charlotte Brontë, Olive Schreiner). I can think of only four (George Sand, Harriet Beecher Stowe, Helen Hunt Jackson, and Elizabeth Gaskell) who married and had children as young women. All had servants.

At first, *Silences* drove me crazy with all its lists. But before you know it I was making lists of my own. I realized that all of my favorite writers from the twentieth century were also childless: Flannery O'Connor, Willa Cather, Gertrude Stein, May Sarton, Anaïs Nin, Harper Lee.

By the second half of the twentieth century, however, several writing mothers emerge. Look at Adrienne Rich, the mother of two sons. The following passage is from page one of Rich's *Of Woman Born* (1976). It is an excerpt from her journals in the early sixties when she was a housewife.

> *My children cause me the most exquisite suffering of which I have any experience. It is the suffering of ambivalence: the murderous alternation between bitter resentment and raw-edged nerves, and blissful gratification and tenderness.*

I never could finish that book. I would get to that passage and slam the book shut, so shocked was I that someone had articulated those emotions.

Sylvia Plath, an example of a writing mother whose life ended tragically, was writing at the same time as Adrienne Rich. As a teen when I was first beginning to write, my favorite poet was Plath, largely because she was available. Of the fifty-four writers taught in my Major American Writers class in the early 1980s, three were women: Anne Bradstreet, Joyce Carol Oates and Sylvia Plath.

When I had children of my own, I returned to Plath because I remembered she had two children, a fact of little consequence to me when I was younger. I found that she had indeed written about mothering, and the poems had gone largely unpublished for many years. In the three years before Plath died, she had two babies and one miscarriage. She was nursing most of that time. When the children were one and three, she separated from her husband and assumed full care of them. In the months before her suicide, she woke at four o'clock every morning. It was the only time she could write before the care of the children and the house consumed her day. The poems she wrote during this period, later collected as *Ariel*, were the most brilliant of her career.

Ravenous for clues about this writing mother's lifestyle, I read back through Sylvia Plath's journals and letters, edited by her estranged husband Ted Hughes and her mother, Aurelia Plath. I found nothing. Unlike her poetry, Plath's journals and letters seldom mention mothering. The last three years of her life seemed to have been edited out. There are shockingly few entries from those crucial years, and even those that are published are filled with telltale ellipses—almost to the point of distraction. It is as if her existence as a writing mother has been wiped out.

Just when I began to despair over the dismal fate of writing mothers, however, I began to find some more. The writing moms on my bulletin board started to add up. Often I'd take a child count: Alice Walker has one child, Louise Erdrich has six, Jamaica Kincaid has two, same with Antonya Nelson. Grace Paley dedicated her book *Later The Same Day* (1985) to her children "without whom my life and literature would be pretty slim."

I realized I was looking in all the wrong places for that dusty old role model. She is right here in my hands. She is on the back flap of a book jacket. See for yourself. There is a new kind of biographical blurb these days, one never seen in literature before. The examples below come from Mary Cahill's suburban mystery *Carpool* (1991) and Katherine Dunn's brilliant *Geek Love* (1989).

> *Mary Cahill lives in Ellicott City, Maryland, with her husband, two children, and a huge slobbery dog. She was born in 1944 next door to the orange grove that later became Disneyland; this set a surreal tone for most of the years that followed . . . She either has been or still is teacher, farmer, quilter, weaver, pastry chef, free-lance writer, and carpool driver.*

> *Katherine Dunn has worked as a journalist, house painter, bookstore clerk, bartender, screenplay writer, proofreader, teacher, and radio personality. Her advice*

column, "The Slice," appears regularly in Willamette Week, *and since 1986 she has been a boxing correspondent for the Associated Press. She is the author of two previous novels,* Attic *and* Truck. *She lives with her son in Portland, Oregon.*

Male writers don't do this. Being a parent is seldom seen as a hindrance to a man's work, but neither have children been considered an integral, inspiring part of men's writing careers—as these blurbs suggest for women. For the writing mother it is second nature to mention her children, her constant disruption and muse through the hectic business of making a living, raising a family and writing. These tiny biographies paint a different picture of the woman writer, surely not one spirited away in a room of her own. These are women writing poetry in school parking lots and supply closets.

There is a story, by now legend in the Bay Area where I live, about the popular writer Danielle Steele. She was at a party in San Francisco. Outside, circling the city blocks, was a limousine. Occasionally Steele would leave the party and hail the limo, where she nursed her newborn in the back seat. I used to think that was a horrible story, so removed was it from my experience. But now I think, that's a long way from Harriet Beecher Stowe.

When I talk to older women about mothering, I say, "Why has it been kept a secret—the enormity of this job? I haven't slept through the night in four years. I am living in a state of shock."

And they look at me and say, "You forget. You truly forget."

This is what defines women, I decide, this amnesia. Talk about self-preservation. We have the remarkable ability to block out pain, in childbirth and otherwise. But it makes our world secret, a cycle of surprise to our children who later have children of their own.

My mother is an artist. I have watched her my whole life try to hang on to her violin music. When I was a kid, my sister and I would tear around the house, jealous that our mother was on the other side of the French doors, standing some other little kid on a chair, teaching him the Suzuki method.

And then there was the time she was playing in a recital at Mills College. We were all going, the three kids and my grandparents too. We arrived late and all piled out of the station wagon. My mother reached for her violin case, but found that it was empty. She had forgotten the violin at home. She screamed, "SHIT!"

She tells that story often, still mortified that she swore like that in front of her parents and kids.

Like most of her friends, my mom went back to school when her kids were grown. Now she is a therapist. Sometimes she has friends over, and they play chamber music together in the living room. A few years ago she realized how much her violin was worth and thought of selling it, but after much thought decided against it.

And yet, until recently I had never thought of her as an artist. Her violin playing was just something about her. It was not until one particular phone call that I hung up and thought of her in a new way.

We had been talking about the work of raising little children. It was a topic we had touched on, but always skirted away from. As usual, it was hard to find the words for it. I broke the ice by saying how I sometimes went bananas over the smallest tasks such as tying pint-sized tennis shoes or negotiating the buckles on the car seats. I told her how I couldn't fall asleep the night before because I was worried I wasn't giving my youngest enough eye contact.

My mother said, "I have never been able to tell you about that time in my life. I have never been sure how to approach it."

My children were asleep. I could hear them breathing, and I could hear my mom breathing on the other end of the line. She said, "There were days when my only contact with the outside world was the mailman's hand coming in the slot."

She told more stories, about getting dressed up just to take the bus to the pediatrician's, about getting us all ready for church, about yelling in the parking lot of the supermarket. While she was talking, I thought, "The stories we don't tell!" And after I hung up, I thought, "My mother is an artist." The words just plopped themselves down in my mind. I understood then this unspoken legacy.

I have spent much of my writing life avoiding the Big I, that is, first person narrative. I thought the true job of writers was to create worlds that were entirely new. Now I have a different motto: in times of crisis, record. Since I have had children, I have written more than ever. My writing is infused with an immediacy it lacked before. And at my desk is something that is new: nonfiction. Suddenly I am writing essays all about me and my kids.

The first essay that I wrote was in response to an ad for a writing contest. The prize was fifty dollars, a small fortune to me. The theme was writing as healing. But the real attractive feature of the contest was the four-page limit. I wrote the essay in one night and mailed it late. It began, "This is one of those crash-and-burn stories, the tale of how my life in one week's time has gone from a shambles to more shambles to a tiny crystal ball I can hold in the palm of my hand." The story described going on a family vacation after discovering my husband's affair.

When they called to tell me I had won the contest, I thought it was a sign that nonfiction was the ticket. These one-stop essays balance my bossy, snobby fiction. And they are easier to publish. I've had numerous tiny articles in *Moms at Home* and *Welfare Mothers Voice*. They are a far cry from the articles I published before I had kids, scholarly pieces complete with footnotes in *Frontiers: A Journal of Women Studies* and *World Literature Today*. Now I write about what it is like having a dog and a baby at the same time or what to do about the problem of TOO MANY TOYS.

So that's what I use nonfiction for: telling stories fiction can't touch, the simplest stories, stories that just say, "We exist." Nonfiction is a relief. It seems more real than fiction because, quite simply, it is. It is truth more easily measured. It comes quickly and completely, written in stolen time.

Now when I think of writing mothers, I think of them more like an army, row upon row, my bulletin board smiling down at me. Often I imagine them late at night. All over the world kids are going to sleep, and writing moms are coming to life. There are thousands of us, women whose voices have been muted by the cries of babies, women who write in bathrooms, in cars, in trees, women with revolution on the brain.

MAASKELAH
KIMIT CHINYERE

Once Wanted:
A Man to Help Me Raise My Son

◆

Kubwa, my eldest child and only son, recently turned eighteen. We've been through a lot together in the last eighteen years, including two stepfathers and an almost nonexistent relationship with his natural father. In spite of it all, Kubwa is a bright, charming, articulate, sensitive and idealistic young man with a future that will be almost entirely of his own making. I still have moments of real concern about what that future will be, but that concern is a habit that began at his birth.

Sixteen and pregnant, all I really knew was that I wanted a child, someone guaranteed to love me and be with me for as long as I wanted and needed. Motherless myself since age nine, lonely and confused—and with the irrational reasoning of youth—I assumed that having a baby would be the answer to my loneliness and would ultimately provide a companion that I could count on.

I remember my father saying two things when I told him of my pregnancy: one was that he decided that I would have an abortion (which, at sixteen, I had the option of refusing); the other was his telling me with fear and concern in his voice, that no man would ever willingly agree to raise another man's child, so what the hell did I expect to do with a baby?

Idealistic and determined, I gave little thought to his concerns since I was sure that all my child would ever need was me. After all, I reasoned, this baby was what I needed to escape what I felt was a pattern of abandonment: first my mother, then my first real boyfriend—the baby's father. My mother hadn't actually abandoned me. She died, at age thirty-seven, of emphysema. Still, I needed her and she wasn't there. Kubwa's father, on the other hand, a seventeen-year-old hormone-crazed adolescent, had proven to be unfaithful, unreliable and uncaring about me, his sixteen-year-old seriously "in-love" girlfriend, and later, his yet-to-be-born child. I had not gotten pregnant to hold on to him, but even if I had it wouldn't have made any difference—six months into the pregnancy it was apparent that my pregnancy in no way restricted him from doing whatever he pleased.

Two years after Kubwa's birth, his natural father and I were history; he had gone on to college and had married another local girl who was, he said, a virgin: a major criterion for him and something I, obviously, no longer was. It was about this time that my father's previous lamentations began to ring in my head. Not only did I have a child to raise, but a man-child at that. After my mother's death, my four brothers and I had been raised by my father. Although I'm sure my brothers missed our mother as much as I did, at least they had a same-sex parent available to them. Daddy took them fishing and hunting and on other types of "male-bonding" expeditions, and occasionally I was allowed to tag along. But by the age of fourteen, I had begun to miss my mother with a force that caused stomach cramps and brought tears to my eyes. I didn't want my son to have to go through the same feelings of loneliness and aloneness that I had fought so relentlessly against, and although I felt confidence in my ability to be a good mother, it occurred to me that this child, my son, needed a father.

Enter Husband/Stepfather No. 1. By then, I was eighteen, had graduated from high school and was pursuing "marketable skills" through a local business college in order to support the two of us. When I met my first husband, we seemed quite compatible, based on the fact that I worked part-time at a record shop, and he liked all the same music that I did. Being the romantic that I was, it seemed like a match made in Motown heaven. Kubwa seemed to like him, too. Kubwa, though, just about to enter that terrible-two terrain, was more than a handful and required much time and attention. I wrote it off as frustration when, after a particularly trying day with Kubwa (he had poured a whole box of fishfood into my future mother-in-law's aquarium, killing all the greedy little tropical fish), my future husband told me that he hated my son. I was sure that he couldn't mean it, since Kubwa was the most adorable, pleasant and lovable baby I'd ever seen. Later, when future Husband No. 1 repented, I agreed to marry him. Thus, we were wed. I was nineteen and he was twenty.

I should have been alerted, if not alarmed, when soon after we were married, Husband No. 1 told me that I "played too much" with my child. Again, I wrote this off as typical "new father jealousy." Dr. Spock talked about it. I thought it was normal. Nevertheless, I rationed my time between the two of them when both were present, and made up for lost time with Kubwa when Husband No. 1 wasn't present. After all, Kubwa's beautiful smile and heart-warming laughter brought joy to my days.

Then came potty-training. My first major confrontation with Husband No. 1 came when he picked up my two-year-old son by his feet to swat his behind after Kubwa had messed his pants. That was his idea of potty-training. I swore that if he ever did such a thing again I would, at the very least, maim him.

Soon after, my second child was born, this time a daughter, Poetry. On the day we brought her home from the hospital, Kubwa, three years old and potty-trained, wet his pants in his excitement. Husband No. 1 again physically punished him for it. I became aware of a developing pattern in which I had to rescue my son from his stepfather's unreasonable punishment.

Seven years and still another daughter later, MyAngel Afrika, the punishment had begun to be taken out on me as well. The day that Kubwa stood in the corner of our family room screaming for us to "please stop fighting!" I knew I had to rethink this stepfather thing. I didn't know exactly how to leave, but I knew that we had to get out of this situation. One night, after spending an entire evening with Husband No. 1's mother and sister in a hospital emergency room after his nephew had fallen off a skateboard, I came home to find my husband in a rage. With the now familiar smell of too many after-work beers on his breath, he terrorized me for over an hour, not allowing me to leave the room, physically threatening me and daring me to defend myself. I had had enough. The next morning, after he left for work, I gathered my children, one still an infant, and as many of our personal belongings as I could fit into my car, and left, never to return again.

Kubwa was twelve at that time. After taking time to handle the business of divorce and resettling myself into an apartment, I made contact with Kubwa's natural father, reminding him that he had a son who hadn't seen or heard from him in over ten years. He now lived out of state, but his mother was still local. He was gracious enough to take time out of his busy schedule to come to town to visit with his first son and to arrange a meeting between Kubwa and his half-brother. He spent some time with Kubwa, but later came back to my apartment at an ungodly hour, supposedly to talk with me about the son he seemed to have all but forgotten until then. Eager to give Kubwa the opportunity to have access to his real father, I allowed the brother in, only to discover that his motives were all but pure and that he had forgotten what I had not. I took the opportunity to "politely" remind him of what a dog he had been and still was, since he was very much married. He had no business, I told him, expecting me to do to his wife what he had done to me. On top of that, I had fallen out of love a long time ago, so it just wasn't going to happen. So much for reunions. It would be five more years, at his graduation from high school, before Kubwa ever saw or talked to his natural father again. In the interim, I met another brother who showed promise of being the "positive male figure" that I still hoped could teach my son what it meant to be a "real man."

When I first met Husband/Stepfather No. 2, I disliked him for what I thought he was. At that time, I was co-founder of a community organization that was considered "radical" for our small-town community. Our organization had invited the national chairman of the African Peoples' Socialist Party to participate in our local Juneteenth festival (a celebration, originating in Texas, to commemorate the end of slavery). Such a move was unprecedented in our conservative, Bible-belt town and brought the attention of every law enforcement agency in the state. Full of energy and zeal, I moved about the park where the festival was being held, selling the newspaper of the Party, the *Burning Spear*. Some of those whom I approached with the paper paid the fifty cents for it either out of curiosity or because they knew me; on the rest I used every tactic from guilt to ridicule to force the paper into their hands. "You're wearing the 'red, black and green'—find out what it means!" No one, other than a uniformed police officer, approached me on their own to purchase a paper. That is, except future Husband/Stepfather No. 2. In my heightened paranoia of the moment, his action indicated to me that he must have been associated with the police, too. And then, he had the nerve to come back and ask questions about something in the paper. I was through with him before he began. I sicked a brother from the Party on him, figuring he would be more adept at handling an undercover cop or an agent provocateur than I. Later, as our organization and Party members gathered to discuss the day's events, we discussed this brother, tagged him as an agent and thought that we should be conscious of his presence at any future gatherings.

I never saw him again until months later, at another community festival. By this time, I was no longer deeply involved with the organization or the Party and my paranoia had lessened in direct proportion to my involvement. My father and I established a black bookstore to provide relevant literature and resources to our community, something that was sorely lacking. The Black Arts Festival was the bookstore's debut. Future Husband/Stepfather No. 2 took this opportunity to approach me again, but not until after he had approached my father to "get permission" to engage me. I found that somewhat provincial, but sweet, and so I agreed to spend some time with him. We ended up spending most of the three days of the festival together and, ultimately, decided to pursue a serious relationship.

As it turned out, brother was Muslim, as are my father and stepmother. My parents have been Muslim since the days of Elijah Muhammad, but after I became an adult, I chose not to involve myself with the religion of Islam, for a variety of reasons. One of those was that, not really being well-versed on what Islam was about, I couldn't see the relevance. Also, I viewed the women involved with Islam—my stepmother included—as passive, submissive and oppressed, something that I definitely was not and had no desire to be. And most of the people in our small community who were Muslim were older, my parents' age. Or so I thought, until I met Husband/Stepfather No. 2. He seemed open to my "womanist" views, and seemed to enjoy my expression of my personal beliefs, even showing me how my beliefs were, in fact, very much in line with what Islam teaches. He informed me that he had been eager to meet me for years, as he had been a regular reader of a column that I wrote for a local community newspaper. I was flattered. He met the children, and they all seemed to like each other. He was raising his six-year-old brother, a child of his father's, whose mother and father had both abandoned him. I found that admirable. I thought: "Now, here's a real man. Willing to take on the responsiblity of another man's child when there's no compulsion and no real obligation. He must be an all right brother." And he seemed agreeable to helping me raise my now teen-aged son. Oh, and did I mention? Brother was tall, dark and *too fine!* And he liked jazz. Thus we began.

I embraced the religion of Islam, not because of him but as a direct result of my exposure to the religion through him. We were married within a year, since Islam doesn't promote "long engagements," and a year after we were married, we went through our first separation. Before our marriage, he had convinced me that Islam was about every family member being valued and strong. After our marriage, he demanded, primarily, that his wife and his children be submissive and obedient to him, regardless of how irrational and impractical his demands were. My efforts at self-expression and any opinions that were not directly in line with his were considered a direct affront to his authority. And Kubwa had been branded early on as rebellious and undisciplined, which bore some truth since Kubwa was a typical adolescent, trying to figure out what it meant to "be a man." Where I had hoped another brother would help him to learn and understand that, instead I found that Husband/Stepfather No. 2 was resentful and angry at having been handed what had to seem like an overwhelming responsibility. I know that it was. I, too, was overwhelmed. That's why I'd sought assistance.

We eventually reconciled, but the relationship continued to deteriorate, based mostly on Husband/Stepfather No. 2's inability and unwillingness to take another man's son in hand and teach him, in whatever ways were appropriate, the meaning of manhood. He, too, expressed hatred for my son and sought to physically discipline him. By now Kubwa, standing six feet tall with peach fuzz on his face, wasn't in the mood. So they fought, and we fought, and our family was nearly torn asunder. My oldest daughter went to live with her paternal grandparents rather than be subjected to the tension, discord and threat of violence that now loomed in our once relatively peaceful home. Because of my unwillingness to submit to what I began to feel was a not-so-benevolent dictatorship, I suffered a fractured rib and immeasurable emotional damage. Finally, after three and a half years and the forced removal of my spouse from our home after the last incident of domestic violence, we decided that it wasn't worth it. And Kubwa, again, was left without a father.

In the midst of both marriages, and afterward, I sought to understand just what was going wrong. Where was I—where were we—falling short? Good at analyzing what is "wrong" with other folks, I looked at both husbands and attempted to get into their psyches.

Husband No. 1 came from a home where his own father was not present, but he had the benefit of a caring and hard-working stepfather who saw him through his own stormy adolescence. His difficulties seemed to stem more from his "difference." A very pale-skinned black man with red hair and freckles, he had revealed to me incidents, as early as kindergarten, where he had been treated unfairly, simply based on his physical features. The mistreatment came from both blacks and whites, thus his anger and resentment was color-blind. Perhaps that was why, as an adult, he resorted to liquor to escape the internalized pain that he wasn't really able to name or otherwise express. Unfortunately, whenever he'd had one beer too many, my son and I became the targets for that expression. He never saw beer as "serious liquor"; therefore, treatment for alcoholism was out of the question. And certainly getting help to deal with the underlying emotional trauma that caused his behavior was never even an option.

Husband No. 2's father was in and out of his life, leaving his mother for a time, then returning and leaving again, saddling his mother with the responsibility of raising seven children pretty much by herself. He and his siblings grew up in stifling poverty, even spending some time in a children's home when his mother was unable to properly care for them. And during those times when his father was present, Husband No. 2 was subjected to painful physical and emotional abuse. He tells of an incident where his father threatened to burn him with a cigarette for misbehavior. His punishment, if not that of his siblings, was always extreme and intense. Strangely, he never talked of his father's treatment of him in terms of it being abusive. He seemed to think that such discipline was normal, if not warranted. Needless to say, his feelings for his own natural father were ambivalent, at best. He never seemed to make the connection between his own father's handling of him and the ways he related to Kubwa. If he had, if he could have named and faced his own pain, I wonder if it would have made a difference in his relationship with my son and with me.

At twenty, Husband No. 2 committed an armed robbery

and ended up in prison for two years. To this day, has never talked to me or anyone in his family about that experience. However, one of his brothers shared with me that he was truly a changed man when he was released: bitter and resentful and full of hate, even toward his own family. While in prison he embraced the religion of Islam, and although there was a period of time when he didn't practice it, he ultimately sought to make Islam the way of life that he followed . . . such as that was.

I don't know the basis for his misogynistic tendencies. His mother is one of the most gentle, generous and even-tempered women that I've ever met. And yet, one day during one of our "disagreements," he made the comment that he understood why his father had treated his mother as he had. "Women have a way of pushing you to the edge," he said.

And what of me and the internal disorder I brought to both relationships? Certainly my need to feel secure and appreciated and my fear of abandonment, combined with my "rebellious" outspokenness, did not sit well with either of the brothers. In spite of that, I, by nature and upbringing, believed (and still believe) that what I think and feel should count for something and that I have a right—and an obligation to myself and others—to express that. Feminist writer and scholar bell hooks calls it "talking back," but I felt that I had that right, since I, too, was an adult and an equal—woman or not. I truly never sought to antagonize—only to "speak my mind" and express my opinion. Husband No. 2, on the other hand, would probably say I deserved to be "slapped in the mouth" for my insolence and for not giving my black man the respect he is due, simply because he is a black man. I was raised by a black man to believe that respect is a two-way street. (Incidentally, neither husband ever liked my father very much either.) For better or for worse, I am raising my children to appreciate their right to their opinions and the voicing of those opinions where appropriate. Unfortunately, Kubwa may have become an unwitting victim of the contradictory values and opinions between me and the men I chose to wed.

What about the other children in this complex familial quagmire? I've talked about Kubwa. Before Kubwa was ever conceived, I had dreams of someday having a dozen children, hopefully a nice mixture of male and female offspring. I enjoyed being raised in a somewhat large family, but I missed never having any females within my immediate family with whom I could relate. Even so, I wished my first child to be a son, so that any subsequent girl-children would have a "big brother" whom they could look up to and who would look after them, when necessary. I have three older brothers and one younger, and enjoyed their love and protection throughout my growing up years. Not far into my mothering, even in spite of my perpetual idealism, I realized that attempting to raise twelve children was a bit unreasonable. I was, however, blessed with two daughters.

I don't want to give the impression that Kubwa has been the perfect son to raise. During his childhood, I dealt with everything from insolence and outright disobedience to fire-setting and theft. I always tried to deal with every incident of misbehavior using consequences that fit the crime. His age at any given time was always considered, as well as his ability to reason and understand. He entered adolescence in a typically rebellious fashion, but there was never a time when I couldn't respond to him in what I felt was an appropriate manner, nor when he didn't ultimately respond appropriately after whatever discipline I imposed. And fortunately, our extended family—his uncles and grandfather—were always available to reinforce whatever principles and values I sought to instill in him.

My daughters, being younger than Kubwa, always had his example (including his "failures") to draw on. Poetry has taken note of many of the poor choices that Kubwa has made, and has declared that she will not make some of the same mistakes. The same is true of the poor choices I have made. It is with mixed feelings that I listen to Poetry swear that she will never marry or have children. I regret that my mistakes may cause her to miss the joy that I've experienced by having children in my life. On the other hand, I do pray that she has watched closely those choices that I have made, and that at some point in her life, she will be able to analyze and understand why I did many of things that I did. I hope she will make better choices than some of mine.

MyAngel is still such a baby. She's a "mama's girl," and her joy is still very much wrapped up in pleasing me. I realize, though, that there will come a time when she will start to ask me hard questions like why I am no longer married to her father. Or why Husband No. 2, whom she absolutely adored and who adored her, is no longer around. I'll answer her as honestly as possible, while also taking the opportunity to begin addressing some of the issues that she herself is bound to face as a young black woman growing up in this society. I think she'll be okay, God willing. I've learned a lot about mothering between Kubwa's birth and today.

And Kubwa is okay. Despite my disastrous attempts to provide him with a male role model, all I seem to have accomplished is to show him the kind of man that I hope he never becomes. I've tried, however, to make him aware of the positive qualities that each of the men in his life exhibited. Maybe, by default, he has learned something positive about manhood, in spite of my imperfect attempts to provide a suitable teacher. Time will tell. For now, he is well. He is currently pursuing a career in graphic design and is working to design and publish a teen magazine for local distribution. He has, so far, managed to avoid peer pressure to become involved with gangs and drugs. The emotional damage, if there is any and surely there is, doesn't appear to be irreparable.

I never meant to harm him. He is my first and only son. I love him. I think he has forgiven me. I think he understands that all I ever wanted was a man to help me raise my son.

◆

DIANE LUTOVICH

Life After Single Parenting

◆

It is four years since my daughter graduated from high school and left for college. When I used to think about my home, daughter gone, me alone, I actually heard the silence— punctuated only by the sound of my own breathing. Though I had lived alone for several years before I was married, I felt unprepared, and unwilling to revisit my single years. As a parent—even without a mate—I had not felt single. And since the last time I was alone, almost twenty-five years ago, my formerly tidy and predictable life had been torn wide open by this child who taught me how to live with another in a way that marriage had failed to do.

I knew her leaving was going to turn my world upside down, just at the point when we had learned, after a painful adolescence—painful to me, at least—to laugh again. A part of me wanted to insist, "don't go." But of course I didn't, and she did.

And her leaving reminded me of all the things I thought I had wanted, would never have, and, for the most part, had learned to do without. Instead of two or three children, I was grateful for one. Instead of having a big family that gathered together, I was grateful that her father and I had joint custody. He shared in the child-raising and we often did things together. For brief moments I had been able to pretend I lived according to the expectations of someone who came of age in the fifties.

It's not easy to plan your life around a child and then, just when the child starts coming into her own and could be fun to spend time with, find her gone. These children who have known us longer and better than just about anyone else are off to start a new life, taking pieces of you with them.

My daughter was the center of my life. From the time I became a "single" mother until the day she left for college, I was not sick. I had too much to do and no one to help. I didn't resent the obligation. I found it a valuable discipline. She kept me healthy. And as much as I hated (as did she) my nagging and pushing, I recognized the energy that disgusting behavior drained off. I used to wonder if I would find myself stopping strangers to tell them to comb their hair, stand up straight, study harder.

I, like most parents, always knew my daughter would grow up and leave home. I knew it in the same vague way I knew I would be old one day or that one day my mother would die. Despite my joking and despite my mother's warnings, I don't think the reality of how my daughter's leaving would change my life hit me until her sophomore year in high school. I don't know why it was then, but I think, in retrospect, it had to do with her pulling away from me, setting the course of her own life. Because our contacts frequently felt so cold and empty, it was fairly easy to imagine the next stage—the absence of her physical presence as well as her emotional presence. And since I'm a natural clinger, a craver of what I know, I felt a sort of desperation. I had fashioned a way of life, albeit improvised, but it included her—at center and periphery. She was such a strong presence in my life I didn't want anything to change. So two years before she left, I wrote the following:

◆ ◆ ◆

Timing

Always too soon . . .
    wait.

Plum blossoms swell,
spread porcelain petals.

Too early

to burst,
ejaculate color,
break the membraned cocoon.

Next week winds,
"easy winds,"
off the Pacific,

will blow petals to
extinction.

Though they were meant to expire
after a day,
make space for plums,
birds, jam,

I want the petals—
a frieze,
me on one side, them on the other.

But the winds came
too soon

like her birth.
I craved the heaviness in my womb,
eyes, I hadn't finished the quilt,

I needed more time.

Still, I learned to love
her rounded laugh
tripping into the ripening body,
bursting all boundaries—
my arms, rules, yard.

Now she's busy packing.
I hear the lids slamming,
no matter it's a day,
year away;
I hear wind off the coast

ready to blow away what is,
make way for the next . . .

Too soon.

Raising a child as a single parent is a lot like riding a roller coaster. Frightening, exhilarating, exhausting—certainly not boring. And as we learn to recognize the rhythm, the ups and downs, the expected and the surprises, it's easy enough to stop thinking about the end of the ride. And then the time is up. The ride is over. A surprise to some, not to others. Certain riders always remember the ride lasts fifteen minutes and are thankful it lasts no longer. Others are actually surprised when the ticket taker says, "Time is up." Some start thinking about the end about halfway through with a mixture of relief and regret. I was one of those.

As her departure got closer, I realized the connection her father and I had maintained ("for the child") was about to change, too. Though divorced, we had a tight connection: this too would change. As if to underline the fragility of our systems, we agreed to her request and, together, drove her to college. Painful, on so many levels.

Round Trip

Near the mouth of the Colorado River,
a mile from the Continental Divide,
we line up the sleeping bags,
our daughter, in the middle.

Divorced years ago, result of
irreconcilable rage, about to turn loose
the last threaded connection,
we enact the myth of family.

Even on this last night,
almost two decades past her conception,
we use her to come close,
to almost touch
in the dark night
beneath stars, half moon,
"Mountains of Never Ending Summer."

*   *   *

We take her bike,
boxes and bags to her third floor room.
She introduces us
as her parents.
It was what she wanted.

After dinner, our hugs, promises still hanging
on the warm still air we head West,
watch her in the rear-view mirror,
small, tearful beneath
the porch light.

She continues to shrink until
again, only two of us
are alone in the car.

Before we've reached
the first pass
the years unravel.

Staring at windows thick with yellow,
red of dead bugs, we talk, over bites
on bruised pears from a stand
in Green River,

try to recall the horrors,
the unspeakable outrages—
anything to stop us

from using departure
the way we used conception
to bond the unbondable,

to shame each other again
in the name of love.

*   *   *

Reno, the last stop before
returning to our separate houses.
He tests his luck at the crap table,
tries for a seven,
I put my quarters in the slots,
hope for three bars,
even two

we come out
even

almost where we started
a quarter century
ago

in the same casino,
the same crystal lights full of dust,
smoke, unable to conceive of the madness
ahead, we drank our celebratory toast
after stumbling out from the judge's
office that Sunday morning—married.

By evening, we're past Tahoe,
roll down Highway 80,
stop for dinner in Davis,
delay home an extra hour

Soon enough bay fog settles thickly
on car windows;
we start fumbling for our bags,
separate, finally,
what's his
from mine.

Despite the fact her leaving was neither sudden nor a surprise, I discovered a lot of empty places that first year—

reminders that I missed her, missed having a child around. Of all things, Halloween was sad. How I envied those parents who accompanied their children. I missed her companionship. In fact, I felt my displacement so profoundly, I wrote:

Ghosts

On Halloween, a parade of dragons,
dancers, clowns, pumpkins,
witches, an old gypsy;
in my empty house,
phantom sounds of teen-agers
and toddlers, even the long dead dog
growling in fear
of marauding
tricksters.

The house is almost
deserted; no
sounds of breathing
except my own—I'm costumed
as a mother,
the easiest disguise.

As each child comes,
I feign horror,
try to recall the motions
mothers make
when children expect you
to hold up their world, no matter
how shaky.

After an hour, I'm tired,
don't want to play.

But when the child who lives next door
pulls off his mask, his eyes
reflecting the shock
he expects to see in mine,

I can't disappoint.

"Tyler, you scared me to death.
I would never have guessed that gorilla
was you."
His giggles roll him
around the porch.

I made it.

But next year, I will dress as the merry widow
or a mother superior,
lock my door,
join the parade,
take all the chocolate and leave
the red licorice.

By the second year, I had started to adjust to my new life—a new business direction, an enormously satisfying lover, a housemate who provided income and a voice to relieve some of the quiet. And my daughter's obvious pleasure with her own life helped, too. I started to find my own rhythm and to see her appearances as gifts. My life had started to grow around the vacuum. It was after her first winter vacation that I wrote the following:

Visitor

The daughter drops in from her college world,
not to reclaim her place
in the orbit of home
but to etch her presence,
spread energy and socks
like uncorked champagne.

  It will be this way . . .

She roams like a he-dog, makes sure we know . . .
a shoe in one room,
purse in another,
sweaters spill into the hall—
uncontrollable.

Always.

One day she collects her art book, makeup, disappears.
But after she's leapt back to her life,
her voice bounces off walls,
shoes seem to creep out
from under the beds,
breath lingers in dust
wrapped around sun.

And finally, this spring when she graduates from college and moves on, I can start to see the larger picture. She was, and is, after all, only temporarily mine. That I was a single parent, more focused, more devoted, more in love did not change the inevitable cycles of life. She liked this piece:

So Hard To Hold On

Hiking with my daughter
along the California coast

we see a bobcat moving suspiciously
across the slope.

Years back, our cat, still unformed,
dropped five kittens under the bed
rolled on her back, bared her nipples.

After five weeks, sucked dry,
Carmen was sent away, long enough
for her milk to dry up, her babies
to new homes.

Back, she wandered
a day or two, seemed to settle,
her chewed nipples her only clue.

*   *   *

Near the end of the trail, the Pacific,
flat and blue, rolls out at our feet,
we talk of big things—her future

I have no news,

only the certainty of my own
insignificance.

On the way to the car, we pass ponds—
she remembers catching tadpoles,
trying to turn them to frogs,
the one that made it as far as hind legs.

I remember my mother splitting open
walleyes, orange globs of eggs slipping
out of the belly
through her hands, onto the floor.

For a time I was confused about just who I was. Not single. Not married. Not childless. Not with children. Was it over or just starting? Recently I woke up from a dream frightened and smiling. My house had been sold. My daughter was happy. Some shadow figure was telling me—go for it. Whatever you didn't get before, you can still achieve. There IS life after parenting.

◆

VALERIE POLAKOW

Contingent Lives

◆

*The following is an excerpt from sociologist Valerie
Polakow's* Lives on the Edge: Single Mothers and Their Children in the Other America. *Polakow interviewed numerous
women for her excellent book that explores the varied realities of single mothers' lives. The women profiled in this excerpt, Anna, Sara, Lori, and Jenny, range in age from teenagers to women in their early thirties. Their names have been
changed to protect confidentiality.*

Anna

I hate being a single mom, but there's nothing I can do about
it. I hate this life! I hate it from day to day—I can't stand it
and everyday I'm thinking what can I do to get away from
this—how can I better myself to get away from this. . . .

All the time I don't think this system's here to help me,
it's just to keep you right where you're at—to be poor—to
make you psychologically dependent. I know a lot of people
who've been on ADC [Aid to Dependent Children] for ten or
twenty years . . . First, I'm like—how can you do that with
your life—it's not good to sit on ADC and have baby after
baby, and people like me we try and want something better
but they don't help—it just doesn't work for you at all. It's
like you're working—well, they want you to work—but then
they take away what you make and they cut you off just as

you get going—so it's like you're never on top. But I gotta find a way out of this—it's just too crazy. . . .

I don't want to be on ADC but I had to get back so I could get caught up on my rent and get Medicaid for my baby . . . so I was working forty hours and since I got back on ADC I had to cut back to fifteen to twenty hours a week—I hate being on ADC, they make you feel so belittled I hate that! I hate going to the office and I hate dealing with the social worker and dealing with every worker that has something to say about my life . . . Sometimes they make you think that they're the one giving you this money and they're not—it's the government and they make me pay taxes so I'm the one giving the money back to myself . . .

And then I was asking what if I wanted to go back to school and the worker said, "You didn't graduate," and I said I graduated! And I want to go to college—I don't want to be on ADC the rest of my life and if I keep doing what I'm doing now I'm never going to get off. I got my high hopes for me and I don't want her [my daughter] to go through the same things I have—it's terrible. . . .

I feel so much better about myself when I'm working 'cos I'm also doing something for myself, and all the time I'm trying to better myself. I'm not just one of those statistics that they say just gets on ADC and sits there—especially about your being black—that's how they think you are anyway, having baby after baby as if you want to just sit all your life on ADC . . . and when you go to the supermarket I get that different treatment when I pull out the food stamps and people look at you and say you're on ADC and you're not trying to better yourself—and then I feel bad, I want to cry I want to tell them don't look like that—you don't know what's going on in our life! Those people who look at you in the line and say, "She's one of them," and I want to tell them—you just don't know—if you have a kid like this and you got no way out—see what you'd go through.

◆ ◆ ◆

Sara

I had graduated from high school and I finished a semester and a half of college; then I had to drop because of my pregnancy . . . When I found out I was like three or four months—the baby's father didn't care, my family didn't care—I never had a real family. I was raised by my grandmother and my aunt and I ran into a lot of problems with that . . . and my aunt passed away when I was sixteen and I was on my own—that's when I had started on my own working at sixteen. So when I had my baby I had to have a C-section and one of my friends was there with me but my family never came to see me in the hospital. I stayed there for five days and after that I came home to my grandmother's house, and I was like sleeping on the floor with my baby—nobody helped me—and then my uncle told me there was no room for us in the house and I had to go—so he gave me $1000 which is not a lot to live off of, so when he said that—it was like I'm grown, I don't care, I'm going to make it okay. I'll leave. I got an apartment and I left and I been out on my own ever since and six weeks later I went back to work. . . .

Then I had like a friend that I thought would be a really good baby-sitter for my son, but I come to find they were neglecting my son. They would like put him in a crib and just leave him in there—they never held him, they never cuddled him. And you know he's very affectionate, he loves you, but I felt that he felt like he was in jail you know and this is a $35 a week baby-sitter and I'm not making that much money at this time. So she would watch him, plus I began to float shift—I would work days, I would work afternoons, midnights, so it was really hard . . . and a lot of stuff later could have been avoided if I could have put him in proper child care but I couldn't afford it. And the place where I worked, they had a child care program, but that's designed for professionals—not entry-level employees. And I'm talking entry level as being at the institution for like five years. I could not afford to send my child there. And DSS the way their program was, it doesn't give you any money because they go by your gross income and I couldn't get any help—Des didn't even qualify for WIC [Women, Infants and Children—a supplemental food program] and with his clothes and milk and Pampers and everything—the only good thing I had really going for me was I was blessed with good insurance from my job that covered all his doctor visits....

Well, he goes to the sitter from 7:45 in the morning and then he goes to school at 12:30 and then he gets out of school at 3:30 and then back to the sitter at 4:00 and then I get off work at 4:30 and catch the bus and get to him about 5 and then we catch the bus again and then we get home about 6, I see Des for bed time...and then we start another day....

I got my vision, I got my dreams, and there are days when I feel down like I really can't make it, I can't go no further, I'm nothing—you know, I'm tired, I'm tired and it's too hard. But it's like I have goals—I want to be something different from what I have right now...I guess to be somebody in poverty, to see that generation that's coming behind us—it's sad, it's real sad, what do they have to strive for? I sacrifice now because when Des looks out the window he sees a family man taking care of his family, where if we lived in the ghetto, if we live where my income allows me to live, Des wouldn't have nothing to strive for—but I just got to believe I only can make the difference...even though obviously the system doesn't really want you to succeed...I can become what statistics has designed me to be, a nothing, or I can make statistics a lie.... Today, I am making statistics a lie!

Lori

Oh God it was hell sitting down there and filling out the forms y'know—it was pretty humiliating. I'm a snob and I'm sitting among the homeless filling out these forms. All these people are driving up in their rusted Chevies and I'm in my '87 Honda. I mean I felt really out of place—it was really horrible...You have to fill out forms and they call your name and there's this security guard and she's real harsh looking. She's maybe thirty and she snaps her gum when she talks to you and it's like—"heh, lowlifes"—y'know what I mean. You talk through windows with holes in them, I don't know, I think it's very demeaning. They tell you to fill out your forms and it's like you should know to stand in this line, or that line, or what forms you should be filling out...I mean I don't know how all these people do it—I really don't—I think it takes a high IQ just to figure out all the forms. And then to get denied—my God!—after dealing with all of that and then they say you make too much money...The caseworker, he filled out my worksheet and he went to work it out on the calculator, so he left the room and I could hear him adding stuff, and he came back and he said, "You make too much money" and I went "You're serious?" and he said "Well at least you have your food stamps for this month."...I don't know what I'm going to do. My dad helped last month, but rent's due next Wednesday and I don't have any money. I mean I don't. I just paid all my bills. It's the end of the month now and I don't get paid for two more weeks. I have $2.50 in my account: two dollars and fifty cents! Rent's $545—I get paid in two weeks again, but that will only be $400...I need help—I feel like I'm sinking....

I had to call this woman at social services who decides whether or not I'm eligible for child care, and every three months I have to give them a total lowdown on my income—where my money's at and whether Jim gives me anything in child support—so I lied—and she said she needs a letter from him stating what money he's given to me, and I said I won't get the letter from him and she said what then—am I denied child care? So she said—technically the letter had to come from him but she'd take it from me—and I only think she did that, and this is probably prejudice—because I was a well-dressed white woman that didn't talk slang and wasn't missing my teeth and looked like I was serious—and I said I really need help y'know...so now I get $77 every two weeks, but even that's not 100 percent of what they can give me, that's 90 percent—according to your income or something like that there's very very low and very low and I'm in the very very....

I scramble for the baby-sitters—I never get baby-sitters unless I'm in school—I can't afford it. Mindy [the neighbor] takes care of Kim whenever I'm in school, and if she can't she'll just say, "Lori, I can't baby-sit Tuesday"; then there's this girl Lee that the woman who cuts my hair recommended, and she just lives down near Krogers' and she's a doll and Kim adores her. She charges only $2 an hour, so I use her quite often. Even to go to school Friday and Saturday nights that's $24 . . . but if I didn't have Mindy I seriously wouldn't be able to make it . . . She's like my savior!

Jenny

When Danny was six months old we left, it was very secretive. I left because I needed to avoid being pursued and followed. It was an awful wife-beating kind of relationship. When I realized that was what it was, I knew I had to leave and when I figured how to do it secretly I did. It was very difficult and depressing. Danny had never been abused and I had to get out before he got hurt. I never thought this would happen to me, but now I see there were many things in my past which predisposed me to this kind of abuse. I came from a rigid Catholic background, my parents were wealthy—they threw me out when I started experimenting with drugs and sex in school—and other people in my family were physically abused—my brother was a healthy, beautiful child who was battered, totally battered, and he went to drug abuse, now he's a very dangerous man to be around . . . So when Dan was born I never left him with his father because I was afraid that he could not handle the pressure, and soon after, I fled. Some abusers will try and pursue a wife who flees. I know the only successful way was to be completely secretive—no communication. . . .

Dan was like no baby I had ever seen. He was like no other. He would not stop crying. He had rashes all over his body—he was allergic to all sorts of things—he was hyperactive—he didn't sleep—I thought what is wrong with this child? At seven months they prescribed phenobarbital which is a barbiturate. I couldn't work, because I couldn't leave him with my sister because he was so intense. Originally we thought we'd work different shifts, but it didn't work out and all this time I'm on welfare—but staying with my sister—she was the only person I could turn to—she was a life saver. . . .

At four years old I had just about lost my mind with this child. He wouldn't listen, was constantly on the move—as much as I loved him I thought I could not deal with this anymore. I was trying to ease him into day care so I could work, but that didn't work. By the time Dan was four I had had it with him. I was still on aid, my house had been broken into twice—everything I did have was stolen, and the social services were threatening to cut me off if I didn't take a job—I told them I was having a terrible time with my child—at one point they were trying to tell me I had to be in a work program for about thirty hours a week. I told them my child and I were at a tremendously difficult point, and so I went to legal aid and they came and represented me and said I had a special-needs child who wasn't able to stay at a daycare center and they wanted documented proof of everything . . . They told me I had to attend some stupid job club for a bunch of uneducated people . . . I didn't want those dead-end minimum wage jobs. I had a 4.0 GPA for my first year at college . . . I wanted to apply for a scholarship to get back in school. . . .

Originally I was getting $170 twice a month, now they've cut it down to two $50 checks. I only make $6 an hour and I'm working twenty to twenty-five hours a week—that's $450 a month and I get $87 in food stamps—add it up that's not much money to live on. Rent was $310 a month here but they gave me a break—if I didn't have that I'd be going out of my mind . . . You can never save money like this and you can't live on $600 a month—all this time Dan and I buy clothes at resale shops—nothing new and I buy almost nothing. If I work through the summer at a temporary job to try and earn a little more, they will cut me off and I will get nothing—then I would have to reapply and they have forty-five days to process the application and for that time we would have nothing. So we can't afford for me to work at a temporary job in summer because we'll get cut off during the fall—so I can't work or I have to cheat to work! And worse, if I find a job and I get cut for longer, after six months they cut Medicaid. So if you aren't covered through your job, which most women aren't, you just stay poor and it's very difficult—you're in a vulnerable position. Oh my God poverty! It's something! You just learn to get by and then they cut you—so you can never get ahead!

SENATOR CAROL MOSELEY-BRAUN

The Silent Constituency

As a United States Senator I am required to spend much of my time in Washington, D.C. It is not the real world. Not only is Washington not the real world but it has a hard time *comprehending* the real world. Washington is all about power, and the measure of power in Washington, as well as in so many other venues, is money. Fortunately for America, however, there is another currency that leverages Washington: votes.

The famed "Beltway" is a deep, psychological, intellectual moat. It can be crossed, but it takes an army—whether an army demanding "choice," an army demanding "health reform," or any other concern. Perhaps one day soon we will see on the horizon an army of mothers demanding that their realities be recognized.

The Clarence Thomas confirmation hearings served as a wake-up call for the women of America. If the men on the Senate Judiciary committee didn't have a clue about sexual harassment in the workplace, what else didn't they have a clue about? My colleague, Senator Patty Murray, elected, as I was, in 1992, brought the issue home when she explained why she decided to run. "I looked at those men," Patty said, "and thought, no wonder we're in a mess. Who among them has ever gone without health care because of no insurance? Who among them worries about getting time off to care for a sick child? Do any of them ever watch the clock to make sure they pick up the kids on time, then grab a pizza somewhere because they haven't had time to think about dinner?"

The government can't solve all our problems; it can, however, ease our burdens. It can work with us, not against us. Yet, to most legislators single mothers are a mere statistic —a growing, some would say, alarming, statistic, but a statistic nonetheless. Somehow this statistic must coalesce into an army, because while there are more of us now in Washington who understand and care about the issues that affect families, we can't go to war without soldiers.

We have an opportunity, and an obligation, to demand that our government prioritize a *family agenda*, concrete and specific responses to a host of issues as they affect families. A first step lies in defining families comprehensively and realistically. A family agenda must be as supportive of the single or non-parent unit as it is of the traditional two-parent unit. Families come in many different forms. We must use our vision of the ideal to shape our reaction to that which is real.

There is nothing wrong with being a single mother, and we must not accept any reduction of status just because this is the circumstance that we have chosen or that life has dealt. As Reverend Jesse Jackson likes to remind some, Jesus Christ, the child of a homeless family, was born of a single mother.

What counts, or should count, is that in our country almost a quarter of all families with children under eighteen are headed by single mothers. That is a statistic, given political life, that would dominate any number of other "special interests" that are accustomed to prevailing in Washington.

I must make it clear, however, that while I demand acknowledgment and respect for our existence, I do not think single motherhood, or fatherhood, is something to be celebrated. Children are much better off with two parents; there is not a bit of evidence to deny that. To glamorize single motherhood is to create another myth where myths already cloud the issues, much to the detriment of the body politic, as well as to each of us as individuals.

In traditional economic theory, the distinction is made between men and women as being a fundamental economic division of labor. For centuries, men have done one kind of work, women, another—the woman being the caregiver, the homemaker, the strong right arm. This allocation of responsibility suggests that the whole burden is too much for one person. And it is.

Moreover, our economy has changed so much since Rosie the Riveter hung up her tools and went back to housekeeping after World War II that now it frequently takes two wage earners in a family to maintain the living standards then purchased by one.

Today forty-five percent of single mothers live below the poverty line, and I suspect, legions more are on the cusp. Nevertheless, single motherhood and its attendant problems are not at all limited to the poor. There is a set of concerns here that cut across all social and economic lines. Despite our differences, all of us are bound together by a universally shared experience: we are mothers alone, loving and striving to create the best possible lives for our children.

I am a single parent but I have been blessed in ways that make my situation almost the exception, rather than the rule. I am a trained attorney, so I have been able to make a comfortable living *in spite of* the fact that my income dropped over sixty percent after my divorce. I was able to recover from the financial free fall that happens to all too many. My son's father has remained a supportive, nurturing parent and is involved in raising his son (that's not to say I haven't gotten a few more gray hairs squabbling with him over just how to do that!). I have a family network that pitches in to help when necessary. No matter how convoluted the child care arrangements had to be, somehow, between formal institutions and family, we have always been able to cope.

Because I have had these life experiences and because I am one of the "sandwich generation," that is, women compelled to nurture both children and an elderly parent (my mother, who was disabled, died in late 1993), I know, first-hand, what is needed.

We need a family friendly government. We need the kind of ethical determinism that drove Lyndon Johnson to create the Great Society. We have a government that sees perfect sense in propping up, through subsidies, tax breaks and the like, everything from beekeepers to merchant ships. But with all the talk of family values, where is the comprehensive policy that says the United States of America values families?

There have been huge economic, demographic and technological changes in this country in my adult lifetime, the increase in single parent households being just one of them. We must take a holistic approach to this problem, addressing these realities:

• that affordable child care for working families is fundamental to the future health of this nation, and that realistic tax and support policies can be part of the solution

• that women making 76 cents to a man's dollar is unconscionable

• that too few companies consider alternative work schedules: flex time, part time, job sharing and the like

• that there is no good reason we can't have systems that both establish paternity where needed (without tedious court involvement) and that enforce collection of child support, perhaps, as has been proposed, with the involvement of the IRS

• that the domestic arts ought to be respected, and that those who need help in order to work and run a home should be able to afford household assistance in which neither worker is exploited

• that personal economic issues, while critical, are not the only determinant in the revitalization of American family life. As the old African proverb tells us, "It takes a whole village to raise a child." Our neighborhoods, our villages, our communities ought to provide socializing assistance through quality education, recreation and training opportunities.

And there is one more thing. The United States led the world in contraceptive research in the 1950s. No longer. In addition, sex education, family planning and reproductive health policies all suffered during the eighties. Public funding of family planning services is one of the most cost-effective roles government can play—according to one study, it can save $4.40 for every dollar spent.

Having said all this, it is of course true that over the years countless programs have been established in an attempt to address some of these problems, many of them funded by the federal government and administered through the states. While there are model programs out there, there are also huge inconsistencies, considerable waste—and not a little foolishness.

Let me give you one example. So much of what we legislate in this area is based on myth rather than reality. Some years ago in Illinois "welfare" became "workfare." This made lawmakers feel good: "We're gonna make 'em work!" they rejoiced. The requirement was that those on Public Aid turn in a piece of paper with a certain number of signatures showing that they had at least sought work, in order to pick up a welfare check. However, education and skill levels—not to mention the minimum wage and lack of affordable child care—being what they were, the economics of the proposal did not work. There was neither time nor money for an individual to improve her status. The program failed because it did not create opportunities for family support.

I was in the state legislature at the time. I thought, why not get some of these folks off this treadmill and instead of giving them credit for collecting signatures, give them credit for going to school? So I introduced legislation to do this, and it passed. Not long ago I ran into a woman who, somehow, knew that had been my bill. She said that she had been on Public Aid and had taken advantage of the new law, gone to school to earn her degree and was now a nurse. Not only that, but she was about to buy her own home. She thanked me for helping her extricate herself from the welfare system and build a life through gainful employment.

Women need to be empowered in this way to take control of their lives. Too many government policies do the opposite: they encourage dependence and extinguish hope. The so-called safety net programs should be designed not to entangle people, but to free them.

1992 was hailed as the "Year of the Woman," and there is no question that Anita Hill triggered an alarm. But let's not push the snooze button. Women are not only a numerical majority in this country, we are a *voting* majority and we need to think about maintaining momentum. From Murphy Brown to the welfare mom, our rallying cry should be, "Value families!"

Nothing will change unless and until that army marches on Washington. There is a saying, "Hell hath no fury like a woman scorned." Well, we are women historically scorned, passed over, put aside, trivialized by *the system that we own.* "'Reproductive choice? Day care? Child support?' Oh, just women's issues." Wrong. These are issues crucial to the security and survival of our country.

Get involved, learn, work, vote, participate in making democracy work. There are seven women in the United States Senate, forty-eight in the House. We need more officers up here in Washington, but more than that, we need an army that's ready to march.

◆

LESLEY SALAS

Venus and Mother Nature
are Actually the Same Woman:
Rough Draft of a New Reality

◆

In the few years since I've become a divorced mother of two, I have been searching for the positive about single motherhood. It has become clear to me that existing images about mothers tend toward being either sickeningly sweet idealizations or the pointed finger of guilt. What is the present-day single mother *really* like? Perpetually tired from working to support a family alone; emotionally strained by having no one to share parenting responsibilities with her; reviled when she expresses herself as a sexual being; and undervalued for the great contribution she makes to the future of society. In racking my brain for a creative solution to some of her problems, I began to notice that a common thread was the old bugaboo of rampant sexism. So, in order to find images of mothers untainted by modern patriarchal brainwashing, I took a crash course in classical women's culture.

My first mind-boggling discovery was that the earliest peoples worshipped only goddesses of creation. *Single mother* goddesses, as it were. To the ancients, women's role in reproduction was miraculous, actually sacred. Since you could always tell who your mother was but not necessarily who your father was, society was matrilineal. Women's efforts as mothers were recognized with more than a sappy Hallmark card once a year. I'm talking some serious respect here. After so many centuries of male-dominated society, it's almost impossible to imagine. Once you learn what to look for, though, you see that there are traces of our glorious past in every part of the world. For example, many rivers, like the Seine and the Danube, still bear the names of Mother Goddesses.

Later the gods came to reign over the earth with a force as hard and unyielding as Moses' tablets; mothers have not gotten a fair shake since then. That's why, when you delivered your child, instead of leaning back in a dug-out pit with a woman sitting behind you massaging your back and stomach, you lay in an unnatural prone position with machines hooked up to your belly, waiting for the male doctor to receive your newborn with a latex spanking. And that was just your first day of motherhood....

My immersion in women's history began to have a strange effect on me. I became so influenced by the fluidity of these women-centered cultures that I devised a rather unusual format for writing about them. With the disjointed logic of a dreamer, I imagined the goddesses of 5,000 years ago getting me out of my present-day jams. The following is my rough draft of a new reality, made possible only by expressing my most longed-for dreams.

One: Our Lady of Perpetual Exhaustion

REALITY: It's the end of yet another wearisome day in which you've worked too hard, too long, for too little pay. You jiggle the key in the lock and finally the front door pops open, to reveal a messier house than you recall leaving. Hyper children pour into the house behind you and pull the pillows off the couch to throw at one another. Your greatest desire is to kick off your shoes, flop into an easy chair and watch reruns of "Roseanne" for a couple of hours. Instead, you will help a child memorize 7 x 4 = 28, sew a button on a sweater, zip open the top of the macaroni-and-cheese box once the water boils and nag someone about taking a shower. WAIT! STOP! Let an alternative vision beckon and engulf you....

(Background music: "Wash Me Clean" by k.d. lang or floaty music of your choice)

ALTERNATIVE REALITY: Your children run to the shore to greet you as you emerge from the sea on the back of a dolphin, like the Chinese goddess Kuan Yin. They raise their short arms to help you down, taste the salt of the water that drips from your hair. The three of you feed on the shrimp and mollusks tossed ashore by the churning surf. The dolphin whispers the secrets of manhood into the boy's ear. The three of you take one last swim in the ocean just before night falls. Your daughter's wet eyebrows reflect the last rays of the dying sun. Your family casts a long darkening shadow on the sand as you walk arm-in-arm down the beach, watching the dolphins one last time as they swim out to sea....

Two: When You Care Enough to Send the Very Best

REALITY: Imagine this time that you are struggling with the Mom-as-Sole-Disciplinarian dilemma. You know, like those times when you are driving the kids somewhere, because you are *always* transporting them somewhere or other, and they begin to bicker and fight. Your son demands that you let him sit in front on a Tuesday, because his sister did the week before. If the noise level grows any higher, you will surely rear-end the Suburban in front of you. You have asked the children to quiet down three times, and you are now contemplating what punishment system to use to get some results. Just as you search for the words to convince the children of your authority, POOF! divine intervention arrives in goddess form.....

(Intro music: "Try a Little Tenderness" by Otis Redding, especially the plaintive saxophone riff and the rough smoothness of his voice)

ALTERNATIVE REALITY: The African mother goddess Maku knocks on the driver's side door. The children are fascinated with her hairdo, long braids with tiny shells laced into them. Unquestioningly they open the door for her. In a steady, lilting voice with a trace of a foreign accent, she begins to speak. "We have a word in Dahomey called *sekpoli*.[1] It means the spirit that lives inside each one of us. It teaches us that fighting is wrong. You are flesh and blood. You must find a way to get along with each other. Woe to those who do not listen to my teachings!

"Let me tell you a story about the monkey who disobeyed me. When I created the world I fashioned a wonderful monkey from clay with the most beautiful hands that could make anything. I gave him a pile of clay and told him he could create all the other animals—whatever he wanted: wings, claws, fur, sharp teeth. I went away for a while, and when I came back, I found the unworked lump of clay and no monkey. He had gone to brag to all his friends about the task I had given him, but he had done nothing. From that day forward I decreed that the monkey would walk on his hands instead of using them.[2] So heed me, and don't forget about the *sekpoli*."

As graceful and self-assured as a gazelle, she leaps out of the car at a red light. Her brightly colored robes flutter about her in the breeze. A busload of children stare as they pass by her commanding figure on the street corner. My kids are quiet the rest of the way home, visions of monkeys dancing in their heads. . . .

Three: Venus and Mother Nature are Actually the Same Woman

One of the most damaging stereotypes of the present is that mothers are only supposed to be sexual beings in a monogamous, heterosexual marriage. This mother/whore dichotomy makes the sexually free lesbian mother an especially reviled being. Come with me to the first meeting of our lesbian mother support group, and I'll show you what I mean.

REALITY: With a lover's familiarity Annette lifts Millie's baggy T-shirt to expose her stomach. "Look how PG she is!" cries out the beaming co-mother, as she teases Millie for either being nauseated or starving at any given moment. It is obvious that this lesbian couple has a satisfying relationship with each other while also raising their little boy, with a second child on the way. Yet, their families on both sides refuse to acknowledge their future grandchild. Only one of us in the group has supportive parents. Most of our own mothers are hoping we're just "going through a phase."

Another artificially inseminated mother shares the dirt about her partner, who couldn't make it to the meeting. "I delivered Diana late at night, Rita congratulated me, kissed me, and showed up again late the next afternoon. I was there all alone trying to get the feeling back in my legs," Patsy reveals. We sit wide-eyed as she describes her partner's fear of changing Diana or holding her as a tiny baby. Suddenly I am struck with a realization—lesbians have been brainwashed into believing that they really shouldn't be around children. As I sit there in all my glorious singleness, I begin to wonder if I will ever find "Ms. Right" and, if so, will she be willing to shuttle my son to his soccer games?

(Background music: the clear, twangy insistence of Carlos Santana's guitar solo on "Black Magic Woman"—minus such lame lyrics as "You're a black magic woman, and you're trying to make a devil out of me.")

ALTERNATIVE REALITY: *Prayer to Xochiquetzal, Aztec Goddess of Sexual Freedom*

Heed our prayer, O Holy One, daughter of Coatlicue, Creatrix of the Earth and Sky. We beseech you, O Butterfly of Stone, patroness of all sexually liberated women, to wrap your wings around us and protect us. Teach us to soar like the spirits of the goddesses of old, who were free to mate and reproduce and enjoy their bodies as they pleased, without losing custody of their children.

With the hard black obsidian you are made of,

Xochiquetzal, crush the centuries of moralistic judgments that have been made against us. We cannot live splintered lives any longer. We know that we should pursue both our desire to be mothers and our love for women, because we feel both impulses with equal urgency. Keep us from trapping ourselves in straight marriages because we cannot reconcile the two. Please, dear Goddess, send your healing powers to those lesbians who have believed the lie and feel they are not fit to be parents and caregivers. Unlock the love inside us, the feelings we have learned to hide.

O Great One, empower us to flit effortlessly among all our different roles, even as the chrysalis transforms to cocoon and then to glorious butterfly. Remind us that it's okay to have both a gay-pride rainbow-flag bumper sticker and one that says, "My child is an honor student at Jefferson Elementary." Give us the dignity to hold our heads high, even as people stare and spit at us in public to shame us. Obsidian Butterfly, the most delicate creature of the air but made from the hardest stone, ever changing, true to all her selves, give us the inner peace to do what we know is right.

Four: Father Does Not Necessarily Know Best

REALITY: Our lesbian mother support group sits in the circle formed by wrap-around couches. My son and the boy of the house are off being superheroes in the bedroom, wisely keeping the noise level down to a respectable din. My daughter, who loves babies, follows the artificially inseminated toddler around for a while.

The mothers and co-mothers look lovingly at the contented children. "Family values," one of us exclaims. "Can't they see how much love and attention we are able to give our very *wanted* children?" But, of course, they can't. We can only demonstrate our interpretation of family when safely inside each others' homes, trying as best we can to shield our children from the hurt outside.

My relationship with the powerful women of the past is second nature to me now. Without the slightest effort on my part, my imagination finds a solution to our plight. The doorbell rings, Annette opens it, and we are witnesses to the largest parade ever seen, curving around the cul-de-sac, goddesses of every nation at its helm. . . .

(Background music: a stirring rendition of "We are Family" by Sister Sledge, played by the Gay and Lesbian Marching Band from Harvey Milk High School)

ALTERNATIVE REALITY: The Celtic goddess Rhiannon, Grand Marshall of the Parade of Real Family Values, shows off her great white steed to the admiring crowds. A blast of fiery breath from the horse's nostril ignites the "RUSH LIMBAUGH FOR KING OF THE UNIVERSE" placard of a protestor on the sidelines. Jerry Falwell and his supporters run to escape being crushed by those mighty hooves. Coretta Scott King, Merlie Evers and Ethel Kennedy lead the contingent of mothers who became single through martyrdom. The homeless mothers look radiant, their children recently fed and fitted in new clothes. The formerly battered wives, right behind them, do a silent demonstration of Aikido that is thrilling to watch.

Oya, the Afro-Caribbean goddess with nine heads, provides a rainbow banner in the sky for the gay and lesbian parents section, which trails for miles. Many gay men and women are hugging each other with surprised looks of recognition. They are heard to exclaim, "I saw you at PTA, but I never knew!"

The largest contingent, though, is the Well-Adjusted Children of Single Mothers. They are all ages, races, socioeconomic groups and sexualities. The President is seen carrying a placard, "So did I turn out all right, Mom?" Adult men and women chant, "I love my lesbian mom." As night falls Coatlicue, Aztec mother of sun and stars, leads the Pleiades, Virgo and other constellations in a belly-dancing display. Their glittering costumes reveal their ample breasts as they shimmy and shake. (Why do you think they call it the Milky Way?)

Exhausted but elated, everyone heads for home. Their ears still ring with the proud pandemonium created by the hordes of single mothers and their children. They will never forget the day they took over the streets, even if it was only for an afternoon.

Conclusion

Thank you for sharing my dreams of liberation with me. I know that each family has its own particular hurts, requiring specific songs and stories of healing. It is my most heartfelt wish that you and yours find the words that honor you.

References

1. Merlin Stone, *Ancient Mirrors of Womanhood: A Treasury of Goddess and Heroine Lore from Around the World,* (Boston: Beacon Press, 1990), p. 137.

2. *Ibid,* p. 138.

General information about historical matriarchies was also taken from:

Grahn, Judy. *Another Mother Tongue: Gay Words, Gay Worlds.* (Boston: Beacon Press, 1984)

Stone, Merlin. *When God Was a Woman.* (New York: Harcourt, Brace, Jovanovich, 1976)

Walker, Barbara G. *The Woman's Encyclopedia of Myths and Secrets.* (San Francisco: Harper and Row, 1983)

◆

MARSHA R. LESLIE

The Gifts of Children and Angels

◆

I do not believe there is any greater moment than holding your baby for the first time and looking into her eyes. There is such a feeling of wonderment and magic—a moment when everything mysterious and sacred in the universe can be seen in one body.

On March 2, 1978, I experienced something I had never felt before and have not felt since. After a long and difficult labor and delivery, the nurse brought my daughter to me for her first feeding at two o'clock in the morning. (My husband, nervously present at the birth, had gone home to recover and to make long-distance phone calls to herald her arrival.) The room was illuminated by a single soft light over the hospital bed.

As I held my daughter for the first time, I felt a strong presence of warmth surrounding us. This presence—unseen, but definitely felt—in the room was that of safe and loving beings—perhaps her ancestors come to welcome her (if you believe in such). I know I was not afraid. There we were, Michaela and I, alone in the world for the first time. I held this little, fragile being as though she were the only gift I would receive in this lifetime. She was a tiny, brown, perfectly round bundle with a head full of black hair and piercing black eyes that looked up at me with complete trust, innocence and an intelligence that I will never completely comprehend. I called her Little Buddha. I believed that she was a gift to be held and cherished in my keeping for only a short time... and then she would leave.

"Mom, why are you crying?" she asks.

"I can't help it, you're growing up so fast...you'll be gone before I know it."

Where has the time gone? It seems like yesterday that Michaela was in diapers...and I wondered whether she would ever be potty trained. She took her first steps at ten months and I worried that she would never talk. She learned to talk at fifteen months and I worried that she would never learn to pause to take a breath.... She learned about racism in preschool when she was told that she couldn't be Superwoman because she is black...and in middle school when she was told that she wasn't black enough because she is smart...and I worried that her soul would be crushed by a world of ignorance and intolerance.

Today, Michaela is a sixteen-year-old honor student, who drives the car, works as an actor and babysitter, and grapples with complex social issues. She is a good friend and a perceptive and caring person of character and integrity. She's more mature in wisdom than her years and often blows me away. And, I still worry about how the world will treat her when she enters it as an independent person in a mere two years.

Meanwhile, Michaela is enthusiastically counting the months until she's off to college. I'm confident that she's ready and has everything she needs to survive and succeed in the world—she knows how to study, how to work, how to cook, how to clean her room (if absolutely necessary) and how to manage her money. I only wish I could have taught her how to take care of her heart.

Of course, the reality is that she's been leaving all along. I remember when she was a toddler and refused to let me hold her hand because she wanted to walk by herself; the scary first days of kindergarten, middle school and high school; when she was thirteen and didn't want me to show her any affection in public. Those instances seem insignificant now.

Today, a stronger force pulls her away from me—the sheer excitement of youth. Though my memories are vague, I recall my teenage years as a time when everything was new—independence, friends, work, driving, dating—and I was busy becoming a woman in the world.

These days I am overcome with a mixture of feelings. I'm excited for her. She's about to set off on the adventure of her life, and she will go places I will never see. And, I'm a bit sad that the time with her has been so brief—that in my forty-six years, I have already lived through my youth and hers. I feel somewhat awkward about my place in the world now that she doesn't need me in the ways she once did.

I remember when I was larger than life to Michaela—her mommy was "super"—could do anything and do no wrong. A time when we would play games under the kitchen table and she would order me to become anything or anybody she could conjure up in her imagination. A time when she would share everything with me—from physical scrapes to psychological bruises. When I always found the right words to make the hurt better or to make her laugh.

Today, she has an emotional life of her own that increasingly does not include me. Although by most standards our communication remains good, we talk more and more on her terms than on mine. There are days when she comes home and tells me that she doesn't want to talk to me right now, but will talk into the early morning hours with friends, or write in her ever-present journal. I do eventually hear the stories of her days, but much later than in her earlier years. I know that most of these changes are healthy separation stuff, but it still makes me cry to know that I am no longer her first confidante.

Not surprisingly, I too, even if sometimes reluctantly, am returning to an emotional life that does not include her. As

Michaela moves out of the center of my universe and finds her new place as an independent young adult, I find myself desperately searching for a new center.

As she discovers her life, I recover parts of mine a little bit at a time and discover a different biological clock ticking. At middle age, with my child almost out of the nest, I feel a surge of creative energy seeking a voice and an overwhelming desire for spiritual, family and community connections. Yet, there are many moments when I am honestly intimidated by the responsibility and courage required to meet those yearnings.

I also feel the uncertainties of starting over, somewhat like after my divorce. I'm not quite sure of my bearings at this stage of the game, and I want some semblance of security and knowing, but realizing in my heart that there is very little that is known for sure. The only thing I'm certain of is that I, like Michaela, will just have to find my way in the world step by step, the way I always have. Ironically, I am more confident that Michaela is well prepared for the next phase of her life than I am for mine.

"Michaela is such a delightful young lady, she's so smart, so outgoing, personable, conscientious—such a great kid.... How did you do it?"

After years of having people ask me how I've managed to raise such a treasure as a single mother, I realize that the compliments have less to do with my accomplishments than the preconceived notions and strongly held definitions of the "single" mother. She is so often portrayed as being a mother without money and without a man, as though there are no other ways she could choose to live and succeed, such as in an extended family or an intentional community.

The gift of parenting one child is that I've had a chance to watch a miracle unfold, with an intensity of observation that I do not believe I personally could have experienced had I more than one child and/or a child and a "husband."

My success in rearing Michaela is not mine alone. There is a history of circumstance, good fortune and mystery.

Until the separation from my husband, I had lived my life pretty much on course, putting one foot in front of the other, (of course, there were a few sidetracks) until I achieved my goals. I got the degrees, got the husband, and got the baby—all the while priding myself in being self-sufficient.

Having been reared by two parents who believed in personal responsibility, financial stability, education, marriage, family and staying close no matter what...I was not exactly prepared for the end of my marriage, parenting "alone," or for accepting gifts from angels.

Angels—those special beings we unexpectedly encounter along the way who share the gifts of their talents and wisdom. These "angels" always seem to have come along at just the right time.

In 1977, before Michaela was born, I met a sixty-eight-year-old woman, with silver hair and deep blue eyes that twinkled. At the time, she didn't seem to be the kind of woman I thought I'd have a significant relationship with. She was an older white woman, who loved opera, wore tennis shoes and was politically conservative. Ruthelma Johnson turned out to be a spiritual mentor and a surrogate grandmother who taught me the essence of parenting. She herself had been a single mother and drew upon her wisdom and her experience of raising a son.

She taught me many lessons that have held me in good stead. One was to spend my time with Michaela one moment at a time—as in, this moment is all I truly have with my daughter, so spend it wisely. Another was to choose my battles. When Michaela was three, I'd often find myself in a battle of the wills with her. There was a long winter when she only wanted to wear sleeveless summer dresses. I fought with her daily to force her into corduroys, an undershirt, shirt and sweater. After weeks of battling, I called Ruthelma for advice. Ruthelma gently asked me whether this was the way I wanted to spend my time with Michaela—arguing over clothing. "Can't you just put a sweater on over the dress?"

"Anyway," she'd say, "will this matter tomorrow, next month, next year or in five years!"

I got it!

Another important lesson, which has given me a reverence for each person's spirit, has been that children come into this world with their own rhythms and ways of knowing, and it's not our right to impose our ways on them; we are only here to help them along their own paths.

"Marsha, you have to believe that Michaela will draw to her all that she needs and that we just need to get out of the way and allow that to happen."

Ruthelma was right, over the years Michaela has magically drawn some of the most incredible people into our lives to help us along the way.

When I look at Michaela, I see the many gifts her father has given her. She's very much like him. Being an outgoing, gregarious, center-stage kind of guy, who adores his first child, Michael was the first to try to communicate with her in playful nonsensical utterances—"oooo, ack, ackiiieee...aaahhh"—on her first day home from the hospital when she cried and cried unmercifully. I thought she had gas...he thought she needed "intellectual" stimulation. In reality, she was hungry. When Michaela was five, Michael taught her to recite *Casey at the Bat* with more vigor and theatrical aplomb than I'd ever heard: "...and now the pitcher holds the ball, and now he lets it go, and now the air is shattered by the force of Casey's blooow." Always her most vocal fan, Michael would wildly cry "Bravo, bravo" for any of her performances—to which she would bow with great theatrical flair and say "Thank you, Daddy."

I'm convinced that these early years of playfulness and many hours of make-believe were critical to the development of Michaela's keen imagination and love of language, sound and drama.

Over the years, even though her father has been geographically distant, the two of them have, sometimes painfully, worked on their relationship with an honesty I admire. Within the last three years, I have seen each of them negotiate their relationship by telling the truth of their pain. At age fourteen, Michaela was finally able to articulate the anger she had at his leaving—an anger that had been bottled up since she was six. Michael, at middle age, was finally able to tell her that he was deeply saddened to have missed so much of her life. I think he has helped her to know that relationships are not static, but can change and be healed.

Mary Ellen entered our lives in a big way just as Michael was leaving. When we entered the clinic for Michaela's first checkup, Mary Ellen, a pediatric nurse, said "This one's mine"—meaning she would take us as patients. She has remained in our lives as a very dear friend and as Michaela's "other mother," co-mom and "my Mary" as Michaela calls her. Mary Ellen has been a compass in our lives, often directing us back to each other, even in hard times. She has always been there for Michaela—no matter what—when I was not able to be present either physically or emotionally. In times when Michaela and I found difficulty communicating (often because of my temperament), Michaela always knew she could go to Mary Ellen. Mary Ellen was the first to let Michaela know, without a doubt that no matter what she feels—sadness, anger, hurt, joy, envy—it's okay to feel and to express her emotions. This gift has helped Michaela be more immediately in touch with her feelings and free in her expression.

Ever the rugged individualist and pragmatist, Mary Ellen has instilled in Michaela a respect and love for nature and the outdoors through gardening, biking, hiking, swimming, skiing. And she, a one-time math major, has encouraged Michaela's interest and competency in math and science.

Lynn, Michaela's third-grade teacher who remains a friend, helped nurture Michaela's writing voice by encouraging her in storytelling and journal writing at an early age. To this day, Michaela still enjoys weaving a good yarn and finds great companionship in her journal, where she records the intimate and routine movements of her days. I'm convinced that Lynn's way of teaching and nurturing the creative spirit in the young is why Michaela has continued to find joy in the written word. Lynn has an uncanny ability to see the creative muse in each student and to nurture each student individually. She gently coaxes her students to unleash their own creative spirit and then she tenderly and compassionately helps them to refine their work—never crushing their enthusiasm and always making sure their voices remain intact. (A far cry from the way most writing classes are taught!) I wish every artistic and passionate child could have such a teacher.

Pat reminds me of "the little engine that could," teaching Michaela the value of perseverance and pushing through the tough places in life—such as the lifeguard training exam, driving lessons and a rigorous history course. She is the person in her life who consistently says "You can do this—keep going!" Pat has also been one of the major sounding boards for Michaela's rapidly evolving social and political consciousness. They can often be found sitting at the kitchen table having heated discussions about the world's social injustices and possible solutions. Having been involved in social service as an advocate for the homeless, Pat has taught Michaela what it means to serve others selflessly, as she and Michaela have volunteered for projects that serve women and children without social advantage.

I think I have given Michaela the gift of dreaming and believing that she can be anything she wants to be.

There are many other angels who have visited our lives as Michaela has grown from childhood into adolescence. These "special beings" always magically appear to help us navigate through our days more fully and gracefully.

"Raising a child is like walking with a toddler on the beach. You want her to experience the spray and surf of the ocean on her own, without the tight restraints of an adult grip. You let her play freely . . . but stay just within reach, so that if she needs your help you can be there." (CJ)

Somewhere between then and now we've both grown in confidence, although at different levels, and are preparing for the next phase of our journey—to separate, to be apart. In retrospect, it's been a very short time together. My hope is that the remainder and majority of our lives together will be as friends.

As much as I am grateful to all the angels in our lives, I know that when the time comes for Michaela to get on the plane, bus or car to leave home . . . it will be I who will miss her the most. It is I who can still feel that moment when I looked into her eyes for the first time; it is my heart that wells up, bursting with love and gratitude, when she tells me "I love you Mom . . . you're such a great mom."

I know that as Michaela and I each take off on our separate journeys, we must listen to and follow our own unique rhythms and ways of knowing and have faith that we will draw to us all that we need.

A few months before her death on August 5, 1992, Ruthelma gave me my final parenting lesson. She said, "If you truly love someone you cannot cling—you must let go."

Contributors

Jeannine Atkins' first novel, *Telling*, deals with a woman's recovery from rape (Sky Room Press, 1994). She is also the author of *Louisa May At Fruitlands*, a book for young adults, and is currently working on a novel about Louisa Alcott's sister, May. She lives with her family in western Massachusetts.

Julene Bair teaches writing and literature at the University of Wyoming at Laramie. She's a graduate of the Iowa Nonfiction Writers' Program. She has published in many journals. Chapters from her memoir, *House Dreams*, appeared in *The Missouri Review* and *North Dakota Quarterly*. She's currently at work on her second book, about her experiences living alone in the Mojave Desert.

Becky Birtha is the author of two short story collections, *For Nights Like This One: Stories of Loving Women* (Frog in the Well, 1983) and *Lovers' Choice* (Seal Press, 1987) and a collection of poetry, *The Forbidden Poems* (Seal Press, 1991). Her work has appeared in a number of literary and feminist journals and in many anthologies. She is the adoptive parent of Tasha Alfrieda.

Julia A. Boyd is a psychotherapist in private and clinical practice. A contributor to *The Black Women's Health Book* (Seal Press, 1990, 1994), she is also the author of *In the Company of My Sisters/Black Women and Self-Esteem* (Dutton, 1993). Her poetry and short fiction have been published in several anthologies and in *Essence* magazine. She lives in Seattle with her son, Michael.

Maaskelah Kimit Chinyere is a freelance writer living in Wichita, Kansas with her three children, Kubwa, Poetry and MyAngel. Co-developer of a National Black Women's Health

Project self-help group, she and her family also operate a local African books and gifts shop. Her primary life goals are sound health, peace of mind, integrity of spirit, and making the opportunity to help others attain the same. She is one half of a performance poetry duet, *Saffire Thighs*, which performs original works of poetry relating life through blackwoman eyes.

Beverly Donofrio is the author of *Riding in Cars with Boys: Confessions of a Bad Girl Who Makes Good* (William Morrow and Co., 1990). She studied at Wesleyan University and received an M.F.A. in creative writing from Columbia. Her work has appeared in *The Village Voice, New York* magazine, *Cosmopolitan,* and *7 Days.* She was born in Wallingford, Connecticut, and lives in New York City.

Wendy Dutton lives in Oakland with her two daughters and fat dog, dreaming of the country. A portion of her essay, "Life as a Writing Mom," appeared in *Moms at Home.* She teaches at Patton College.

Linda Hogan is a Chickasaw poet, novelist, and essayist. Her novel, *Mean Spirit* (Atheneum, 1990), received the 1990 Oklahoma Book Award and the Mountains and Plains Booksellers Award. It was also one of three finalists for the Pulitzer, 1991. Her book, *Seeing Through the Sun* (University of Massachusetts Press, 1985), received an American Book Award from the Before Columbus Foundation. She is a professor at the University of Colorado.

Barbara Kingsolver is the author of the novels *Pigs in Heaven* (1993), *Animal Dreams* (1990), *The Bean Trees* (1988), and the short story collection *Homeland and Other Stories* (1989), all published by HarperCollins. She is also the author of the bilingual (Spanish/English) collection of poetry, *Another America* (Seal Press, 1992), and the non-fiction book, *Holding the Line: Women in the Great Arizona Mine Strike of 1983* (ILR Press, 1989). She has contributed articles and reviews to the *New York Times* and many other publications. She lives in Tucson, Arizona with her daughter.

Anne Lamott is the author of *Operating Instructions: A Journal of My Son's First Year* (Pantheon Books, 1993), as well as four novels: *Rosie* (Farrar, Straus and Giroux, 1989), *Hard Laughter* (Farrar, Straus and Giroux, 1987), *Joe Jones* (North Point Press, 1985) and *All New People* (Bantam Books, 1991). A past recipient of a Guggenheim Fellowship, she has been the book review columnist for *Mademoiselle* and a restaurant critic for *California* magazine. Lamott lives in San Rafael, California, with her son, Sam, now four years old.

Diane Lutovich, a single parent for twenty-one years, has lived the experiences about which she writes. A professional writer, poet and teacher, she has been published in journals and magazines, including *The Seattle Review, Viva,* and *Elippsis.* For fourteen years, she and her business partner have been developing and delivering training materials to people in business.

devorah major is a poet, fiction and essay writer, an actress and dancer. She released her first book of poetry, *traveling women,* with Opal Palmer Adisa, in 1989 (Jukebox Press). In 1992 the two released a recording of poetry and jazz, entitled *Fierce/Love.* She has received Pushcart recognition for her short story, "A Crowded Table." She lives in San Francisco with her daughter, Yroko, and her son, Iwa. Her first novel, *An Open Weave,* will be published by Seal Press in 1995.

Kathleen Moore writes from the experiences of "real lives— her own and other people's." She has been writing for five years. Her own experiences, including growing up in Detroit, being a Peace Corps Volunteer in Ethiopia, raising a son in Minneapolis, provide ample material for her work. She is currently writing about the lives of elderly women.

Jenny Morris is a feminist and freelance writer/researcher. She is the editor of *Alone Together: Voices of Single Mothers* (1992) and *Able Lives: Women's Experience of Paralysis* (1989) as well as the author of *Pride Against Prejudice: Transforming Attitudes to Disability* (1991), all published by The Women's Press. She lives with her eleven-year-old daughter, Rosa.

Carol Moseley-Braun, a native Chicagoan, attended the University of Illinois at Chicago and received her law degree from the University of Chicago. She was elected to the Illinois General Assembly in 1978 and served for ten years. In 1987, Ms. Moseley-Braun was elected Cook County Recorder of Deeds, becoming the first woman and the first African American ever to hold executive office in Cook County Government. She was elected to the United States Senate in 1992, and is the first African-American woman to hold a Senate seat. A long-time legislative leader in education, health care, the political empowerment of women and minorities, and family-centered issues, she currently lives in Chicago and Washington, D.C. with her sixteen-year-old son, Matthew.

Valerie Polakow is the author of *Lives on the Edge: Single Mothers and Their Children in the Other America* (1993) and *The Erosion of Childhood* (1982), both published by University of Chicago Press, as well as numerous publications about single mothers and children in poverty, public policy and family entitlement issues, educational inequality, the child care crisis and child advocacy. She is a Professor in the College of Education and the Institute for the Study of Children and Families at Eastern Michigan University.

Mary Plamondon was born in Washington State in 1948. She was a single mother for thirteen years, including four years on public assistance. She lives in Seattle with her family. She has a B. A. from Seattle University and a Ph.D. from the University of Washington. She has been a teacher and administrator in alternative higher education for two decades. "Unwed Mother, 1970" is her first published story.

Michelle Ramsey is a single mother of one son, Kevin. They reside in Seattle, Washington. Michelle wrote essays about being a single parent when she enrolled in college to pursue a degree in Medical Records Technology. She graduated with honors in June of 1994.

Sheila Rule is a reporter for *The New York Times*. As a journalist she has been foreign correspondent and has written about events in Africa and Europe. She currently writes about popular music and lives in New York City with her five-year-old son, Sean.

Lesley Salas is a lesbian mother of two children of Cuban and European descent. She has lived in Chicago, Iowa, San Francisco and Mexico. She currently resides in the Republic of Texas where she awaits the day when the world is run by post-menopausal women.

Bonnie Tavares is the Executive Director of the New Bedford Women's Center and is actively involved in the women's movement. An advocate for women's health issues, she is currently developing housing for HIV-impacted women and their children. She lives in Rochester, Massachusetts with her husband Paul and their three children.

Barbara Earl Thomas lives, writes and paints in Seattle. Her artwork has been exhibited in galleries and museums around the U.S.—and on the covers of the Seal Press books *Gathering Ground* (1984) and *Angel* (1988). Since 1989, she has worked at Seattle's Elliott Bay Book Co.

Mayumi Tsutakawa is an independent writer, editor and art curator. She has edited four multicultural anthologies of literature and art, including *The Forbidden Stitch: Asian American Women's Literary Anthology* (Calyx, 1989), which received the Before Columbus Foundation American Book Award in 1990. She also curated "A Room of One's Own: Asian American Installation Art," an exhibit held at Seattle's Bumbershoot Arts Festival in 1993.

Barbara Walker works as a music teacher in an inner London primary school. In between being exhausted she enjoys cycling, walking, canoeing and playing duets with her son, Tom. Living next to the Walthamstow Marshes by the River Lea in East London, the experience of nature and the profuse wildlife to be found in this ninety-acre "piece of countryside" is an important part of their lives.

Carol Weir is a practicing attorney and lives on a farm in upstate New York. Her story, "Applesauce Apples" was selected for syndication in 1991 by PEN. In 1993 her story "Tile" won first prize in The International Fiction Contest sponsored by The Writers Workshop in Ashville, North Carolina. Additional stories have appeared recently in *Other Voices* and *Jewish Currents*. She has just completed her first novel about a single mother running for political office.

Marsha R. Leslie is a writer and associate producer for public television and is a contributor to *The Black Womens' Health Book* (Seal Press, 1990, 1994). She is the mother of a sixteen-year-old daughter, Michaela, and lives in Seattle.

Selected Titles from Seal Press

THE BLACK WOMEN'S HEALTH BOOK: *Speaking for Ourselves,* expanded second edition, edited by Evelyn C. White. $16.95, 1-878067-40-0. More than fifty black women write about the health issues that affect them and the well-being of their families and communities. Contributors include Marsha R. Leslie, Faye Wattleton, Byllye Avery, Alice Walker, Angela Y. Davis, Zora Neale Hurston, Audre Lorde, Julia A. Boyd, bell hooks and Toni Morrison.

HARD-HATTED WOMEN: *Stories of Struggle and Success in the Trades* edited by Molly Martin. $12.95, 0-931188-66-0. Vivid and inspiring accounts of life on the job by twenty-six trades-women.

GETTING FREE: *You Can End Abuse and Take Back Your Life* by Ginny NiCarthy. $12.95. 0-931188-37-7. The most important self-help resource book of the domestic violence movement.

THE ONES WHO GOT AWAY: *Women Who Left Abusive Partners* by Ginny NiCarthy. $12.95, 0-931188-49-0. This book takes us directly into the lives of more than thirty women who left abusive partners and started their lives over.

YOU DON'T HAVE TO TAKE IT!: *A Woman's Guide to Confronting Emotional Abuse at Work* by Ginny NiCarthy, Naomi Gottlieb and Sandra Coffman. $14.95, 1-878067-35-4. This comprehensive guide provides practical advice and exercises to help women recognize abusive situations and respond with constructive action, including assertive confrontation and workplace organizing.

THE THINGS THAT DIVIDE US: *Stories by Women* edited by Faith Conlon, Rachel da Silva and Barbara Wilson. $10.95, 0-931188-32-6. Sixteen feminist writers present vivid and powerful short stories that explore difference and commonality between women.

SEAL PRESS, founded in 1976 to provide a forum for women writers and feminist issues, has many other books of fiction and non-fiction, including books on health and self-help, sports and outdoors, mysteries, translations and memoirs. You can order the books listed above by writing to 3131 Western Avenue, Suite 410, Seattle, Washington 98121 (please add 15% of the book total for shipping and handling). Write to us for a free catalog.